Wesley is a very zealous man who has experienced many aspects of the prophetic ministry in his local church for more than ten years. He has struggled with the inevitable tensions and has gained insight that will benefit the body of Christ. His thirst for revival and his fearless courage make him a gift to the church in these days.

Mike Bickle, senior pastor
Metro Vineyard Fellowship
Kansas City, Missouri

In this current outpouring Wesley has been wonderfully used of God as a fire lighter and fire stoker. This book reflects his heart and passion for all that the Spirit is calling forth. *Welcoming a Visitation of the Holy Spirit* is grounded in Wesley's nine years of experience pastoring the prophetic and serves as a practical and instructive guide for renewal churches.

Guy Chevreau, author
Toronto, Ontario
Canada

In the last two or three years the spiritual landscape has been altered by the work of the Holy Spirit. Wesley Campbell's well-researched and carefully documented book will help us understand what He has done and why.

Gerald Coates, leader
The Pioneer Church International
London, England

Wesley Campbell is a man saturated with purpose and desire. That desire has set him on a pilgrimage in pursuit of the operation of the Holy Spirit during times of special visitation. His historical research has established the well-known maxim that nothing is new under the sun.

Wesley is without a doubt a Holy Spirit apologist who has a talent for gathering information on a popular front which God has used to ignite a fire in the hearts of thousands of believers around the world.

This book is dynamite!

Ken Gott, senior pastor
Sunderland Christian Centre
Sunderland, England

D0645680

Wesley Campbell's burning heart for God is felt in his expert account of the guidance and events leading up to the dynamic refreshing currently being experienced by God's people. More importantly he talks about where it's all headed. And with the proficiency of a scholar, Wesley also tackles the tough questions regarding its biblical basis, the unfamiliar phenomena and the place of the prophetic in the church. This book is bold yet balanced. It should be read by skeptics as well as those seeking a clear and in-depth substantiation of this powerful move of God.

Melody Green Sievright, cofounder
Last Days Ministries

Welcoming a Visitation of the Holy Spirit by Wesley Campbell is a welcomed book pertaining to the present outpouring of the Holy Spirit. It is not just related to the Toronto Blessing but deals with the greater outpouring of the Holy Spirit which is occurring around the world. Wesley's writing is very helpful in understanding what God is doing.

Randy Clark, senior pastor
Vineyard Christian Fellowship
St. Louis, Missouri

Wesley Campbell is well known for his unique style in effectively communicating from the platform. He achieves the same in this refreshing book — racy, reflective, good teaching and a wealth of fascinating illustration. I commend it for its observations, insight and wide-ranging testimonies coming out of the most recent move of the Holy Spirit.

David Pytches, bishop
St. Andrews Church
Chorleywood, England

I believe Wesley Campbell has captured the essence of the impact the Holy Spirit has imparted through His manifestations in Toronto. He has also given us some very practical input on how to pastor subjective manifestations in a highly objective church environment.

John Paul Jackson, senior pastor
Shiloh House Community Church
Fort Worth, Texas

Theologically trained, pastorally seasoned and world traveled, Wesley is at the white-heat center of renewal. His own story is woven into the fabric of past and present outpourings of God's Spirit. This book answers critics and advances the discussion: Where is all this going? Read for biblical balance, prophetic direction and above all, elevated faith in God's purpose to engulf this planet with His power and mercy.

Don Williams, author and senior pastor
Coast Vineyard Christian Fellowship
La Jolla, California

Wesley has done a marvelous job in combining what the Lord is doing through this present outpouring of the Spirit with solid Bible teaching and many examples from church history. This book is easy to read, and it quickens us to open up to the presence of the Holy Spirit.

Martin Buhlmann, senior pastor
Berne, Switzerland
Vineyard Director of German Speaking Europe

Wesley and I have walked many miles together along the pathway to renewal. This book is filled with stories and insights from the twists and turns along the way. Conclusive answers to issues arising out of a visitation of God are hard to wrestle down at the best of times. We still have a lot to learn, but Wesley's book is a helpful tool in processing an encounter with God's power.

David Ruis
Vineyard worship leader and
recording artist

Welcoming a Visitation of the Holy Spirit captures the interest from page one! It is well-documented, informative and essential reading about what God is doing now. This breath of fresh air is most needed in the present atmosphere of uninformed, prejudiced and frantic attacks upon the visitation and the visited. It is a vital piece of the puzzle.

Victor Richards, senior pastor and director
Vino Nuevo Ministries and national director of
Intercesores for Mexico, Juarez, Mexico

For those who know Wesley and Stacey Campbell this is exactly the work one would expect: a book contagious with a love for God, His presence and His Word — both the written and spoken. Just as Wesley and Stacey do, this book will encourage many to seek God and to make His love known to many.

Marc A. Dupont, conference speaker and author
Mantel of Praise Ministries International

Writers could be divided into two broad types. Some assemble facts and arrange them logically. Others write out of deep experience — out of what their own lives have taught them. Wesley Campbell belongs to the latter group. Wesley knows revival *from the inside,* which is the only way it can be known.

John White, author
Surrey, British Columbia
Canada

I wish every person on the planet had this book in hand in order to react properly to moves of God in many places. I believe it will be a valuable aid as a point of reference to somewhat controversial manifestations accompanying renewal now and in the future. No one is more credible in passion, disposition and scholarship than Wesley Campbell to write this book.

Jack Taylor, president
Dimension Ministries

Campbell's book is an intensely personal and practical study of revival manifestations written from the perspective of a Vineyard pastor with Baptist roots. Its warm and positive historical approach will be helpful to churches and pastors in the midst of spiritual renewal.

Vinson Synan, dean
School of Divinity
Regent University

Welcoming a Visitation of the Holy Spirit

WESLEY CAMPBELL

CREATION
HOUSE
Orlando, FL

To Stacey

A wife of noble character who can find? She is worth far more than rubies. Her husband has full confidence in her and lacks nothing of value. She brings him good, not harm, all the days of her life... She is clothed with strength and dignity...She speaks with wisdom and faithful instruction is on her tongue...Her children arise and call her blessed; her husband also, and he praises her: "Many women do noble things, but you surpass them all"...a woman who fears the Lord is to be praised.

Proverbs 31:10-12,25-26,28-30

ACKNOWLEDGMENTS

Of course in everyone's life and work acknowledgments are in order. To some they are merely an endless traffic of names. But to those in the trenches together they represent real live heroes — the stuff life is made of. Throughout the Bible even God could not resist acknowledging a job well done. Those long lists of names that now one today knows, but they were known to Him.

First, I want to acknowledge an incredibly great church as well as the entire leadership team who made it possible to forge the stuff of this book.

To those who have been with us over the years at New Life Vineyard who comprise (in my opinion) one of the best churches in the world. It has been my privilege to work with the senior leadership team, Roger and Gail Helland, Gord and Jan Whyte, and Ralph and Donna Bromley, for more than ten years. A special thanks to you, Roger, for helping with the manuscript in the early stages and gathering material data.

I also want to acknowledge a faithful group who have prophesied in season and out of season for over nine years. I affectionately call you "the prophetic group." You know who you are.

To Joerg and Ingrid Wagner. You are a couple who have always been there when we've needed you, and in so many ways you help to make our life that little bit easier.

To those outside our own church, including David and Anita Ruis, who were an integral part of pioneering the first five years.

To John Wimber. You opened our eyes to the theological understanding and reality that there was something more.

To John and Carol Arnott for inviting us to share in the joy of the party and being our friends.

Last, to Mike Bickle for being an example and inspiration by his very life. When there were no visible models of radical devotion, your flag pointed the way.

Thank you also Stephen Strang at Creation House for being patient with me.

God bless you all.

CONTENTS

FOREWORD

A great deal of the literature about revivals that is available on bookstore shelves today is written by scholarly authors who quote credible historical sources as well as Christian leaders involved with revivals throughout history — such as John Wesley, George Whitefield and Jonathan Edwards. This literature witnesses to the Great Awakening 250 years ago. Others refer to Charles Finney, whose generation experienced revival 150 years ago. Their insights have been tremendously helpful to those who are trying to understand the dynamics of renewal today.

While a historical framework is indispensable, something that would be most helpful is a current perspective on what revival would look like in the nineties if it were happening in our own churches.

Such was the situation that confronted Canadian pastor Wesley Campbell of Kelowna, British Columbia. While Wesley was endeavoring to start a new church in the late eighties, a series of untoward events took place that literally shook the body of believers at his young Baptist church. Suddenly New Life Baptist Fellowship was in the midst of a powerful visitation of the Holy Spirit, and yet no one had any idea what to expect during such a visitation.

Wesley, whose church background was traditional and noncharismatic, had to address all the issues associated with revival based on theological and historical evidence. Some of the most pressing questions were: How do you explain the manifestations? Are they of God? Are they demonic? Are they biblical? Wesley observed that in almost every case, the fruit was very good.

Welcoming a Visitation of the Holy Spirit, in part, tells the story of how Wesley Campbell successfully pastored his congregation through an incredibly challenging time so that the New Life Vineyard, as it is now called, is a healthy and vibrant church. With no modern reference points against which to measure the experiences of his congregation, Wesley was forced to "do his homework" in terms of church history and theology. Wesley and his congregation pressed on through uncharted waters to where both he and his co-pastor, David Ruis, gained amazing and helpful insights into what the Holy Spirit wants God's people to do as He brings revival and renewal in our day.

With his own keen perspective, Wesley has chronicled events which, I believe, will help welcome a visitation of the Holy Spirit among hungry pastors and ministers throughout the world. Many leaders are desperately seeking help and insight that is based on experience, especially since we are in the midst of what has become a worldwide visitation of the Holy Spirit.

I believe this book is unique in that regard. There are few Christian leaders with whom we could consult today who are as well qualified as Wesley. This book reflects his veteran experience with pastoring, evaluating and documenting a church's experience with renewal and the prophetic. He also describes the good fruit which has resulted from all of the wonderful prophetic blessings that have flowed forth from the visitation of God in Kelowna, British Columbia.

In spite of the fact that our church, the Toronto Airport Christian Fellowship, has been experiencing renewal for many months now, I still find this book very helpful. It serves as a reference point for what a modern renewal experience should look like in practical terms. The book is filled with many deep insights on how to nurture the wonderful prophetic giftings that God is so graciously bestowing upon us. We are endeavoring to apply these insights in a similar manner among our congregation while also continuing to value God's words and letting none of them fall to the ground. Our goal is to pastor our people responsibly so that this present visitation of the Holy Spirit can bring life and blessing.

We owe Wesley a debt of thanks and gratitude for his persistence and perseverance as he walked his congregation through all the difficulties associated with the unknown, long-term effects of a powerful visitation of the Holy Spirit.

This is a significant and timely book that belongs in the hands of pastors, church leaders and believers who are partaking in the refreshing move of God that is sweeping the world today.

Carol and I count Wesley and his wife, Stacey, among our dearest and closest friends. They are a very important link in our renewal team.

John Arnott
Pastor of Toronto Airport Christian Fellowship
March 1996

INTRODUCTION

The church of Jesus Christ around the world is currently experiencing what may become one of the most massive visitations of God in salvation history. Like a fast-moving fire overtaking a forest, impartations, empowerings and times of refreshing are breaking out in church after church. There has been laughter, tears, joy and repentance! All this is becoming commonplace as people experience powerful manifestations of the Holy Spirit and are physically shaken or struck motionless. Brand-new believers are being empowered to prophesy with the boldness and eloquence of the previous mystics. What is happening in the church around the world as we enter the next millennium? How are we to pastor and be pastored in the midst of the fastest outpouring of the Holy Spirit since the 1906 Azusa Street Revival? What are we to do in services interrupted by holy laughter, punctuated with shaking declarative prophecy and culminated with many staggering under the power of God as if soberly intoxicated?

The following accounts and related teachings will deal primarily with the visitation of the Holy Spirit that I have been privileged to be a part of. This is in no way meant to minimize the great work that God is bringing about in other streams and locations. I am aware that these times of refreshing have already been developing in Argentina and other isolated spots for some time, but they were not of worldwide proportions. I also want to acknowledge the catalytic work in this present outpouring by other men such as Claudio Freidzon and Rodney Howard-Browne. But to bear testimony to the many thousands of locations now ablaze with the Holy Spirit would occupy more time and space than is permissible. Please accept our stories and testimonies as typical of many others. Even as I write this book, reports of renewal and, more recently, revival pour in from everywhere. Holy Spirit hot spots are flaring up in every corner of the globe. Thirsty believers are drinking deep from the river of God and in turn are being refreshed, empowered and filled. History is being changed, and many of you have been privileged to be a part of it. Praise God!

Because I usually like to know where I am going, I assume you do, too. *Welcoming a Visitation of the Holy Spirit* is divided into four main sections.

In section 1, "Welcoming a Visitation of the Holy Spirit," the goal is to awaken faith. You will read of the inception of the widely publicized Toronto Blessing and how it has spread throughout the world. Many people are asking how they can prepare themselves and their churches for this blessing. Based on the model of the Toronto Blessing, six principles have been noted that are transferable to your own context. In the fourth chapter of this section, I address what you may expect to see in a visitation of God, and what it is that God is doing by way of refreshings, impartations and empowerings. The last chapter in section 1 also contains the actual account of our own church's initiation into the reality of God's visitation upon His people.

In section 2, "The Bible and a Visitation of the Holy Spirit," I emphasize teaching in order to provide a reasonable defense for the current visitation of the Spirit. Many born-again Christians have belief systems tainted with a cessationist, anti-supernatural bias. They desire to enter into what is happening but need an intellectual as well as biblical basis in order to welcome a visitation. This section deals with the subject of how to interpret the Bible and how biblical presuppositions can produce not-so-biblical outcomes. Then we will take a fresh look at the Bible and examine it for evidence of spiritual and physical phenomena that we are not normally accustomed to. There are three chapters devoted to what I call "Holy Spirit apologetics." These deal with the subject of why this current move is of God and not of the devil. For those who have questions about the hope of a visitation, and ultimate revival, this section is most helpful.

In section 3, "The Prophetic and a Visitation of the Holy Spirit," our desire is to provide pastoral help so that people can lead and be led more effectively through the current visitation. The purpose is clearly to encourage and empower people to be involved — to go for it. Through observations, principles and illustrations gleaned over seven years of pastoring in the midst of a visitation, I will share on both facilitating the advance of a visitation and the pastoral issues related to it. As pastors, we lead people and meetings (or church services). My hope is to give away what we have learned so that it might help you to lead people and meetings in such a way as to produce the most fruit possible.

Section 4, "Where to Go With a Visitation of the Holy Spirit," addresses the fundamental question: "Where is this move headed?" As with every visitation, what comes down must go out. In this section I focus on our responsibility to apply what God has given us. The ultimate purpose for the Spirit's visitation is far greater than just to provide us with good meetings. Rather, it is to direct us to the "main and plain" things of loving God and loving our neighbor — a passion for Jesus, evangelism, unity, prayer, the gifts of the Spirit, mercy and missions. This is where the current visitation must go in order for it to become a full-blown revival. This section is an exhortation in that direction.

When I was younger and first began to preach, I used to think, *Who are you to preach? Sit down! You ought not to do that.* But then I looked around and evidently everybody else must have felt the same way because they weren't preaching either. So I thought, *Maybe my message won't be as good as others, but at least it will be a voice.* In a similar way, I now find myself years later thinking, *Who are you to write this account?* And while it might not be as good as some, at least it will be a voice. But I do know that mine is a voice that has witnessed things which must be spoken. My prayer is that this book will encourage your heart to seek heaven, to welcome a visitation of God on earth and to walk in the power of the Holy Spirit. Amen.

SECTION ONE

Welcoming a
Visitation of the Holy Spirit

1

WELCOMING A VISITATION OF THE HOLY SPIRIT

*Repent, then, and turn to God, so that your sins may be
wiped out, that times of refreshing may come from the Lord.*
Acts 3:19

"Yes, Wes! Where are you, Wes?" The excited voice on the other end of the phone was John Arnott, pastor at Toronto Airport Christian Fellowship in Canada, and he had "revival fever." *What a dumb question,* I thought. *I'm right here at home in bed where I should be at 6:45 in the morning!* But by the time I was coherent enough to answer, John was already talking again. "I've been trying to track you down for days. It's all happened, Wes. Everything that was prophesied, it's all happened." Still not with it, I asked rather ignorantly, "What has happened, what was prophesied?" Slowly John began to relate how the prophecies he and his wife, Carol, had received from Marc Dupont and my wife, Stacey, months earlier were just now beginning to happen.

John described the past events. "Do you remember last summer when you and I and Marc Dupont were walking across the parking lot and suddenly Marc began to prophesy?" How could I forget? Marc, who was a prophetic teacher on staff at John's church, had already received a lengthy word about a coming visitation to Toronto. On that particular day as we walked from our car, he received another spectacular word for John about a coming revival. He described how in less than six months John would begin to visit the cities of the earth and be used to release thousands of people into the things of the Spirit. We didn't know what to do with that word at the time.

John continued, "Do you remember what Stacey said in October?" That one was hazy to me. "No, I don't," I said. "Refresh my memory."

John recounted Stacey's prophecy: "The Lord is going to come in a wave of miracles...with His great power and with His great celebration...For I am telling you that the day is coming when miracles will be common-place...And it [will go] not only from this place, from the interior of this province, but it [will] go from nation to nation to nation to nation...And...the deception of that day will be to focus on the power." Then John received an exhortation to be like Jesus, who, when the seventy-two returned, laughed and rejoiced with them. But He also taught them not to forget that their names were written down in the Lamb's book of life. "Wes," John said, "it's all beginning to happen. God has come upon our church in mighty power."

What John was saying sounded good, but I needed to hear more. John went on. He spoke of people falling in love with Jesus and others being smitten to the ground for hours. Young people were getting saved and canceling their ski trips so they could go to church. Even though it was now only 7 A.M., I was interested. Abruptly John stopped, "Here, talk to Randy."

"Hi, Wesley," said a slow, gentle voice. "I'm Randy." I later would find out all about pastor Randy Clark, but for now he just sounded like a real nice guy who was more excited about God than I was. Randy told me that he and a team from St. Louis, Missouri, had traveled to Toronto for four nights of meetings. But without warning they found themselves in a full-blown visitation of the Holy Spirit. He related story after story about what God was doing and the blessings they were experiencing.

John came back on the line and said, "All that stuff you were telling me about last summer is happening here, now! The filling, the laughing, the falling, the violent shaking, the prophecy — it's all breaking out. You've got to come and help us, Wesley. Can you come immediately?"

I sputtered in protest, "I can't just drop everything and fly right out there."

"Well, do the best you can," John encouraged. I promised I would and we said goodbye. By the time the call ended, I was late for work, but somehow I didn't care. Something was up, and it sounded awfully good. Within a week Stacey and I were on our way to Toronto.

Firsthand Experience

Stepping off the plane, a blast of arctic air stung our noses. Toronto was in a deep freeze, and just a few minutes out of doors would make your teeth chatter. Someone met us at the airport, and we were whisked directly to the renewal meeting. As we drove in the dark cold, I thought, *Who would be out to church on a night like this?* I remembered an old saying from the days of the American circuit-riding preachers. When the weather was particularly bad they would say, "There is nothing out today but crows and Methodist preachers!" As we drove along in the freezing cold, I thought, *There will be nothing out tonight but polar bears and rabid renewalists!*

A jubilant John Arnott met us at a large rental facility. Already, within two weeks, they could no longer accommodate the crowds in their tiny warehouse church. Four or five other meetings were going on simultaneously in nearby cities and still the crowds nearly filled their rented facilities. John proceeded to introduced us to some people, including Ron Allen. Ron smiled weakly and sat rather still. I later found out that he was absolutely incapacitated by the glory of God. When we finally entered the auditorium, the buzz was incredible. More than one thousand people were giggling and talking excitedly to each other as if the greatest show on earth were about to begin. Personally, I had been in good meetings before, and I hoped that this would be more than just a good meeting. After all, we had flown clear across Canada to get there. Fortunately we were not about to be disappointed.

The meeting began with exuberant celebration. After a good time of that, John Arnott came to the front and shared various testimonies that had occurred in the past forty-eight hours. Then he called for a few people to come up and publicly testify about what God was doing in their lives. The first spokesperson was to be Ron Allen. The crowd yelled and cheered as he made his way to the stage.

The first thing I noticed was that Ron was not walking very well as he padded up in his stocking feet. He then looked at the crowd for a long time without speaking. We just waited. Slowly Ron began to talk, but his speech was slightly slurred. "Let me take out my hand," he said, as he brought his hand up to his face. "Ever...since...this renewal hit...I can't remember things very well. I have to write them on my hand." I thought, *Oh well, I guess that's OK.* Ron lifted one finger upwards slightly and began. "Point number one." His speech was getting worse and his thoughts were disjointed. I couldn't really make sense of what he was trying to say. The second finger went up. "Point number two." He rambled on. Quietly, I said to myself, "This guy can't even speak! How did he ever get to be a pastor?" "Uh...point number three..." He was laboring now and I thought, *He would never make it as a pastor in Canada!*

Just then Ron looked up and mumbled, "I...I...I can't take this anymore!" Instantly, with no thought of where or how he would fall — he fell! No one on the stage was ready for this. Even John Arnott, as big as he is, was nearly pulled over on top of Ron as he made a valiant effort to catch him and lessen his fall. Microphones were pulled out, piano stands knocked over, and general dishevelment reigned. The audience cheered, and John regrouped. I looked over at Stacey in disbelief. "Did you see that?" She had, and God had our full attention.

The next people to testify were a Baptist pastor named John Freil, and his wife, Ann. As they cautiously took their place on the stage, John said, "Tell the people how you have been renewed in the last couple of weeks." Smiling like high schoolers, they told of their fresh love for God, for each other and for the Lord's work. Their excitement was contagious, and everyone felt it. After a time of testimony John said, "Can we pray for you?"

The look of joy on their Baptist faces quickly changed to concern as they protested unconvincingly, "Oh no, no, no. I don't think you had better do that."

Arnott was already moving toward them, "Oh yes, just a little more blessing." Freil was now backing up, shaking his head, but John's big hand reached out and touched him. Suddenly, as if kicked by a horse, Freil's whole body was jolted back and upward. The ushers, assuming what would probably happen, had flanked him from behind. They caught him and laid his now jolting body on the stage where he would lay shaking virtually nonstop for the entire service. Ann only had time to say, "No, no, no," and she was also down on the stage. Now there were three of them who never moved (other than the shaking) for the next hour and a half.

Next, a prophetic person by the name of Larry Randolph ministered in the most exact words of knowledge I had ever seen. He called out specific words of knowledge and illnesses, matching the person's name to the ailment and even pointing out the area where the person was sitting. From time to time he would call out ailments as individuals walked forward. Or he would say, "And you're Susie, and you're Kathy." They would nod in disbelief. After Larry had about thirty to forty people assembled at the front, he asked for help from the prayer teams and moved the crowd to the ballroom bar area which had affectionately been dubbed, "Joel's bar." The people received prayer, and some were healed; others were suddenly knocked to the floor; some shook; and some rested quietly in the Spirit. Some tried to hold it back but just burst out laughing, even to the point of rolling on the floor. Joy was everywhere.

Now it was Randy Clark's turn. Randy had been there every night for two and a half weeks. As he preached, laughter rippled across the auditorium, but the people seemed intent on not missing anything he said. Whenever Randy said something that appeared to ring a spiritual bell, shaking would break out here and there. After his message an altar call was given for those individuals who wanted salvation and then for individuals who wanted personal ministry. Almost the whole crowd of one thousand people came forward.

Stacey and I were fully encouraged and leaped into action. I prayed with individuals, and she prophesied. Before the night was over, we had prophesied to many people, led a young Iranian Muslim to Christ, prayed through a demonic deliverance and ministered for more than two hours. We were exhausted but thrilled. At about 2 A.M. we dragged ourselves out as the last of the worshipers were winding down. John looked at me with a big grin and said, "Oh Wesley, isn't this wonderful? What do you think?"

I had to admit the weight of glory was thicker and heavier than anything I had ever seen. I said, "Praise God, I love it!"

The next day we gathered to debrief and strategize for the weekend meetings. John decided Larry and I should make a circuit run to the other four locations, which had already entered into protracted meetings. Stacey would remain at the Airport meetings to help with prayer ministry, and Randy would stay for another weekend. Larry nonchalantly said, "Yeah, this is what the Lord said was going to happen — beginning in the fall of 1993 and breaking out into a full-blown visitation in 1994." I would later learn what he meant by that statement. The following days of meetings were every bit as powerful as the first one. At the end of the week, I was ready to go home with a fresh fire in my spirit to believe for revival.

The Fire Spreads

The faith-igniting nature of the Toronto Blessing was astounding. It seemed that whoever visited and got prayed for or touched in some way, became a carrier of the "virus." Prior to going to Toronto we had received a number of very specific prophecies describing how the Lord was going to move significantly in our lives and in the life of our church. One Vineyard pastor had just prophesied that he saw me with forceps about to deliver a "baby of revival." Six years earlier we had experienced a move of the Holy Spirit similar to what was now taking place in Toronto, after which our church had gone through some very difficult times. We were just getting to the stage of daring to believe again. Our visit to Toronto was like a spiritual wake-up call to say, "See! It can happen again!" I flew back to my home church in Kelowna with a renewed sense of vision. It was time for the baby to be born.

Since new faith had entered my heart, I could now preach with full confidence that God would move again in our midst. Within four weeks we experienced the most powerful move of God in our history. Our church was scheduled to dedicate our newly acquired facilities, which had been obtained only after a very difficult process of fighting to inherit a prophetic promise. On the weekend of the dedication, the Holy Spirit fell on many people. Prophecy again broke out in the public meetings, and hundreds of individuals were prayed for and received refreshing, impartations of gifts and major empowerings. One exciting result has been that our church has sent out an average of one ministry team a week to help spread the renewal worldwide from that time to this.

The Lord of the States, East and West

During the next few months, thousands of stories just like ours surfaced everywhere as pastors and laypeople from around the world flocked to Toronto to "catch the fire." There was a cumulative attendance of about two hundred thousand persons in the first year alone; including more than ten thousand pastors and Christian leaders, and seventy-five thousand first-time visitors.[1] The first people to come from outside the southern Ontario region were mostly from Vineyard churches. News began to spread through the Vineyard grapevine; "Something was up — and it was of God."

Initially, Ron Allen had intended to come to Toronto as a critical overseer. But as he packed a notebook for the trip, the Lord stopped him and said, "If you go to criticize, I will lift my anointing. You go to receive."

Needless to say, Ron put away his notebook.

The Sunday morning after the impartation I witnessed, Ron told his own church in Indiana how he had been impacted, inviting those who wanted prayer to come to the front. He was surprised by a stampede — almost the entire congregation came forward! The power of the Spirit fell on them and soon more than one hundred people lay on the floor! When people arrived for the second service, they couldn't believe their eyes. Bodies, overcome by God, were strewn about on the floor. Some people were laughing; some were shaking. The second service was a repeat of the first. At 1:30 P.M. it was decided that an evening meeting should be held. The news spread, and that night about five hundred people arrived. The same thing happened again.

Ron's church held meetings nightly for nine weeks. After the seventh week the Lord led them to get a large tent where more than a thousand people gathered nightly. They were touched by God's power repeatedly. The renewal spread, and calls poured in requesting Ron and his associates to minister at other churches. Wherever they went, the presence of the Lord went with them, bringing renewal, refreshment and impartation to more than two hundred churches in six months.

Next the Lord instructed Ron and his church to "take the tent to the streets." They were to go to the roughest gang areas in town and set up the tent on an empty lot. Per capita, Fort Wayne is one of the most dangerous places to live in America. It is located in a triangle of large cities where there are territorial gang wars and many drive-by shootings. Even so, with a new faith in their hearts, they set up their tent. One night a ten-year-old black boy, the son of a Pentecostal preacher, asked if he could share his testimony. His friend had been killed recently in a drive-by shooting. The young boy got up to speak and soon his burdened heart could hold back no longer. He fervently preached a "turn or burn" message. There were gang members in the audience that night. He called them to repent and to give their lives to Christ! When the young boy finished, he gave an altar call. You could hear a pin drop, and no one moved. No one did anything.

This was too much for the boy preacher, who suddenly dropped to his knees and burst into tears, crying, "Oh God! Open their eyes, or they'll die and go to hell." He began to plead with the audience as though they were slipping into hell right then and there. This time, it was too much for the convicted gang members. One by one they began to run forward, crying out "I want Jesus!" They pulled off their colors and threw them down in front of the boy. Fifteen gang members came to Christ that night. Before the week was over, fifty-five gang members had gotten saved!

Meanwhile, back on the West Coast, the fire of God was breaking out in another location — the Anaheim Vineyard church. In April 1993 John Wimber, the founder and leader of the Vineyard movement, discovered that he had cancer in his nasal area. He underwent forty-three radiation treatments which were, as he describes it, "horrific." During the treatment and in its aftermath, John couldn't eat. In eight months he lost more than one hundred pounds. During this time of incredible weakness the Holy Spirit spoke to Carol, John's wife, and said, "John is to go to the nations." John Wimber later said, "I understood that to mean to go to the church in the nations, as opposed to go and evangelize the world. This in my mind meant a ministry of renewal and revival." [2]

Carol responded with a question, as well as a request. "Lord," she prayed, "my husband is sleeping twenty to twenty-two hours a day. He has no voice. Tomorrow, pastors from all over the world are going to be here for a pastor's conference, and John won't even be able to participate. If this is indeed Your will, touch him tonight. Please give him back his voice so that he may minister." The next day we were all shocked and surprised when John Wimber came to the conference and delivered a profound and powerful message. His voice and body were weak, but the presence of the Holy Spirit was strong.

By October 1993 God had spoken twenty-seven times confirming again that John was to go to the nations. Seventeen times the Lord said that this would be a "season of new beginnings." The Lord was saying, "I'm going to start it all over again. I'm going to pour out My Spirit in your midst like I did in the beginning." That November, at the Association of Vineyard Churches National Board and Council meetings, John Wimber brought this message to the national leadership of the Vineyard. This leadership laid their hands on him and encouraged him to go and stir up the church.

Paul Cain, a prophetic man who ministers to the larger body of Christ, was unaware of all this when he came to visit John and Carol Wimber. Paul prophesied to them and said, "The Lord is coming again to visit the Vineyard, and He is also going to move dramatically in Toronto, Canada, through a John and Carol — not Wimber." At that time, John Wimber was only briefly aware of John and Carol Arnott.

On Sunday, December 5, 1993, the Holy Spirit again spoke to John Wimber and told him to stir up the gifts of the Spirit so that His people would have a greater hunger for the Giver, Jesus. The church began to do this with a great sense of expectancy. Six weeks later, on a Sunday afternoon when John was preparing for the evening service, the Holy Spirit gave him the word *Pentecost*. John Wimber wrote:

> I spent the rest of the afternoon asking the Lord what He meant by it. No answer. At that evening's church service, the Lord gave me a vision of young people in a certain set and order. During the ministry time, from the pulpit, I asked the young people to come forward. They did and the Lord came, consuming them in a beautiful and powerful way. It began a significant increase of the outflowing of power at Anaheim that has continued until this writing. [3]

With both the move of the Holy Spirit at the Anaheim Vineyard and the protracted nightly meetings at the Toronto Airport Vineyard, two-thirds of all of the Vineyard churches were flowing in the renewal in the first six months of 1994. One Vineyard pastor in Atlanta phoned with joy to report, "We're having more than one thousand people a day coming to the meetings and more than three hundred pastors. What should our next step be? What do we do?" Wimber's answer was direct: "Do more of it! Just do it with everything you've got in you, as hard as you can, as fast as you can and as for as long as you can. Do it!" Wimber organized a conference with those involved in the Toronto Blessing as the keynote speakers: John Arnott, Randy Clark, myself and Lance Pitluck. More than five thousand people came on short notice. Within the first six months of 1994, more than one hundred thousand people throughout the Vineyard movement alone had been touched by the renewal.[4]

Not Great Britain, But God's Britain

It was not until the renewal fires jumped the Atlantic waters to Britain and ignited thousands of churches there that the secular media began to take notice. By May 1994 I was back in Toronto. I had come with two prophetic people from our church — Cathy Graham and Jan Steffen. We were just about to return to Kelowna when we met three ladies who were friends of the Arnotts. The Arnotts insisted that we stay overnight with them so we could pray for their friends in the morning. The friends were Penny Fulton, Carolyn Allen and Eleanor (Elli) Mumford. By the time the ladies arrived the next morning, we had only an hour until we had to catch our plane. We decided to dispense with breakfast and went directly to prayer. The first one to receive prayer was Carolyn Allen. Her entire body began to shake violently as Cathy prophesied that Carolyn would be released in prophetic gifts. Carolyn was instantly touched by God, fell to the floor and received a mighty impartation. We later learned that this impartation intensified over the weeks and shortly thereafter Carolyn was released in prophecy.

The next one to be prayed for was Eleanor Mumford. Elli and her husband, John, pastor the South West London Vineyard church in Putney and oversee the Vineyard churches of England. Elli later testified that she had come to Toronto feeling "spiritually burnt-out and longing for a fresh understanding and vitality in her relationship with Jesus."[5] Eleanor prayed out a great burden for Britain while we all gathered around and agreed in prayer with her. Again Cathy took off in a prophecy, only this time it was sweeping in its scope. It was to Eleanor, but it was about England: God was going to bring England to its knees and back to Him. Then Cathy proclaimed in a loud voice, "It's not 'Great Britain.' It's 'God's Britain.' It won't be 'Great Britain.' It will be 'God's Britain.'" A deep, groaning intercession was taking place all over the room, and we all knew something was happening in the Spirit. Over the next few days Eleanor spent much of her time on the carpet, prostrate before God, praying for herself and her country. Little did she know God was going to use her in part, to answer her own prayers.

Upon arriving home, Eleanor's testimony electrified all who heard it. On the Tuesday morning of May 24, 1994, John and Elli gathered some staff members and friends to share what God was doing. Elli described how she had seen God move and how He had met her. With fresh faith, they all prayed, asking God to come and fill them. Within moments everyone present was powerfully touched. Nicky Gumbel, curate at Holy Trinity Brompton Church, was present at this meeting which had lasted through his church's scheduled staff lunch. He rushed back to his own office just in time for the closing of that meeting. They asked Nicky to give a concluding prayer. Again the power of Holy Spirit working in the transference of ministry was undeniable as now, in his Anglican church office, the staff members fell under the weight of God. The church newspaper, *HTB in Focus,* wrote:

> The Holy Spirit touched all those present in ways few had ever experienced or seen. Staff members walking past the room were also affected. Prayer was still continuing after 5 P.M.[6]

Somewhere during the course of this holy outpouring, a secretary managed to get an emergency call off to the senior vicar, Sandy Millar. "Sandy," she sputtered, "I know you said not to bother you and that you are in a very important meeting, but Sandy, I just thought you should know that your entire staff is incapacitated and lying on the floor."

Furtively Sandy asked, "Is it good?"

The voice on the other end said, "I think so."

Sandy questioned further: "Then what are you doing up?"

"I crawled on my hands and knees," came the answer from the office.[7]

Shortly thereafter, an excited Sandy Millar arrived to survey the goings on. It was decided that Elli would be asked to speak the next Sunday.

Rumors of renewal and revival had been circulating in England ever since Paul Cain had announced at one of Wimber's meetings that revival was going to break out in Britain, and that "tokens of revival [would] come in October 1990."[8] Already manifestations such as the ones previously described were breaking out in isolated pockets. To use the description of a revivalist of a day gone by, Eleanor Mumford was "like a particle of radium in our midst." As she described her own reignited faith and love for Jesus in simple, unabashed terms, the description proved irresistible. Elli declared, "I have a greater love for Jesus than I have ever known; a greater excitement about the kingdom than I ever thought possible; a greater sense that these are glorious, glorious days to be alive. I am thrilled about the Scriptures...I haven't had this appetite for ministry for years. Jesus is restoring His joy, and His laughter is medicine to the soul."[9] Elli asked the congregation to stand while she prayed that the Lord would bless them and touch them afresh with His Spirit. In both the morning and the evening services, the response was the same. Soon hundreds were laughing and weeping, receiving a visitation of the Holy Spirit.

The secular press was not long in taking notice. On Saturday, June 18, 1994, about half a million London readers of *The Times* saw the headline, "Spread of Hysteria Fad Worries Church — 'Toronto Blessings.'" The article described that a "religious craze" originating in Canada had come to England and was worrying some church officials. The next day, *The Sunday Telegraph,* with more than a million readers, headlined, "Faithful Fall for Power of the Spirit — Revival of Evangelism Sweeps Round the World from 'Airport Church.'" On June 20, the *Daily Mail* read, "Laughter and Tears in Church as New Revival Spreads 'The Party Spirit.'" And the day after that, the front-page headline in the London section of *The Inde-*

pendent announced, "The Holy Spirit Hits South Kensington."

Within weeks news of the "times of refreshing from the hand of the Lord" appeared on television and radio, and in newspapers and magazines. Shortly after the British Broadcasting Company aired a program, the Canadian Broadcasting Company featured a spot on its evening news. On July 6, *The Globe and Mail* of Toronto read, "Pilgrims Worshipping on a Different Plane." The *Toronto Star* declared, "Mighty Wind from Toronto Blows Faithful Away." Even *Time* magazine featured an article entitled "Laughing for the Lord" (August 15, 1994). One vicar, whom the reporter described as "benignly wary," was quoted as saying, "We are watchful. One does not want something to be blown up that then proves to be a letdown." *Time* observed that there was no sign of a letdown, since, for months, long lines of people gathered outside Holy Trinity Brompton Church for an hour and a half before services just to make it in. This practice would continue to be the case for months afterward until, in desperation, Holy Trinity Brompton went to two Sunday evening services to try to accommodate the crowds. The summer closed with the *Jerusalem Post* running an article on the "Evangelical Trend Reaching Rural England" (August 25, 1994). The last sentence of the article quoted Gerald Coates of England: "I believe we are on the edge of what could be the greatest thing to hit our nation this century." How ironic that the testimony of this present-day visitation had made its way back to the original site of the very first visitation — Jerusalem.

Out of Toronto and Into the World

It seemed that Elli Mumford's testimony was like a lit match hitting the dry grass of the churches of England. As the spread of "Holy Spirit fever" hit London, it burst the Toronto Blessing into worldwide notoriety. Within months fires burned everywhere and so did the news of them. The world was taking notice that it was in the midst of a visitation of God. Rodney Howard-Browne and Claudio Freidzon continued their relentless pace of spreading the laughing revival in other streams with similar results. Like the circuit riders of old, scores of freshly renewed pastors traversed their denominations spreading and further facilitating the renewal. Randy Clark, knowing he was called to be a "fire starter," conducted meetings in city after city. In December 1994 Randy told me about upcoming renewal meetings he would be involved in at the Tabernacle church in Melbourne, Florida. He said, "Wesley, I believe this will be another Toronto." True to his predictions, Melbourne received a powerful visitation of God, renewing multitudes and drawing six hundred new converts to Jesus Christ.[10] Melbourne continued to hold protracted meetings for the next ten months.

Churches, believing they were called to become renewal centers, moved into protracted meetings, sometimes with astounding results. In Boston, the Christian Teaching and Worship Center, a church of about 450 members, felt the Lord spoke a very clear word to them in late 1993 about revival. The word was, "Set aside everything you had planned to do and flow with revival." Revival became their main theme. In the following year, pastors Paul and Mona Johnian ministered to about sixty thousand people during their church's three weekly services. At least twenty thousand of those people came from out of state or even out of the country.[11]

In July 1994 Ken and Lois Gott of Sunderland, England heard about the move of the Holy Spirit at Holy Trinity Brompton. Ken decided to check it out in person. At a leaders' meeting led by Anglican Bishop David Pytches, Ken and four others received a simple prayer of blessing. Later Ken told me, "We were smug Pentecostals. Immediately all five of us were on the floor just laughing our heads off. This had never happened to me before, and it started a refreshing that was to change our lives. I tell you, Wesley, I laughed for ninety minutes straight." Upon returning home similar manifestations began to break out in their church. The church decided that the Gotts should travel to Toronto, and on August 6 the couple was "on the floor again" (to put a new twist on an old Willie Nelson song).

Their story, although amazing, is too intricate to chronicle here. Suffice it to say, Ken and Lois went home as walking carriers of the fire of God. They began protracted meetings with no advertising or special speakers. Soon there were more than five hundred people at their nightly services. At this writing, they continue two years of virtually non-stop meetings. People continue to pour in, many of whom are making first-time decisions for Christ. John Arnott recently visited the Gotts and relayed this humorous story to me. He said that Sunderland is known for being the car theft capital of the world. In a recent conversation with a police chief, Arnott was told that in the last few months the most amazing thing has happened. Police noticed that car thefts have declined by 44 percent in Sunderland and they can't figure out why. John spoke up boldly, "I can tell you why. It's the revival!" The police chief just nodded thoughtfully.

Other streams around the world are also seeing unprecedented signs of a visitation of God. Even though a great deal is traceable to the Toronto outpouring which began on January 20, 1994, the realization is that revival fire is beginning to fall everywhere at about the same time. The whole world is experiencing a move of God such as it has not seen since the beginning of this century during the Welsh Revival of 1904 and the Azusa Street Revival of 1906.

On July 1, 1994, at the North American Conference for Itinerant Evangelists. Billy Graham said, "America is at the center of a great revival. Seldom has the soil of the human heart and mind been better prepared than today. I've never seen so many come to salvation in such a short time." His exhortation to the evangelists was to "not sleep through it." And, as if sensing the fresh wind of the Spirit blowing, the seventy-five-year-old man of God said, "I am praying for a new touch of the Holy Spirit."[12]

An example of what Billy Graham was saying can be found in Bethany World Prayer Center, a three thousand-member church in Baton Rouge, Louisiana. The church intended to host an evangelistic drama for three days. The drama was called *Heaven's Gates, Hell's Flames*. On the first night, one thousand people came forward to respond to Christ. The church decided to extend the drama. People kept coming and thousands more came to Christ. Over a twenty-one-day period, more than eighteen thousand people came forward for either firsttime decisions or recommitments to follow Christ. The church grew from three thousand to six thousand overnight, and the number of cell groups meeting regularly in the church doubled to more than three hundred.

In Modesto, California, a similar occurrence took place in January 1995. Calvary Temple, a Pentecostal church of about twenty-five hundred members, decided to host the same drama for four nights. Pastor Glen Berteau began preparing the church months prior to the event. The church engaged in a rotating forty-day prayer and fasting event. Members were directed to write down on three-by-five-inch cards the names of unsaved friends and family members and then lay these cards out before them as they prayed for them daily by name. Opening night saw the church full. At the end of the drama when the call was given for those who would like to give their lives to Christ there wasn't enough room at the altar for all the people who responded. More than one thousand people came forward on the first night. The next night was the same and again the night after that. They decided to extend the event.

By the second week so many people were trying to get to the church that the streets nearby experienced traffic jams. On one occasion the traffic helicopter came on a local radio station announcing what was thought to be a car accident somewhere near Calvary Temple Church. The announcer said, "We've never seen a traffic jam like this. As soon as we find out the cause we'll get back to you." Moments later the announcer exclaimed, "We've found out what's going on. All those cars jamming the road are trying to get to church. There's a church down there that's holding a drama, and we hear it's pretty good!" In the days that followed, cars showed up in the church parking lot at three and four o'clock in the after-noon for tailgate parties. The people barbequed and ate dinner in the park-ing lot while waiting for the church to open. Even when the weather was so bad that there were record-breaking rains the people were so desperate for God they parked more than a mile away and walked to the church, standing in line for three hours in the rain. Even so, the church still had to turn away thousands.

Senior pastor Glen Berteau told that two teenagers brought 181 of their classmates to the play; about eighty of them received Christ. "The other night there were four generations standing at the altar receiving Christ: a little girl, the mother, the grandmother and the great grandmother — all getting saved in one night." Glen said to me with a big grin, "You should see the gang kids. I just have to show you my bag of rags. I said to them, 'You're carrying rags in your pants, but you've got Jesus in your hearts — get rid of the rags.' They did!" Drug addicts handed over their needles and drugs to prayer counselors. Whole families were restored after coming to the front of the church to receive Christ. One family begged the pastor not to bring the campaign to a close because twenty-three family and extended family members had come to Christ in two weeks. People even came forward uninvited during the Sunday morning announcements, requesting to be led to Christ.

Before the drama was over, every church in the city that had supported this event was showing signs of growth. In all, about eighty thousand peo-ple attended the drama during its twenty-eight-night run. Documented reg-istrations of first-time decisions for Christ numbered more than ten thou-sand, with another fifteen to twenty thousand either rededicating their lives or praying for assurance of salvation. Events such as these have been almost unheard of, except in times of extraordinary visitations of God.

Another addition to the rising tide of revival news was found in the headlines of the *National & International Religion Report* which reported that "a spontaneous spiritual revival has begun on college campuses in the United States."[13] The phenomena, which includes open confession of personal sins, began at Howard Payne University in Texas. The *Baptist Standard's* top story described how Southwestern Baptist Seminary suddenly shut down classes after a forty-minute chapel service sparked what its president called "a genuine moving of God and the beginning of authentic spiritual revival."[14] Within weeks the student revival spread throughout several states, affecting colleges and universities such as Criswell College in Dallas, Texas; Houston Baptist University in Houston, Texas; Morehead State University, Morehead, Kentucky; Olivet Nazarene College, Kankakee, Illinois; and Louisiana Tech University in Ruston, Louisiana. Wheaton College, in Wheaton, Illinois, had an evening service that lasted all night as students formed lines at the microphone to confess their sins. When the service was over, students had filled five large garbage bags with alcohol, pornography and secular music. More than one thousand students were involved.[15]

Even in previously hard-to-reach areas such as Mexico, senior church leaders of that nation's largest network of evangelical churches called to say that the renewal has just begun to hit churches. In April 1995 Marc Dupont arrived in Finland to lead a prophetic conference with about four hundred registrants expected. They were shocked when five thousand people showed up, hungry for God. Countries affected by this awakening now include North America, Britain, Chile, Argentina, Switzerland, France, Germany, Scandinavia, South Africa, Nigeria, Kenya, Japan, Korea, New Zealand, Australia, Indonesia and many more. Christian leaders in the United States declare that there are more than six thousand significant hot spots where dramatic moves of God have taken place in the span of two years. As of November 1994 reports indicated four thousand churches in England had been affected — including two thousand Church of England parishes (Anglican). By the end of 1995 the number was up to seven thousand churches affected in England. Since then global statistics have become virtually impossible to track, yet one thing is certain: The world is experiencing a mighty visitation of the Holy Spirit. Perhaps by proportion it will exceed the Pentecostal revival of the early 1900s.

2

PROPHETIC FORECASTING OF GOD'S VISITATION

As He approached Jerusalem and saw the city, He wept
over it and said, "If you, even you, had only known on this day
what would bring you peace — but now it is hidden from your
eyes. The days will come upon you when your enemies will
build an embankment against you and encircle you...They will
not leave one stone on another, because you did not recognize
the time of God's coming [visitation, KJV] to you."
Luke 19:41-44

The phrase "visitation of God" is taken from the words of Jesus in Luke 19:44. Jesus described His coming to the earth in the flesh as the *kairos* or "the time, the season, the day," of God's visitation. Two main concepts in Jesus' indictment of Jerusalem are time and visitation. God had chosen an appointed time to come close to His people, but they did not recognize it. *Kairos* carries with it the idea of a season of opportunity as in Hebrews 11:15, or even the idea of some decisive event or crisis.

The Greek word for *visitation* in Luke 19:44 is *episkope*. Its root meaning is "to look over, to oversee." This gives the idea of a gracious visitation with demonstrations of divine power manifested in protection and care. English terms related to this root are *episcopal* and *overseer*. The term for elder or overseer in the New Testament is the derivative *episkopos*. Jesus was saying to Jerusalem that God had come to look over her with care and power, but she did not acknowledge it. She didn't "recognize the time of her visitation."

Thus, the phrase "welcoming a visitation of God or the Holy Spirit" can be used to describe our embracing of an extraordinary time when God visits individuals and groups in such a way that His presence and its effects are intensified. Yet from Scripture and experience we also see there are exceptional times when God chooses to come closer. He moves in *kairos* action, producing dramatic effects and results. Christians everywhere are asking how they may prepare themselves to welcome a visitation of God.

God often prepares His people for times of visitation and will even indicate these times through prophetic revelation. Amos 3:7-8 declares, "Surely the Sovereign Lord does nothing without revealing his plan to his servants the prophets. The lion has roared, who will not fear? The Sovereign Lord has spoken, who can but prophesy?" As introduced in the first chapter, a great visitation has been in progress since before 1994. A major part in preparing ourselves to receive a visitation is to recognize the *kairos* time forecast by God's servants, the prophets. This will provoke us to a revived spiritual state and will fill us with the faith needed to welcome and embrace His visit.

Prophecy and a Visitation of God

Bible examples

Prophecy can play a strong role in preparing us to welcome a visitation, as seen in both the Bible and church history. In past revivals prophecies inspired faith in believers thereby empowering them to act. A biblical example of this is demonstrated in the life of Josiah, the boy king of Judah. When Josiah was twenty-six years old he ordered the temple to be repaired. During this time workers found the lost Book of the Law. When the contents were read to him, Josiah was amazed to learn he had been prophesied and written about approximately three hundred years earlier. A prophet had come and cried out against the altar on which King Jeroboam was making an offering, saying:

> O altar, altar! This is what the Lord says: "A son named Josiah will be born to the house of David. On you he will sacrifice the priests of the high places who now make offerings here, and human bones will be burned on you" (1 Kin. 13:2).

35

Many years — and kings — later, Josiah was born. Seeking to obey the Lord, he stumbled upon his own destiny. The impact of the Book of the Law and the scrolls foretelling Josiah's life three hundred years earlier had an overwhelming affect on the young king. Josiah ripped his clothes and wept in the presence of God. He went on a holy rampage, renewing Israel's (or Judah's) covenant with God. He gathered all the idols from the temple of God and burned them. He tore down the houses of the male cult prostitutes. He desecrated all the high places and smashed the sacred stones. Ashtoreth poles were cut down and their sites covered with human bones. The fact that Josiah was cognizant of his three-hundred-year-old personal prophecy is evidenced by the biblical reference made to the prophecy during his clean-up operations just days later. In wild abandonment Josiah deliberately acted to fulfill prophecy (see 2 Kin. 23:16).

Revival resulted as Josiah fulfilled the word on his life and reaped a spiritual reward. The epitaph of Josiah's life as recorded in Scripture, states:

> Neither before nor after Josiah was there a king like him who turned to the Lord as he did — with all his heart and with all his soul and with all his strength, in accordance with all the Law of Moses (2 Kin. 23:25).

Historical examples

Even the last worldwide revival, which began in 1904, was fueled by the contemporary word of prophecy as laid hold of by Evan Roberts. I was shocked recently to realize that revivalists of the past believed and exercised prophetic giftings. As a Baptist, educated in a Baptist college and seminary, I had often heard teachers lament for the days of Evan Roberts and the Welsh Revival. During that extraordinary time of visitation, whole cities were brought to Christ. Taverns were closed due to the immediate and severe financial losses in the liquor trade. Crime was reduced dramatically, and Bibles were sold out. Every social venue became a religious occasion as prayer meetings sprang up in coal mines, trains, trams and places of business. Yet despite the obvious spiritual fruit, my conservative mentors selectively edited out the supernatural component. I was surprised to learn that Evan Roberts was referred to as "the young prophet."[1] Furthermore, his faith and belief for the soon-to-come Welsh Revival was due in part to personal visions and dreams.

In the spring of 1904 Evan Roberts experienced a series of unusual spiritual experiences. For about four months, each night Evan was awakened by the Lord for hours of communion. In an interview with W. T. Stead, the British editor of *Review of Reviews,* Evan testified of one of these times.

> I found myself with unspeakable joy and awe in the very presence of the Almighty God. And for the space of four hours I was privileged to speak face-to-face with Him as a man speaks face-to-face with a friend. At five o'clock it seemed to me as if I again returned to earth...And it was not only that morning, but every morning for three or four months.[2]

During this season of refreshing Roberts received a specific vision that propelled him forward with faith for revival. He had a vision of the moon, which appeared with greater brilliance than ever before. Historian Eifion Evans recorded:

> In a matter of moments the moon seemed to reflect the divine presence and there appeared an arm outstretched towards the world, claiming something for itself before being withdrawn. At another time, the arm and hand were indistinct, but the piece of paper which it held had the figures '100,000' written on it. After that, whenever he prayed, he had no peace until he had asked God specifically for that number of souls.[3]

From then on Roberts had faith for revival. His confidence was unsettling to his family and friends and brought criticism from others. Even before the actual outbreak of revival, so strong was his prophetic confidence that on November 4, 1904, Evan Roberts wrote to the editor of a Sunday newspaper to ask for an estimate on printing notepaper, explaining, "We are on the eve of a great and grand revival, the greatest the world has ever seen. Do not think that the writer is a madman."[4]

It is an established fact that after the commencement of his mission on a Monday night, October 31, with only seventeen in attendance, Roberts believed it was the start of a movement that would win a hundred thousand people to a vital Christian faith in the little principality of Wales alone, not to mention its impact farther afield.[5]

Within days revival fire gripped all of Wales and later the entire Christian world. "Totals of converts added to the churches were published in local newspapers, seventy thousand in two months, eighty-five thousand in five, and more than a hundred thousand in half a year."[6] The revival movement went on to sweep the rest of Britain, Scandinavia, parts of Europe, North America, the mission fields of India, the Orient, Africa and Latin America. There is no question the Welsh Revival was also the soil out of which the famous Azusa Street Revival sprang, and which set in motion the greatest century of Christian expansion in the history of mankind.[7] This move was spurred on by the faith drawn from prophetic confidence.

Prophetic Forecasting of the 1994 Visitation of God

As people ask how they can position themselves to welcome a visitation of God, it is important that they understand the "times and seasons" — the *kairos* time of God. My belief is that God is willing to tell us His will if we will ask (see John 14:29; 15:15; 16:13-14). The following modern-day examples of specific prophetic words are astounding in light of what has happened since their proclamation and initial fulfillment which began in 1993.

The main point of the following material is to highlight what God has done so you have a grid to believe for what God may do in your own personal setting. The Holy Spirit wants to reveal what the Father is doing. Let's make sure our spiritual eyes are open. The chronicling of the following prophecies is not meant to be exhaustive, but only to represent a portion of that with which I am acquainted.[8] In some cases, space does not allow for the entire prophecy and detailed interpretation to be given.[9] Still it is my prayer that by just reading and believing God's holy intentions for this time will cause your faith to ignite and burn in your own heart and church.

Mike Bickle

In 1983, shortly after Mike planted his church in Kansas City, he had a dramatic experience at a prayer meeting on April 13. Mike heard the internal voice of God, saying, "Call the people together and come before Me and fast, even as Daniel fasted in chapter 9." God directed Mike to lead his church in a twenty-one-day fast, just as Daniel, who through prophecy understood the timing concerning promises to come, then prayed and fasted to apprehend them. At this time the church was only six months old, and Mike was twenty-seven years old.[10]

The next morning Mike called Bob Jones, a man in his church who moved in a strong prophetic gifting. Mike said, "Something happened last night that will change my life. I heard the voice of God." Bob surprised

Mike by saying, "Yes, I know. The Lord already told me what He told you." Mike replied, "I'll be right over." Mike called some of his friends and together they drove to Bob's house. In the car Mike talked about how God mentioned Daniel 9 and how the purposes of God are won through fasting and prayer.

At the house Bob announced that he would tell them what the Lord showed Mike the night before. Bob said he had a very profound vision the same night. "I saw in a night vision literally the angel Gabriel. And Gabriel said, 'Give the young man Daniel chapter 9, and he will understand.'" Mike nodded in agreement. Then Bob said, "The Lord is going to confirm this with a sign. A comet unpredicted by scientists will appear in the heavens when the time of prayer and fasting begins as a sign to you that He will hear and act to accomplish His own purposes."

"What was the day the Lord told you to begin?" Bob asked.

Mike replied, "We are to start our fast on May 7."

On May 7 the fellowship began their twenty-one-day prayer and fasting. Many were on water only and praying for eighteen hours a day. When a newspaper — the *Independence (Mo.) Examiner* — was brought in that day, everyone was stunned to see the following headline: "Comet's Pass to Give Close View." The paper reported that the comet had been unpredicted by scientists and that the IRAS said, "It was sheer good luck we happened to be looking where the comet was passing."

Finally on the last day of the fast Bob told Mike he had bad news. "The Lord spoke to me in a dream last night and told me that He is not going to break loose in the revival in the way that we all thought. God never said that it would begin after the fast. We only assumed it would. The Lord says 'No! There is an appointed time and appointed season for America, and when the Lord says *it's time,* it will not be one day late.'"

Bob continued, "But God is going to help you by giving you another sign. There will be another sign in the heavens. Over this city there will be a three-month drought. And there will be a drought in America in the Spirit until God's appointed time. On August 23 — mark the date — rain will come on August 23. And when the rains come on August 23 you will know of a truth that there is a day and an hour that God has already determined that the rains will come in the Spirit. Know that all that God has promised this nation which you have participated in praying for for these twenty-one days will surely come to pass."

This occurred on May 28.

Sure enough, by the end of June Kansas City was locked in a serious drought. Newspapers said it was the third driest summer on record for approximately one hundred years. Mike and the fellowship continued praying six hours a day for a revival visitation. On the morning of August 23 — the appointed day of rain — the sky was still clear. But as people gathered for the evening prayer meeting, rain clouds began to form. Just as the prayer meeting started there was a tremendous downpour for about an hour. The group was ecstatic; the rains had come. The drought continued the next day and lasted for another five weeks making it a total of three months.

Though the physical drought had ended after three months, the spiritual drought remained alive and well. Prayer was hard and the people not very buoyant. Then in November another word came. Bob called Mike, "The Lord spoke to me in a dream last night concerning what happened on May 7, 1983. God says that in eight days, on November 15, you will receive a message from heaven. When you receive this message you will never doubt again that a visitation unprecedented in history is coming to America."

At the nightly prayer meeting on November 15, nothing was happening — flat. At ten o'clock Mike went to his office to pray and wait. Anxious, he picked up a little fifty-page booklet on his desk about a man named Howard Pittman who had been a Baptist pastor for thirty-five years. In August 1979 Pittman had a massive rupture of his stomach arteries and died on the hospital bed. His spirit left his body, and he went up to converse with God before being resuscitated and sent back to his body. (Space permits only a brief outline of this story; for a full account read Pittman's fifty-three page booklet *Placebo*.)

God told Pittman that this was the Laodicean age and various things relating to that. Then God said, "Go and tell them I am raising up an army who will go to the ends of the earth. And this army will do signs and wonders — greater works than even My Son did."

By 11:50 P.M. Mike had reached the final pages of the book. He was still waiting to hear from the Lord about May 7, 1983. To his amazement, the book began to discuss an "announcement in the sky related to a supernatural event." Pittman wrote, "My three-year limitation (which began May 7, 1980) was a ministry of prophecy of an earthshaking event that would occur at the end of my three years. The event itself would be supernatural. The announcement from the sky...represented the worldwide event that would start immediately."

Pittman went on to write that this event was no less than the recruitment for an end-time great revival spoken by Joel and begun at Pentecost. The whole process was to start with a "worldwide regurgitation" as the Lord set about "spewing out of His mouth" the so-called "lukewarm."[11]

Suddenly the realization hit Mike. *It's ten minutes before midnight, and I'm receiving a message from one who has been to heaven.* The message, in short, was that on May 7, 1983, a sign in the sky would announce a new season concerning the purposes of God relating to a Gideon's army preparing for a great harvest. This is the same topic that Mike and his church had been praying for, and now he knew their fast, commencing May 7, 1983, had been part of it.

Now only one question remained: When would revival come? The answer came months later on an ordinary Saturday morning in April 1984. Mike was in his bedroom when the room filled with the presence of the Holy Spirit, and Mike heard the audible voice of God. "His voice sounded like thunder both near and far at the same time. It shook me to the depths." The Lord said, "I have a revelation for you." Then the Lord said, "Call Bob Jones." Mike intuitively knew that the Lord was giving the same word, as well as the timing of the revival, to Bob Jones.

When Mike composed himself he called Bob. Bob was also shaken and said, "You will not believe what just happened to me this morning." Mike responded, "I bet I will!" The Lord had taken Bob into an open vision and showed him Genesis 40, the story of the baker and the cupbearer who were put in prison for offending Pharaoh. The baker was beheaded, but the butler was delivered to again serve wine to the king. The Lord also gave Bob the meaning of the vision.

The church would undergo ten years of divine restraint or restriction, like being in a dungeon or confinement. The two men symbolized two types of ministries. During the ten years the Lord would deal with the baker ministries, that is, those that served the bread with the leaven of hypocrisy. Many teaching ministries which sowed the Word and produced pride and arrogance instead of humility and lowliness before the Lord would lose their heads. A purging was going to take place. On the other hand, ministries that served humbly before the King would be kept hidden and in restraint for a season. Then in ten years there would be a mighty visitation of God in the church. Many of these cupbearers/servants who had strategically been held back would emerge from the prison and begin to serve new wine to the King. This move would go global, and it would crescendo in the end-time move that the Lord spoke about on May 7, 1983. The timing was to be ten years — 1994.

Later Mike said, "People in 1994 think this is a tremendous word, but it was a lousy word in 1984, especially if you had just planted a church." Nevertheless they received the word and began to pray about the ten years of divine restraint. They prayed that the Lord would help the church during its time of desolation and that He would prepare ministries in secret for the time when they would begin to serve this new wine in 1994.

It is no coincidence that after ten years of what could be described as a tragic decade of scandals in the church in North America a mighty outpouring and visitation of God was unleashed in 1994. Since then we have witnessed the largest worldwide renewal since the Welsh and Azusa Street movements at the turn of the century. Though many good ministries have functioned over the years with some significant localized results, historians and church watchers are now beginning to record that the year when the world began to be served this new wine was 1994 as it was poured out at the Toronto Airport Christian Fellowship.

Then in the spring of 1994 the wine began to flow internationally as England exposed the move to the rest of the world. After eighteen months virtually the whole Christian world knew of the move dubbed the Toronto Blessing, which by then had already impacted tens of thousands of churches. At the time of this writing, over two hundred nations have been touched by the new wine.[12]

The leadership of Metro Vineyard received further revelation in 1985 concerning the coming visitation. The Lord told them to "keep your eyes open for a great flood. When you see the Mississippi flood and even change direction, this is the signal that a mighty move of the Spirit is about to begin." In the next section about Larry Randolph, you'll learn more about this prophesied flood.

Larry Randolph

Another prophetic leader, Larry Randolph, didn't know about the prophecies recorded above. He was living in Arkansas praying for revival in his own life and in the church. In 1986 Larry had an encounter with God and was told to move to California. Within a week of moving to California, Larry received a very dramatic visitation from the Lord. In his own words he recounts the story:

> I was anticipating God answering me. One night I was on my
> bed listening when all of a sudden I was, what seemed like, in
> the spirit. I was still in my body, but I was in the spirit...I was

being rained upon. I could smell, feel and hear rain. I thought, *Maybe this is God, maybe not.*

I jumped up and ran to the window, but the sky was clear. And the stars were shining. I thought, *This is strange*, and went back to bed. A few minutes later the same thing happened again. I jumped out of bed, opened the window and saw the same clear sky. This time, like Samuel, I said, "God, what's happening? It's not raining outside — speak to me." As I lay on my bed, the Lord spoke to me in an almost audible voice. The Lord said, "As it was in the days of Noah, so shall it be in the coming of the Son of Man. I'm going to bring an unprecedented outpouring of My Spirit upon the church and the world. Just as Noah received a rain that was unprecedented in his generation, I'm bringing a rain of My Spirit unprecedented upon this generation."[13]

God described how He was about to rain His Spirit on the earth. Larry asked, "How long?" The answer: "Seven years." The Lord said this would start in the fall of 1993 in embryo form and develop into great revival.

Larry began to share this message all over America, Europe and everywhere else he went. Laughingly, he told me, "I even developed a three-part series on the life of Noah — the rain, the levels in the ark and all the different kinds of animals."

On January 1, 1993, Larry said, "OK, Lord, it's coming. This is the year. Give me a sign." The next day he received a call from Fred Price of Crenshaw Christian Fellowship in Los Angeles, who invited Larry to share on his radio broadcast what he felt the Lord was saying about 1993. While live on the radio, Larry felt the following words come forth:

> The Lord is bringing an unprecedented revival. The fall of 1993 is its beginning. A sign will be that the nation is going to have one of the wettest years ever in the last hundred years in this nation. It's going to rain in the Midwest, it's going to rain in California. It's going to rain, rain, rain.[14]

After the broadcast, Larry hung up his phone and thought, *Gee, there were millions of people listening to this.* By February 1993 mudslides brought devastation in California. Torrential spring rains pounded the Midwest! Newscasters in St. Louis were saying, "This is the worst flooding in one hundred years!" Floods of the century were the talk on people's lips. So great were the floods in the Midwest that the Missouri River overflowed its banks and spilled into the Mississippi River. Whole sections of the area were flooded and major roads were shut down because of the flooding. The merging of the two great rivers even caused the Mississippi to change its direction at various places. As had been prophesied, "The waters are going to flood, and when you see the Mississippi River change its direction, that will be the signal for the beginning of the time of visitation."

Ironically the heavy rains in St. Louis flooded Randy Clark's new church basement three times that spring. Months later, in September, Randy and his church would experience a flood of a different kind when the Lord visited them with His first installment of the renewal. In January 1994 they would travel to Toronto Airport Christian Fellowship and the blessing would begin.

John Paul Jackson

John Paul Jackson, a pastor in Fort Worth, Texas, said for years that there was going be a major move of the Spirit in the mid 1990s. In 1989 *Charisma* asked John Paul what God had revealed was coming in the nineties. One of the things that John Paul wrote was that the Lord was going to return the "passion of Pentecost" to the church through a massive outpouring of the Holy Spirit.

In September 1993 John Paul had a prophetic dream in which he was taken high above North America.

> I was up above North America looking down on it. It looked much like a road map was superimposed on the terrain. I saw a thick golden band begin in St. Louis and go east toward Terre Haute, Indiana. It suddenly swung up toward the northeast and went into Canada. The Lord then told me that from this golden band He was going to raise up "power tools," and many "power tool stores" would open because of His golden band.[15]

John Paul wrote Randy and told him he felt something was going to begin in St. Louis and would spread all over North America.

Paul Cain

The prophetic history of Paul Cain is absolutely amazing.[16] Paul is a major prophetic leader who predicted this current visitation of the Spirit. In 1989 Mike Bickle was teaching an introduction to prophecy series where he quoted Paul as saying:

In the fall of 1993 and in 1994 the Lord is going to begin to release sovereign vessels across this nation, and it will stagger the minds of the church. Ministries that are going around in first or second gear will instantly go into tenth gear. Like Malachi 3:1 where it says, "Suddenly the Lord you are seeking will come to his temple," Paul said, "The Lord told me specifically, that in 1993 and 1994 He would release these sovereign vessels. Everything we have seen before will begin to draw back in obscurity because of the glory of what is going to happen in that day."[17]

At the Anaheim Vineyard on New Year's Eve 1993, Paul Cain prophesied concerning the soon-coming move of the Spirit. A full three weeks prior to the first meeting at Toronto, Paul announced, "There is coming a fresh release and visitation of the Spirit to John and Carol." He also said, "This new move of the Spirit will bless the whole Vineyard." Everyone cheered and thanked the Lord. Later Paul went to John and Carol Wimber and told them that the Lord had said, "John and Carol, not Wimber!" John Wimber began to ponder. The only other John and Carol he knew of in the Vineyard was John and Carol Arnott. By July 1994, seven months after Paul Cain's prophecy, two-thirds of all the Vineyards had been blessed by the outpouring which had fallen upon John and Carol Arnott and their church.

By the end of December 1994 more than four thousand churches in England had been dramatically impacted by a visitation of God. Leading evangelical leaders today say continually in the press and magazines that England is hotter than they have ever known it to be. Definitely the church has been revived, and anticipation is everywhere that lost souls will begin to be saved en masse.[18]

Marc Dupont

Marc Dupont, a prophetic leader on staff at the Toronto church, received a two-part revelation concerning the 1994 outpouring. In May 1992 Marc and his wife, Kim, had relocated to Toronto from San Diego, California. On Marc's very first day at work, the Lord gave him a tremendous vision and prophetic word of what would eventually take place in that city. Part of the vision was as follows:

I had a vision of water falling over and onto a large rock. The amount of water was similar to Niagara Falls. I felt that Toronto was the rock over which much living water would flow with great power. Like Jerusalem, Toronto will end up being a sending place to the nations on all continents. As the rock began to be raised up it took the shape of a huge dam, which to some degree stored living water. The water began to pour out of the dam and flow west all the way to the Rocky Mountains. Then it ran north along the eastern edge of the mountains and back east across the prairies of Canada.[19]

On July 5, 1993, while in Vancouver, British Columbia, Marc felt a sense of urgency from the Lord. He believed the Lord indicated an increase in evangelism, a move of the Holy Spirit and a call to Christians for prayer to happen in the summer and autumn of that year. The pace would accelerate into the new year.

Marc saw that there would be two basic stages to the process illustrated in Ezekiel's vision of dry bones (see Ezek. 37). The first would be a prophetic stage where the church and leaders would seek the Father and cry out to Him for a sovereign move of His Spirit. The other would be an apostolic stage of power and authority coming to the church in the Toronto area. There would be a move of the Spirit on the city that would include powerful signs and wonders.

Marc felt God was going to do a unique work in Toronto and southern Ontario. The winds of the Spirit would blow from there to all corners of the earth. He saw artists and musicians going out into public places. Church unity would increase and pastors would cooperate as they worked together for outreach and prayer.[20] Various cultural groups would be touched. Traditional denominational pastors and churches would move right into the forefront of the move of the Spirit.

The next month, in August 1993, Marc, John Arnott and I were walking across the parking lot at their family camp when suddenly a spirit of prophecy came upon Marc. He told John that within seven months a move of the Spirit would begin catapulting John and Carol onto the major platforms in the earth. Marc described how John would travel to capital cities around the world and speak to thousands. The power of God would be released through his hands and his presence as he prayed and released people into the mighty things of the Spirit of God. The prophecy was so grandiose that we didn't know how to even compute such a thing. John was pastoring a three hundred-member church, and speaking invitations were not exactly pouring in. It was a prayer, but there were no signs of reality. Within seven months everything prophesied began to happen and be set in place.

Randy Clark

The day before Randy Clark was to leave for the first meeting in Toronto he was feeling nervous. What if God did not move? That day Randy received a call from Richard Holcomb. Richard was a Baptist friend who had no idea what was about to happen. He told Randy, "I have a word for you that is the clearest word I have ever had."

Randy asked, "What is it?"

Richard prophesied, "The Lord says, 'Test Me now. Test Me now. Test Me now. Do not be afraid. I will back you up. I want your eyes to be opened to see My resources for you in the heavenlies just as Elisha prayed that Gehazi's eyes would be open (2 Kin. 6:17). Do not become anxious because when you become anxious you cannot hear Me.'"

Randy said later, "A peace came into my heart, and I knew God was going to move. I even told my team: 'Get ready! We are going on an apostolic mission to Canada.'"[21]

Summary

Through the various spokespersons God had revealed a time: 1994. Through prophecy a specific place had been revealed: Toronto, Canada. God had identified some sovereign vessels: a John and Carol from Canada who would be used to bring a great wave of refreshing to the Vineyard. Finally, the Lord said it would go out to touch the entire world. Never before in the history of Canada has anything like this ever happened. Even after more than two and a half years the meetings continued. Throughout year two about one thousand people attended every weeknight to be blessed, and about two thousand attended on weekends. Virtually every nation in the world with a Christian witness has been affected directly or indirectly by this one specific visitation. God had said it would happen before it ever happened, so that we would not doubt that this is His *kairos* time — His season to bless the earth.

In the days of Evan Roberts, the *Quaker Journal* of 1905 wrote, "What we have seen in Wales is Quakerism rebaptized!...The iron in our Welsh valleys is hot. Let us strike before it cools."[23] We would do well to take a lesson from our Welsh brethren. A realization that this is our *kairos* time should dramatically alter our attitude, faith and activities. Just one word is sufficient: "More!"

3

HOW TO PREPARE FOR A VISITATION OF THE HOLY SPIRIT

Men of Issachar, who understood the times and knew
what Israel should do.
1 Chronicles 12:32

The billboard in front of our church read, "Day 17 of 21 days of Prayer and Fasting — Praying for Revival in Kelowna." Perched thirty feet up in the air on a platform made of scaffolding, I was praying, "Lord, bring revival." I also was mighty hungry! After our initial experience in Toronto, the questions resonating in our souls were, Why not here? Why not now? So as a church we had decided to enter into twenty-one days of prayer and fasting with meetings every night and prayer meetings every weekday at noon in order to pray and preach for revival. Fasting was optional, yet many people chose to do the full twenty-one days, and scores chose alternate fasts of plain rice and vegetables (no soy sauce!), or fasting two meals a day or fasting for one solid week. Adventuresome teenagers even fasted television.

Before I continue, I'd better mention that the idea for the scaffolding came from an example of an ancient desert holy man, Symeon the Stylite, who lived from A.D. 390-459. When he reached the age of Christ at his crucifixion, Symeon began to practice dying daily as he turned away from everything earthly and built himself a pillar which he mounted in devotion unto God. The pillar, which was situated forty miles east of the famous church of Antioch, eventually reached a height of thirty-six cubits (fifty-four feet or eighteen meters). The top platform was only three feet in diameter with a railing around it. The extraordinary saint would sleep standing up or kneeling. Because he was such an oddity, he began to attract onlookers and curiosity seekers. The crowds who braved the two-day journey into the wilderness to see this unusual "wonder of the world" became Symeon's congregation. From this pulpit, hung between heaven and earth, he preached twice a day to the masses gathered below. The celebrated Theodoret, an eyewitness of the life of the saint, reports that Symeon was accredited with converting thousands of onlookers to Christianity, settling controversies, counseling kings and emperors, healing the sick and even producing miracles in the name of Jesus. Devoted disciples would send up all his worldly needs by way of a rope ladder. Symeon lived out his days in this manner, devoting himself daily to God for the entire remaining thirty-six years of his life until his death in 459. So revered did he become that at his death, his body was carried in a solemn procession to the metropolitan church of Antioch. His example initiated a movement of pillar saints who dotted the ancient Middle East and Mesopotamia for the next seven hundred years.[1]

Although I had no notions of such extreme asceticism in mind, Symeon's example had grabbed my attention. As one sympathizer from Symeon's day had maintained, "God often uses very striking means to arouse the negligent, as the history of the prophets shows."[2] I thought maybe this could be a means of provoking others to "come and see" and thereby challenge them to pray and labor toward a visitation of God. We did have lofty goals, and a great deal of spiritual good was secured, not the least being our prayer goal of fifty salvations in twenty-one days. Many in our fellowship testified to a time of renewed commitment unlike any they had ever known. The prayer was good, and the meetings were great. Yet for all that, we did not move into months of nonstop continuous meetings. We did experience pronounced church renewal but we did not see revival. Why?

People everywhere are now asking similar questions. They are asking how they may position themselves and their churches to welcome a visitation of God. Jesus indicted Israel because it did not recognize the season of God's divine visitation. Obviously today's believers do not want to be guilty of the same oversight. Literally hundreds of thousands of Christians are asking, "Why Toronto? Why now? Why not here?" As a participant and one intimately acquainted with the Toronto and Vineyard segment of this worldwide visitation, I have observed common denominators from the Toronto Blessing that have ramifications for every Christian and church as they seek to welcome a visitation of God.

It is worthy of mentioning that since the time of the Welsh and Azusa Street revivals there has been no visitation that could be classified as a worldwide move of the Holy Spirit. The Azusa Street Revival ran for three years of night and day protracted meetings. When coupled with evangelistic movements such as the Christian Missionary Alliance and others, they ushered in the largest missionary and church growth expansion the world has ever seen. Today's Pentecostal/charismatic Christians comprise the largest body of Protestant Christians in the world.

On July 20, 1996, the Toronto Airport Christian Fellowship had completed two and a half years of protracted meetings. They had prayed and ministered to more than one million Christians from most nations of the world. Most of the representatives from other countries who were sent to receive the Toronto Blessing have taken it back and spread it throughout their own countries. Thus, in this way, the present outpouring has already distinguished itself as the biggest wave of refreshing since that last worldwide outpouring in the first decade of the twentieth century.

The Principle of God's *Kairos* Time

As demonstrated in the previous chapter, God does nothing without revealing His plan to His servants, the prophets (see Amos 3:7). The great renewal of 1994 had been prophesied by many reputable prophetic speakers during the last decade. The Toronto Blessing and worldwide renewal was on God's prophetic timetable. You can be safe in assuming that the spread of this renewal is also God's will for your church. However you must seek God further and ask Him what the specifics of His *kairos* timetable looks like for you. Not every church will be a Toronto, Melbourne or Sunderland. The question is, What is God doing with your fellowship and maybe more specifically, in you right now?

The Principle of Prayer — Yours or Another's

A second common denominator I have observed is prayer. Whether it's your own or another's, somewhere in the process prayer has to go up to heaven. The debate has raged for years: Does God initiate revival, or do righteous servants press in, storm heaven and earth, and say, "I will not let go until You bless me." The late J. Edwin Orr said, "Whenever God is ready to do something new with His people, He always sets them to praying."[3] As a modern authority on revival, Orr believed the early twentieth-century worldwide evangelical awakening did not begin with the Welsh Revival of 1904-05.

> Rather its sources were in the springs of little prayer meetings which seemed to arise spontaneously all over the world, combining into the streams of expectation which became a river of blessing in which the Welsh Revival became the greatest cataract.[4]

Such a view need not render God dependent on our prayers. Instead, He is the initiator provoking us to pray for His holy intentions. The main thesis of David Bryant's new book, *The Hope at Hand*, is that we are on the verge of worldwide revival, and prayer has and is, playing a huge part in it.[5]

What began as a "voice in the wilderness" calling the church to united prayer has now become a roar louder than Niagara Falls. In an article titled "Talking to God," *Newsweek* magazine wrote: "This week, if you believe at all in opinion surveys, more of us will pray than will go to work, exercise or have sexual relations."[6] Bryant cites David Barrett, the leading demographer of the worldwide Christian movement as saying:

> 1. Worldwide there are about 170 million Christians who are committed to praying every day for spiritual awakening and world evangelization. 2. Of these, twenty million believe that praying in that direction is their primary calling in ministry within the body of Christ (what we might otherwise call 'prayer warriors'). 3. Worldwide there are at least ten million prayer groups that have as a major focus every time they meet to pray to seek God for a coming world revival. And finally, 4. Worldwide there are an estimated thirteen hundred prayer mobilization networks that are seeking to stir up the church to accelerated prayer for world revival and mission.[7]

Examples of this are everywhere. They may be bold and visible like 1994's A Day to Change the World, which saw the greatest coordination of prayer in history as an estimated thirty million Christians prayed in unison over a twenty-four-hour period for the closure of the Great Commission by the year 2000; or the Meet Me at the Flagpole prayer movement that draws about two million high school students in America to gather around their school's flagpoles on a day in September to intercede for revival on their campuses; or the Promise Keepers men's movement, which desires to bring one million men together in Washington D.C. in 1997 to, among other things, pray for national revival.[8]

On the other hand, it may be more personal and church-based as in the case of Mike Bickle. When Mike received the prophetic word described in the previous chapter, he began to pray. He prayed privately three to five hours a day, seven days a week for more than seven years. He mobilized his entire church to pray, with prayer meetings happening three times a day, six days a week. They prayed thousands of hours for revival.

John and Carol Arnott, frustrated with ministering in their own power for so many years, decided in 1993 to give their mornings to God. They spent most of their mornings that year in personal prayer and devotion to the Lord. This has been true for so many believers all over the world. Like an irresistible siren's call, the Holy Spirit is wooing worshippers everywhere to prayer.

This great prayer momentum came into laser beam, pinpoint focus on January 21, 1993, at the National Consultation on United Prayer.

> Three hundred leaders, from 166 denominations and Christian ministries, representing nearly half of the Protestant churches in America, from thirty-five states came to convene on a common goal: to inaugurate a new era of spiritual leadership in the body of Christ, calling the church to united prayer for revival until revival comes.[9]

As the multitudes have engaged in prayer, the "golden bowls of incense, which are the prayers of the saints," have also begun to fill (Rev. 5:8). Exactly one year minus a day after the new era of united prayer was inaugurated, the golden bowls over Toronto tipped and the Toronto Blessing began. The bowls tipped over in London and soon the flow of the Spirit was flooding "God's Britain." In August 1994 Sunderland, England, began protracted meetings which continue even to the time of this writing. On January 1, 1995, the bowls tipped in Melbourne, Florida, when Randy Clark helped kick off what has now become known as the Melbourne Renewal. Originally scheduled to last two weeks, the Tabernacle Church continued holding meetings six days a week for eight months. They had more than eighty-five thousand people attending their meetings and have seen more than a thousand conversions and rededications, which is phenomenal for any church. The bowls tipped over Brownsville Assembly in Pensacola, Florida, on Father's Day 1995. One year later more than twenty thousand people had received Jesus Christ in one local church. The nightly meetings continue up to the time of this writing.

The bowls continued to tip as the Pasadena Vineyard church launched a twenty-one-day prayer and fasting vigil to pray for revival in Pasadena, California, and greater Los Angeles. The meetings continue five nights a week with daily prayer meetings every weekday. The bowls are tipping. Many nations are recording the flow of the Spirit and salvations in anticipation of full-scale revival. The application is obvious — to prepare to welcome a visitation of the Holy Spirit, begin to pray, and pray some more.

The Principle of Blessing What the Father Is Doing

It takes faith to let God be God — and faith to bless what He *is* doing, not what we *want* to see Him do. We have all been in churches where leaders have said, "Oooohhhh to have God come down." Then when God does come down they try to change or stop it. Why? Because it looks different than the way they thought it should look or different than the way we believe God would do things. But we must remember: God is God, and we're not. He is the Lion of Judah, and as C. S. Lewis said, "He is not a tame lion." G. Campbell Morgan, who was an eyewitness of the Welsh Revival, writes, "In what seemed supreme confusion, one was conscious of splendid order."[10] In a sermon at his own Westminster Chapel, Morgan affirmed, "It was a meeting characterized by a perpetual series of interruptions and disorderliness; it was a meeting characterized by a great continuity and an absolute order."[11] However we want to describe it, God wants His church back.

A major theme of John Wimber's teaching over the years has been to "bless what you see the Father doing," which is based on John 5:19. John Arnott told me, "The first time the Lord moved like this years ago, I got scared. I watched all these people, and it looked so messy that it scared me. I felt that I had to start to direct this thing, I had to organize it. What I actually did as I started to control the thing, is that I controlled Jesus right out the door. What I resulted in doing was eventually shutting the move down." Arnott is fond of saying that later his prayer came to be, "Oh God, if You ever do it again, I'll take my hands off."

Sometimes during a meeting Arnott will look at the congregation and say, "Don't you just love this? Oh I love it!" He has often lamented how pastors ask him why the move of the Holy Spirit seems to last for only a short while and then gradually fizzle out. He said to me, "You know at first I used to sympathize with them. Then I began to realize that so many of them wanted the Holy Spirit but they didn't want His package. Wesley, they have to love it!"

As mentioned earlier, many leaders are already saying we are in the fastest worldwide move of refreshing since the turn of the century.[12] Can we have eyes of faith to believe and then act like it? Leonard Ravenhill, the soldier saint, said at the end of his life, "Now I can go in peace. I've seen it. It's come." He prayed all his saved life for revival. In the last year of his life on earth, he saw the beginnings of the outpouring of the Spirit in 1994 — and he blessed it. Can you? If so, it will produce a change in attitude and action. This is one of the principles I've observed in welcoming a visitation of the Holy Spirit.

The Principle of Faith: Believe for More of What God Is Doing

Some years ago we were trying to write a new vision statement for our church. We locked ourselves in a ski cabin and tried to achieve the perfect vision statement. Imagine eight strong male bulls all shouting out at once what they thought the vision of the church was to be. Every word was an issue. Nothing seemed to fit. Like Goldilocks' porridge, every word was either too hot or too cold; nothing was just right. Finally someone turned to me and said, "OK then, what's your vision statement?" I thought for a moment and said, "If I were really to say what I believe is my vision statement, I would have to say that it is...'more!'"

They all looked at me, "More? More what?"

"More everything! Whatever it is, just 'more'!" I answered.

"More," someone mused, "More. I like that. Now that's just right." In a moment we had our vision statement, and it has been the same ever since: "More!"

The theology of the apostle James is that the outcome of faith is works or action. What we truly believe will affect what we actually do. Therefore, if we really believe God is visiting the earth in a special way today, why would we stop it? Why wouldn't we go for it all the way? Why should we settle for the alternative of sitting at home to watch a movie?

When the prophet Elisha was prophesying victory for the king of Israel, he told the king to take his arrows and strike the ground. So the king struck the ground three times and stopped. The Bible says, "The man of God was angry with him and said, 'You should have struck the ground five or six times; then you would have defeated Aram and completely destroyed it. But now you will defeat it only three times'" (2 Kin. 13:19). We do not know the correlation between hitting the ground and achieving victory, but the parallel is obvious. Whatever you were going to do, do more! Better to err on the side of striking the ground too many times than not enough. As we look at the testimonies throughout the earth, it seems God smiles on that type of faith.

In the early days of the Toronto Blessing I remember meeting in the back of an old Greek restaurant called the Olympic Flame. This little restaurant had become our war room where strategies and plans were drawn up for the next day's meetings. John Arnott would look at the rest of us bantering back and forth and ask seriously, "What if this thing (the renewal) continues for a month or even three months? What will we do?" John would press Randy hard, "Randy, are you prepared and ready to keep coming here over the next month...over the next three months?" We all thought it was wishful thinking. Yet John had the expectancy and the faith to take it higher and longer than anyone else.

As Toronto reached its one-year mark of straight meetings, Mike Bickle joked, "This is either conference purgatory or conference heaven, depending on how you like meetings." To John and Carol Arnott it was heaven.

The Principle of Proclamation: Good News Is for Sharing

Good news is for sharing. When a couple has its first baby, no one can keep them quiet. "Our baby has been born! Come and see!" Information that something is happening has been key in both the spreading of renewal and revivals. In Orr's description of the fast-spreading Welsh Revival, he points out the role that the printed page played in alerting the nation that "no ordinary gathering was taking place." This only seemed to spread the news and the fire. Before a blaze has time to go out, more people must come to be ignited.

John and Carol were so excited about their love for Jesus that they were unabashed in their telling of the work of God. Good news is for sharing, and they told everybody who would listen. God is here! Come and join the party! Come and drink! Come and be a part!

At first most people were cynical. Ho hum, yeah sure, we've heard that before. But then they began to come. For every ten who were called, maybe one would come. Then they would be powerfully touched and phone their friends. The news continued to go out. First from their own fellowship and then from other local churches and their friends. Within weeks, the word was out: Something is happening in Toronto.

When Martin Buhlman, senior pastor at Basileia Bern Vineyard in Switzerland, first heard the news, he thought, "Yeah, sure, I've heard this before." As reports kept coming he grew envious and agitated, "Why do I have to go all the way across the world to be touched by God? Can't God just do it here?" Finally Martin and his team flew to Toronto. In his own words Martin describes his visit.

> The meeting began very unspectacularly. I had already started asking myself why I had traveled so far, seeing that nothing unusual was happening. After the sermon, all were invited to come forward who wanted to be touched anew by the Holy Spirit. I thought, *You'll make those last ten meters after coming five thousand miles,* and went forward. When I caught John Arnott's eye I was pulled to the ground. I stood up again, only to fall again after a couple of minutes. This continued five or six times. Later Carol Arnott came to me and prayed for me as I lay on the floor. The presence of the Holy Spirit flowed like power streams through my body. I was electrified. Today I think that on that first evening I felt the power of the Holy Spirit. God wanted to say. "Not your power, but Mine! Not your will, but Mine! Not your ideas, but Mine!" During the following evenings I experienced different phenomena. Every evening something else. One evening I had to laugh. Without any reason, I screamed with laughter. Another evening I experienced the peace of God very deeply.
>
> Another evening I experienced strong empowerment (authorization). When John Arnott asked me to share...I couldn't speak.[14]

Martin returned home on Sunday, May 8, 1994, for an afternoon meeting at the French Church in Bern. On the train he was overcome by fear that God wouldn't pour out His Spirit in the meeting. "I had inner struggles, *Is this all from God? What will happen? How will we cope?*" He further testifies as to what happened.

> At the beginning of the meeting, after a time of worship, I shared a bit about our journey. Following that, I had the impulse to ask all those forward for personal prayer who had experienced a physical change while we were sharing. I

expected about ten people to come forward, instead more than one hundred came for ministry. I thought they must have misunderstood me, so I repeated the call. No one returned to their seats. After I had invited the Holy Spirit to come, those who had traveled with us started to pray.

The Holy Spirit fell in a powerful way! Dozens lay on the floor, many trembled, cried, laughed, shook or screamed. I couldn't preach anymore. We couldn't collect the offering. The more we prayed for the people, the stronger the manifestations were. Around 7 P.M., the children returned from their own program and a few asked for prayer. My own nine-year-old son received prayer, fell and lay about a quarter of an hour completely calm on the church floor. When he got up, I asked him what he had experienced. "I was in heaven, and I saw Jesus and the Holy Spirit! It was bright there, and I want to return." The experience was something natural for him. For me it was a shock! Since that Sunday, the Holy Spirit hasn't stopped moving like this among us.

John Arnott later told us that the Lord had spoken to him, saying, "Don't worry about the criticism or being respectful because I'm going to take this thing and I'm going to throw it in the face of the world." The next thing John knew, the media was visiting and splashing the news over the world — all over television, all over the newspapers and all over the magazines. Before long the whole world had heard about it. Why? Because good news is for sharing. As the world heard that God was visiting, people first came in trickles. Then they came by the busloads, then by airplane loads. In time the nations were coming. Good news is for sharing. Don't keep a visitation quiet. When God shows up, tell everybody. Sharing the good news affects the next principle.

The Principle of Fresh Wood

The final major observation in facilitating a move of the Holy Spirit is "fresh wood." In Kelowna where I live, our geographical area is very susceptible to forest fires. It is crucial for the logging industry that firefighters know how to put out a fire. Firefighters are trained to go ahead of the blaze and burn the upcoming area in a controlled way so when the fire reaches that area there is no more fresh wood. A fire needs fresh wood in order to keep going. In the same way, the fire of the Spirit must be touching new people every day in order to keep blazing. One of the initial prophetic words given to the Toronto church was, "You get to keep what you give away."

In the first few months the meetings burned hot with the fire of God. Within a few weeks more locations had to be opened up to handle the crowds from cities all around Toronto. But shortly they found out they could not sustain all these meetings because the interested people could only keep up the pace for a few weeks. After some weeks all the satellite locations shut down and merged with the Toronto meetings. Then, even the Airport meetings began to lag. They questioned whether the rocket could stay airborne. Yet because the publicity had gone out so far, new people kept coming from even further and further distances. Just as North America was waning, England took up the torch. Again the good news was being shared. Soon hundreds and then thousands of pilgrims were coming from the United Kingdom. By the summer of 1994 many more inquisitive seekers began to book their summer holidays to come to the renewal meetings. They lined up for church two and three hours early to get a chair in the small warehouse. More and more fresh wood was piled on the fire and the blaze continued to burn.

In October 1994 the first Catch the Fire conference was held and publicized worldwide. Since then thousands of renewal seekers have come from Asia, Africa and Europe. Within a year, a thousand a night were attending the extended meetings. At just the right time — exactly one year — the Toronto church secured a larger facility. The space kept up to the demand, and the rest is history.

There is a message in all of this for the rest of us. The same principles apply to everyone. We can all position ourselves to welcome a visitation in our own lives and the lives of our churches. But there is a danger in measuring our success or so-called blessing of God by whether or not we can sustain indefinite protracted meetings like Toronto. In our case we fasted and prayed for twenty-one days straight, yet we did not have months and months of meetings. In reality we met for thirty-five nights. The problem in our town was that its population was only one hundred thousand. After approximately eighteen nights, everybody that wanted to come had come and was already saturated. Literally hundreds and hundreds of people were touched. But once they were renewed, they were renewed. For the time being our town was done. The fire now had to be directed to walking the renewal out into the community (see section 4). It didn't mean that we were not dedicated enough, or had not sought God enough. We did what was in our own hand to do. Renewal is for everyone, but what it looks like in each individual life and church will be slightly different according to your own context and what God wants you to do. Let the fire burn according to the fresh wood you have, and after that cook a good meal on the hot coals.

58

4

WHAT HAPPENS WHEN
THE HOLY SPIRIT VISITS?

*The Spirit of the Lord will come upon you in power,
and you will prophesy with them; and you will be changed
into a different person.
1 Samuel 10:6*

Stacey stood on one side and another prophetic minister stood on the other. John and Carol Arnott were in the middle. With arms flailing and head shaking back and forth, Stacey prophesied, "You are a father. You are a father, John Arnott. The Lord is going to come and bless you!"

John and Carol didn't know what to make of their first experience with ecstatic utterance. They wanted more of God, but was this what more looked like? John and Carol, like many other pastors, desired to see God move powerfully in their congregation. But what if Jesus did show up? Would His people recognize Him? Would they be prepared for what He might do in their midst?

O Jerusalem, Jerusalem, you who kill the prophets and stone those sent to you, how often I have longed to gather your children together, as a hen gathers her chicks under her wings, but you were not willing! Look, your house is left to you desolate. I tell you, you will not see me again until you say, "Blessed is he who comes in the name of the Lord" (Luke 13:34-35).

Recognizing Jesus

God visited Jerusalem many times. His voice came through His prophets. His glory came in *kairos* events such as the building of the temples. Finally, He came through His Son, Jesus Christ, who boldly stated: "Anyone who has seen me has seen the Father" (John 14:9). However, after only three years of ministry, Jesus was forced to declare that enemies would raze the holy city of Jerusalem to the ground as judgment for not recognizing Him, even when He came in the flesh (see Luke 19:41-44). The prophesied judgement happened in A.D. 70 when Jerusalem was destroyed by the Roman invader, Titus. Sadly, God judged the nation of Israel because they rejected His visitation. The astounding fact is that though God Himself came, He went unrecognized by His own people. They didn't recognize Him in the stable because He didn't come as a king. They didn't recognize Him as a boy because "What good thing could come out of Nazareth?" They didn't recognize Him when He came to Jerusalem because they didn't understand the mysteries foretold by the prophets. Instead, they stoned the prophets! Then, after killing them, they built memorials to them (see Luke 11:47-48). Throughout the Bible and church history we can read of God's special visits. Interestingly enough, what we discover is that God generally comes in ways that people don't expect. The lesson to be learned is this: We must be open to a visitation of God, no matter how it happens and no matter what it looks like.

Jesus Desires to Visit His Church

If it is true that every generation is in danger of missing a visitation of the Holy Spirit, legitimate questions would be, "What exactly are we looking for, and what might it look like?" For answers to these questions we must search the Scriptures to find examples of the Holy Spirit coming upon the people of God.

The first issue one faces is that there is no static, concrete description of what the Holy Spirit might do in a visitation. Biblical descriptions of His activities are wide and varied. As one example, He came upon Saul at one time and upon Elisha at another time, causing both men to prophesy (see 1 Sam. 10:10; 2 Kin. 3:14-19). At another time He caused Samson to have superhuman strength (Judg. 15:14-16). David attributed his ability to kill both a lion and bear in hand-to-hand combat to God's deliverance and empowering (see 1 Sam. 17:34-37). Miracles, grace, wisdom, superhuman strength, prophetic ability, boldness and even artistic ability are some of His manifestations (see Ex. 28:3; 31:3). In fact, the impact of a visitation encompasses virtually everything a child of God does. So how are we to know what it is we are looking for?

Three Aspects of a Visitation

Over the years I have had opportunity to interact with hundreds of pastors and leaders who have been touched by renewal. In addition to this interaction, I have personally observed and ministered in the midst of this present move of the Holy Spirit in Canada, America, Mexico, Europe and Asia. In every place I have been, at least three primary works have been prevalent. These include times of refreshing, the impartation of gifts (especially revelatory gifts) and empowerment from the Spirit for works of service.

In both the Old and New Testaments we observe the same three works. The premier example is the early church when the Holy Spirit was poured out on them at Pentecost and afterward. The people of God were refreshed, imparted with gifts of the Holy Spirit and empowered for witness.

1. Times of refreshment

After the initial outpouring of the Holy Spirit, many wonders and signs were taking place by the hands of the disciples. One such healing miracle was recorded in Acts 3 and happened to the man born lame. This incredible miracle produced a wide open door to preach the gospel. Peter's message to Israel was, "Repent, then, and turn to God, so that your sins may be wiped out, that times of refreshing may come from the Lord" (Acts 3:19). Both Jesus and the prophets dealt with Israel as God's people. Now Peter declares that times of refreshing are ready to accompany the visitation of God.

The metaphor of rain is used to describe the work of God. The Holy Spirit comes to refresh His people. Dry, discouraged and burnt-out individuals receive water from the Lord. I cannot count the number of pastors who have told me they were ready to quit and throw in the ministry towel just prior to getting refreshing in this renewal. Some even testified to receiving deliverance from deep depression and even thoughts of suicide. Randy Clark himself testified to burnout, depression and what he describes as being on the verge of a nervous breakdown. In 1993 God refreshed Randy with His touch at a Rodney Howard-Browne meeting. Amazingly, in the following two years, Randy has been used to spread this refreshing to literally hundreds of cities and churches.

2. Impartation of gifts

The most noticeable work at Pentecost was the impartation of the gifts of the Holy Spirit. The disciples spoke in other languages as the Spirit gave them utterance, declaring the wonderful works of God (see Acts 2:11). When Peter stood up to explain the event, he labels it "the last days outpouring" which had been prophesied by Joel. Quoting Joel he declared:

> No, this is what was spoken by the prophet Joel:
> "In the last days, God says, I will pour out my Spirit on all people. Your sons and daughters will prophesy, your young men will see visions, your old men will dream dreams. Even on my servants, both men and women, I will pour out my Spirit in those days, and they will prophesy.
> I will show wonders in the heaven above and signs on the earth below, blood and fire and billows of smoke. The sun will be turned to darkness and the moon to blood before the coming of the great and glorious day of the Lord.
> And everyone who calls on the name of the Lord will be saved" (Acts 2:16-21).

For years I believed that Pentecost was about tongues. But in this present renewal I have noticed many people receiving an impartation for prophecy, or at least some form of revelatory ability. I went back again to study Acts 2. I was surprised to realize that prophecy, or revelation was the main evidence that the Spirit was poured out on all people. The interpretation that Peter assigns to the miracle of tongues is prophecy, visions, dreams and prophecy (vv. 17-18). Four different times a type of revelatory impartation is described as being the result of a spiritual outpouring of the last days. The age, sex or maturity of the receivers was of no concern; they were young and old, male and female, new believers, old believers.

The dispensational line of interpretation might say that Pentecost was a one-time event, not to be repeated. While we agree that Pentecost will not be repeated, does that also mean the properties of a visitation of the Holy Spirit are also to stop with the apostles? I think not. Verses 18 and 20 have not yet had their fulfillment and therefore must still be applicable to us. Furthermore, the outpouring which historically occurred at Pentecost was to continue all the way to "the great and glorious day of the Lord" when all who call on His name will be saved (vv. 20-21). Prophecy existed pre-Pentecost and will continue until "the perfect comes" (1 Cor. 13:10). Almost all modern scholarship is now unanimous in acknowledging that the perfect — or *teleios*, meaning "having attained the end or purpose" — is the second coming. Contrary to the opinions of some, Pentecost did not result in a limiting of the work of the Spirit, but in the increasing of it. After Pentecost, revelation became a gift for the whole church (see 1 Cor. 14:1,5,24,31,39).

Today every person who receives Christ also receives His Spirit. The Spirit has the ability to impart and release revelation. As Paul taught many years later, the imparting and releasing of gifts is the manifestation of the Spirit.

> Now to each one the manifestation of the Spirit is given for the common good. To one there is given through the Spirit the message of wisdom, to another the message of knowledge by means of the same Spirit, to another faith by the same Spirit, to another gifts of healing by that one Spirit, to another miraculous powers, to another prophecy, to another distinguishing between spirits, to another speaking in different kinds of tongues, and to still another the interpretation of tongues. All these are the work of one and the same Spirit, and he gives them to each one, just as he determines (1 Cor. 12:7-11).

"Now to each one the manifestation [*phanerosis*] of the Spirit is given..." or as the Good News Bible renders it: "The Spirit's presence is shown in some way in each person" (1 Cor. 12:7). It appears that each of the nine gifts are a "showing of the Spirit" in the gathered church context. Paul is not saying that every single person will receive a manifestation gift, but that to each person to whom one of these gifts is distributed, the Spirit's presence is being made known (continuous present tense). In times of visitation, these nine gifts are especially intensified as they give tangible expressions of the presence or manifestation of the Spirit.

Where the Spirit of God comes, charismatic activity is normal. For example, Paul declares that, "When you come together, everyone has a hymn, or a word of instruction, a revelation, a tongue or an interpretation. All of these must be done for the strengthening of the church" (1 Cor. 14:26). Note the term revelation. When the presence of the Spirit is shown, supernatural revelation is a normal manifestation. It can come through prophecy, words of knowledge and wisdom, mental pictures and so on. In hundreds of different settings, we have personally witnessed and have heard reports of every gift listed in 1 Corinthians 12:8-10.

Spiritual gifts are called *pneumatikon* (literally "spirituals") derived from the Greek, *pneuma,* meaning "spirit" (1 Cor. 12:1; 14;1.) Generally speaking, it refers to an expression or embodiment of the Spirit. Spiritual gifts are also called *charismaton* (literally "gifts") derived from the Greek *charis* "grace" (1 Cor. 12:4; 1 Tim. 4:4; Rom. 12:6), which is where we get the word *charismatic*. This is a more specific term referring to an expression or embodiment of grace. There is a connection between spiritual gifts and God's grace. In fact, we could say that all Christians who experience the Spirit are "charismatics."

These manifestations of grace release the gifts, ministries and effects of God's Spirit when He is present in a gathered assembly. The grace, service and effects of the Spirit are His power and presence applied through nine "manifestation gifts." In a visitation of God the following gifts intensify in the church, precisely because they "show the Spirit."

3. Empowerment from the Spirit

A third and common work of the Holy Spirit during a time of visitation is that of empowering for witness and service. Jesus Himself said, "But you will receive power when the Holy Spirit comes on you; and you will be my witnesses in Jerusalem, and in all Judea and Samaria, and to the ends of the earth" (Acts 1:8). This is exactly what happened. The Holy Spirit fell and all the disciples became witnesses. Thousands began to be saved. After the disciples were persecuted by religious leaders who could not recognize their day of visitation, they went back to the other believers and began to pray. Luke writes, "After they prayed, the place where they were meeting was shaken. And they were all filled with the Holy Spirit and *spoke the word of God boldly"* (Acts 4:31, emphasis added). Boldness for witness is a common fruit of special visits of God's grace.

Stories by the thousands abound today of ordinary Christians getting prayed for at renewal services and then, like Saul, "becoming changed into another man"! (1 Sam. 10:6). Ron Allen (chapter 1), who initially went to Toronto to criticize but was actually empowered with a new unction for evangelism, said to me six months later with eyes flashing, "Wesley, I've led more people to Christ in these last six months than in the last fifteen years." Believe it or not, he had seen more than six hundred people make professions of faith through the ministry of their church immediately following his Toronto encounter. Everywhere I go, the story is the same. People touched by the renewal have experienced a refreshing in their walk with the Lord, or they've received an impartation of revelation or some other gift. Some have received a new boldness and power for service. This is the fruit and the expectation of a visitation of the Holy Spirit.

Our Story: New Life Fellowship Baptist Church

As a living example of these three primary works, I want to share the story of how our Baptist church experienced a visitation for which we were totally unprepared. The exciting thing is that our story is becoming the story of others. Like the wind, the Holy Spirit is blowing on thousands of churches who now share a similar testimony of their own visitation of the Holy Spirit. To be sure, we were hungry for more and were calling out to God as best as we knew how. However, we were really not ready for our own fulfillment of Malachi 3:1: "Then suddenly the Lord you are seeking will come to his temple."

In 1985 David Ruis and I were fresh out of Baptist Bible college. With our wives, we decided to plant a Baptist church in Canada with a very conservative Baptist denomination. In May 1986 New Life Fellowship Baptist Church was born. Although the church grew rapidly, after eighteen months of ministry we felt eager but empty. We believed there was more, and we wanted it! That was the spring of 1987. It was during this time that David Ruis attended a Holy Spirit conference led by John Wimber in Anaheim. During the ministry time Wimber invited pastors forward for prayer and infilling of the Holy Spirit. Then with great authority he invited the Holy Spirit to come.

As he said, "Holy Spirit, come," David began to shake violently, and in an instant was powerfully filled with the Spirit and began speaking in tongues. He was overcome and fell to the floor shaking, jerking, bouncing and shouting. He was seized so violently that he literally bounced onto the stage. His glasses were askew, and his nose was pushed into the carpet. Wimber looked down and smiled blithely. David managed to sputter, "I can't get up. I'm stuck." This three-hour encounter overcame David with power, wonder, weeping and an overwhelming love for God. Needless to say, nothing like this had happened in his Baptist life before! Unbeknownst to us, John Wimber had called a sympathetic pastor in our area, saying, "Watch out for this guy. I've hardly ever seen someone get hit by God that hard. Something is up!"

A Christmas party we'll never forget

And something was up. Upon his return home, we met with David to find out how the conference had gone. We could hardly believe his story. "What do you mean you shook? You actually bounced up onto the stage? You mean you couldn't stop it?" I was really excited. I said, "Do you think you could do it now?" David didn't know what he could or could not do. We were "green" but full of anticipation.

From that time on, strange things began to happen. Seeking advice and encouragement, we visited eighty-three-year-old Bob Birch, who was considered to be a charismatic father in Canada. After hearing our story he laid hands on us and prayed that God would do in David what He wanted to accomplish in Kelowna. Again David erupted in violent shaking as he jackhammered around the study for more than ten minutes. Later, Stacey, while praying in a small meeting, had the same phenomena come upon her. We were Baptists, and we were wondering, "What is going on?"

Then an event happened that changed our lives. It was during a Christmas house party in 1987. Our leadership team was celebrating the goodness and blessing of God. At about ten o'clock Roger Helland suggested we spend a short time in prayer. Because it was a Christmas party we all felt more like playing than praying, but at his insistence we capitulated. We were neither prepared for, nor could we ever conceive of, what would happen next.

Within minutes, a powerful presence of God swept into the room. Without warning, David Ruis began to shake. Suddenly, one of the elders was struck down into the couch as if hit on the top of his head by a huge fist and was then rocketed up into the center of the room. He was shaking and speaking in tongues. Next, to my astonishment, my own dear wife was catapulted off the couch into the center of the room where she began to shake violently and speak in tongues. They were seized as if by some unseen hand and shaken like puppets on a string. As they were bouncing in the center of the room, another burst of power hit them simultaneously. At the exact same moment all three of them jolted. Their legs flew out from under them, and they were thrown onto the floor on their backs — all the while speaking in tongues.

Fear and awe gripped us. We wept, repented, rebuked any possible false spirits, plead the blood of Jesus and cried out for protection. Although we knew this was God, we had never experienced anything even remotely like this before!

Next, the three who had been shaking began to prophesy and speak the very secrets of our hearts to the group. They spoke words of exhortation, praise and rebuke. The sense of dread and awe that filled the room was indescribable. We were in shock. Sometimes we laughed and sometimes wept. Sometimes we were on our faces with our noses pressed into the carpet. Steve Clarke, an elder from an exclusive Brethren background said, "Surely I would have run out the door, but 'they' were between it and me!" The encounter lasted over four hours. We were spiritually wrung out by the time it ended. When we staggered out at 2:30 A.M. I knew we would never be the same.

One month later a similar event took place with the same group, only this time with more and varied phenomena. Prophetic motions began to be enacted by those prophesying. Blowing, chopping and waving motions were directed to the individuals receiving prayer. Sometimes the one prophesying would be bent over backwards. During an exhortation or rebuke, the speaker would sometimes laugh, clap his hands or sharply kick. At this second outpouring we received a word from the Lord to record the prophetic messages so that we would not exaggerate what had been said, and we would have them for future evaluation. Since then we have been recording prophecies faithfully for nine years.

Eventually about fifty individuals were anointed in a similar way; they were seized by the power of God and physically shaken while they spoke forth prophecy. Later, they testified that they were overwhelmed and engulfed by a sweetness of God. During and after these impartations, almost all testified to sensing a direct communication with God through the Spirit via revelation in the form of visions, pictures and words.

Some began to move strongly in the gift of the discerning of spirits and became competent in naming the spirits and praying them out. Some could even see spirits with their physical eyes and could describe their appearances. Others could see angels who directed them in words of knowledge and healing. Still others had anointings of great spiritual power and open visions. Almost all of these manifestations came in the context of worship and prayer.

Ongoing renewal (and even a mini-revival) resulted, with the demonized being released, the lost saved, and the noncommitted convicted to a deeper walk with the Lord.

However, we had a problem: Our group was almost entirely conservative evangelicals. There were only a few Pentecostals and charismatics in our midst. This outpouring had happened in house meetings and only on small numbers of people who had witnessed these things. We had a sense that if this got out to the church, people would panic. We didn't know what to do, so we went into hiding. We continued to have these incredible meetings where the Lord would move, and the people would shake and prophesy, but still we never brought it into the church. Then one night the Lord spoke prophetically and rebuked us saying, "Take Me out of the back room!" He prescribed a church-wide "repentance night" to do it.

God visits church on a Friday night

In obedience, one Sunday in February we explained to the entire church what had been happening and announced that the Lord had called for a church-wide repentance night. The designated night saw the church packed. As we began to worship, the Lord moved mightily upon a number of people with prophecy and shaking. For the first time it was public, right in front of the church. Some people screamed and cried out, wailing on the carpet for hours. Several were impacted and went down under the power of the Spirit. Some repented and at least two people got saved on the spot. Others were alarmed. At one point David Ruis shouted out in a thundering voice while under the unction of prophecy, "On your face!" The entire room was filled with a holy fear. Later many testified to that night being the beginning of personal revival in their own lives.

As this visitation of the Holy Spirit became public, it spread like a summer brush fire. We began having prayer meetings virtually every night throughout the week and special ministry nights on weekends. The Lord so absolutely captivated us that prayer was all we wanted to do. For the next six months we were involved in prayer and refreshing meetings an average of twenty-five to forty hours a week. Every time we would worship and pray, powerful displays of God's presence would take place.

Repentance spread out to everyone who came. A number of Bible college students were so convicted that they went to their dean and college president and confessed serious sins. Though some had to be expelled from school for a time, they counted it worthwhile since they were "coming clean before God." More people were saved. We held a series of baptism services with as many as seventy-five baptisms in a day. In our church we experienced a revival.

The heat of this visitation lasted about eight months and thrust our church into a two-year period of blessing. We experienced ongoing ministry in prophecy, word of knowledge, healing, physical manifestations, deliverance and repentance. The church grew to more than one thousand adults and children in the next few years. Eventually the move waned due to the manifold circumstances of church life. It was the newfound vision received at Toronto that again opened our eyes of faith to strive for yet another move of the Spirit. Faithful to His word, the Lord revisited us with an even broader outpouring in March 1994, during the dedication weekend of our new facilities. Since then on average scarcely a week goes by without our teams going out to carry and transfer this renewal to other locations throughout the world. And, true to form, whoever catches the fire also begins to give it away.

Steve Clarke's testimony

Recently I was reunited with one of our former elders who had been with us during our initial outpouring of the Spirit. Steve and his family had since gone out to serve in missions and other things. As we reminisced about all that had happened to us and reflected on our spiritual pilgrimage, he said to me, "You know, I probably would never have accepted any of this stuff, but it was the credibility of the people. I knew these people. They weren't flakes. They were deeply spiritual and thinking people. They were my friends. I just praise God that He allowed me to observe it first in people I knew before I had to see and hear about it secondhand."

Unfortunately many of you who read this book will not have the advantage of knowing the many godly people who make up this testimony. Yet God in His grace spread out this work of His Spirit to thousands of churches of every denomination in every country. Find someone near you who has been touched. Interview them. Ask them how God refreshed, imparted or recently empowered them to serve Him. Ask them how God visited them and changed their lives when they welcomed Him.

SECTION TWO

The Bible and a
Visitation of the Holy Spirit

5

INTERPRETING
THE BIBLE

*And my speech and my preaching was not with enticing
words of man's wisdom, but in demonstration
of the Spirit and of power.*
1 Corinthians 2:4, KJV

As mentioned earlier, in the spring of 1994 our church entered into twenty-one days of prayer and fasting as well as thirty-five consecutive nights of meetings in order to seek the Lord for more — more outpouring and more salvations. One evening, after an exceptionally good time of worship, one of our prophetic persons indicated that she had a corporate word for the body. After giving a brief explanation of the strong type of shaking manifestation that often accompanies these words, I invited the individual to speak. The Holy Spirit moved strongly and suddenly she began to shake and speak in a loud voice as an oracle. It was a profound word concerning the Lord's pleasure that we had sought Him so earnestly; He was delighted in being found by His people. Many people were visibly moved and a number began to weep. Most thought that it was a high point in the service, and we carried on.

Approximately a week later I received a letter from a young man who had attended that service. He identified himself as a serious and committed Christian of three years and said that prior to his conversion he had been exposed to things in the New Age movement. He was concerned about what he had witnessed at our church. He wrote:

> First I must say that I was edified and refreshed during the worship time, but I must also say that I seriously question some things that took place that night. During the service you told the congregation that a lady at the front had a word from the Lord. You gently said that we should not be concerned by the shaking that was going to take place, as it had been happening for years. As this lady spoke inspired words from the Lord she burst into *violent* convulsions. I just stared in complete *shock*. Her head shook back and forth so quickly that I couldn't even see her facial features. I wondered if my eyes were playing tricks on me as her face manifested in a total blur. Dear Wesley, manifestations in the New Testament like this only took place when Jesus was confronted with demonic spirits.
>
> I urge you to stop people from falsely prophesying in the name of the Lord, "Do not believe every spirit, but test the spirits to see whether they are from God" (1 John 4:1).
>
> In closing, I met you personally at a young adult service at our church early last year. One of the ladies on your worship team prophesied over me, and I felt it was very accurate and was very edified by her words. At the close of that service you prayed with me, and I was most encouraged.

I was not offended by this letter because I knew that years before I held similar views and may have reacted in the same way. But what this letter does illustrate is the great distance that exists between opposite views of the same events. Of course this is nothing new. A brief survey of church history will reveal that godly men have always differed, both on what the Bible says — exegesis — and what the Bible means — interpretation. Attitudes also have been heated concerning how we are to apply what the Bible says and means: application. The process for interpreting and applying the Scripture is called hermeneutics. Without a common hermeneutical process the end product is usually worlds apart. It is like studying an animal from opposite ends: same body, different conclusions.

The young man's interpretations of both the data he was observing and what he believed Scripture taught led him to assume that these activities were demonic. His previous exposure to the New Age movement led him to associate this phenomena with New Age. As a result, the feelings of fear, concern and disbelief are the natural follow-through of a person with a presupposition that a practice is demonic, anti-scriptural and New Age.

But what if I told that young man that the lady he was so concerned about was my wife, a Christian of eighteen years, with seminary training, and the mother of five small children? And that the ladies who prayed for him a year before also prophesy consistently in the same manner that alarmed him so much that evening at our church. Suppose I told him that we also have witnessed demonic manifestations, but after thousands of hours of observation we know the difference between what is demonic and what is not. Suppose I also said that we have studied the Bible thoroughly as it relates to this whole subject and after eight years of working experience we are more convinced than ever that this is God. Suppose I said that we have prayed, tested the spirits, measured the fruit and monitored the character. Suppose we did all that and, after all these years, we still love God, and we still have not been taken over or led into gross doctrinal error by demonic delusion. And despite the controversy, thousands of recognized leaders in the corporate body of Christ do testify to these activities as being inspired by God. Then what?

The impasse is really a question of hermeneutics. As the largest Protestant body in the Christian world, the Pentecostal/charismatic Third Wave, and now more recently, renewalist, persuasions continue to grow, there will be an even greater need for Holy Spirit hermeneutics. An adequate study of this subject could easily fill a book all on its own, which is not my purpose.[1] However, a brief mention of issues that have a bearing on the hermeneutical process and its application of this position sets a context for this entire section. I hope this will help to answer such questions as those posed by the concerned young man and others.

Hermeneutics: Principles of Biblical Interpretation

Hermeneutics is the study of the principles for interpreting and applying the Scripture. It is both a science and an art that involves exegesis and exposition. Our hermeneutic is affected by our worldview and experience as we study Scripture to formulate our understanding, theology and practice. Ultimately exegesis should shape our worldview, theology and practice. Unfortunately this is not always the case.

Exegesis

According to Gordon Fee, exegesis seeks to "draw out" the meaning of the biblical text with what the biblical author wrote (content) and why he wrote it (context). The task of exegesis is to determine the meaning that the writers intended to communicate and what their readers were expected to understand. Exposition seeks to teach or preach that meaning and apply its significance to the contemporary audience.[2]

The exegetical task involves the biblical languages with their grammar, syntax, figures of speech and idioms; the types of literature (genre); the historical and cultural background; the purpose, life setting, occasion and structure of a biblical book or passage; and the overall theological message of the author. If we seek to apply Scripture to or give a biblical defense for a visitation of God, we must engage in proper exegesis. If we want to determine whether the gifts, miracles and manifestations of the Holy Spirit that often accompany a visitation are for today, we also require proper exegesis.

This entire process makes it possible to determine what is normative and for today against what is not normative and relegated to cultural contexts or history.[3] It would be nice to say that this process is as easy as reading the text and determining its straightforward meaning and application. While we all wish it would be that easy, it isn't. The primary problem is that most everyone has poor spiritual eyesight and wears thick interpretive glasses. The one lens is called worldview and the other, experience. The subtle danger is that those who think they don't wear or need any glasses are those most likely to be wearing the thickest ones. They are like the proverbial absent-minded professor who is frantically looking everywhere for his glasses, not realizing they are already on his head. In this next section I will deal mainly with the way worldview and experience tend to influence the exegetical process.

Worldview

The other day a friend asked me a question, "A man was found dead in a cabin on the side of a mountain. How did he die?"

I said, "What do you mean, 'How did he die?' How am I supposed to know?"

He grinned and said, "Just think about it, and you will figure it out."

I suggested one theory and then another. Every wrong answer seemed to tickle my friend more. Finally I said, "OK smarty, how did he die?"

He shrugged and said, "The man died in a plane crash."

I stared at him.

"You know, the 'cabin' of the plane."

I groaned, but his riddle did what it was supposed to do: sneak up on our line of defense, which is called worldview, and catch us in our blind spot.

Our worldview is our set of assumptions, values and commitments (conscious and unconscious) about our perceptions of reality and the basic makeup of our world. It is the grid through which we process and explain reality as we perceive and experience it. Worldview is especially relevant when it comes to interpreting scripture as it relates to the Holy Spirit and manifestations of revival. (See John Wimber's book, *Power Evangelism,* for an entire chapter on this subject.[4])

We see what we are taught to see by our culture. Perception influences our interpretations and responses. We perceive selectively, accept things that confirm what we have been taught and believe what we think is possible. For example, as the young man saw a person shake during the worship time, his natural, learned perception would ordinarily lead him to conclude that this person was experiencing a convulsion, epileptic seizure, electrical shock or demonic manifestation. We are not taught and usually do not believe that people can shake violently as a genuine reaction to God's presence. Therefore, our worldview can unconsciously screen out God as even being a possible option.

When we read Scripture, we approach it with our basic assumptions about what we think the text means or what we expect it to say. We interpret the Bible according to our presuppositions, prejudices, experiences and theologies. We carry a "pre-understanding" shaped by what we believe about reality — that is, our worldview. Our worldview affects our ability to welcome a visitation of Holy Spirit and to explain the supernatural phenomena and manifestations that often accompany one. Our worldview governs what we think the Bible says and what we believe is possible. As Jack Deere says, "There is no such thing as purely biblical objectivity."[5]

Anti-Supernatural Western Worldview

So what is a Western worldview, and where does it come from? The dominant Western worldview has evolved out of the so-called Christian nations of Western Europe and North America. As a product of eighteenth-century Enlightenment philosophy, deism infected Western theology and culture. Deism reduces God to "the first cause." Like a clockmaker, God created and wound up His world clock leaving it to run on its own natural momentum without His further intervention. You could say we become endarkened by the enlightenment.

The natural outflow of deism was materialism and rationalism. Materialism assumes that only matter is real. Truth is arrived at through empirical means of measuring with the senses, testing, observing probabilities, and developing laws and principles. Rationalism seeks a rational explanation for all of life. Something is true if it makes sense. Inherent within this system is a fixation with control and knowledge. If we can control or at least know a cause, we can probably determine the outcome — become sort of masters of our own destinies. This is seen in our approach to medicine, economics, science, socialization and so on.

For better or worse, the Western worldview did lend itself to becoming the lead culture. That is, it became the main culture to be measured against. Language, money, education, technology, medicine, military might and even pop culture. While benefiting certain disciplines, the Western worldview has had disastrous effects on others, especially in areas of faith and the supernatural. Ironically the worldview of the so-called Christian West came into conflict with not only the worldviews of other cultures but even the worldview of the Bible itself. Harry Blamires, a former student of C. S. Lewis, believed that the dominant element of the modern Western worldview is secularism. "To think secularly is to think within a frame of reference bounded by the limits of our life on earth: it is to keep one's calculations rooted in this worldly criteria."[6]

The long-standing theory in conservative church circles is that miracles, exorcisms and healings happen out on the mission field because they need it more out there than we need it here. The truth is, however, the mission fields are now sending their missionaries here because of the lack of penetration of the gospel in our own Western countries. The supernatural has nothing to do with who needs it more (if anything the West needs it more because we are so gospel-hardened). It has everything to do with who believes that the supernatural is a normal part of their worldview.

In the non-Western world, the view of reality includes a working relationship with the supernatural world. Not surprisingly, they can operate in it. To a great extent the Western church does not and has not believed for or cultivated a ministry of the supernatural.[7] In the West we have an anti-supernatural worldview that lacks the "believing is seeing" kind of faith. Thus, it leads largely to a powerless Christian practice (see Matt. 13:58).

Many Western Christians are practicing deists due to their cessationist, anti-supernatural worldview which affects their beliefs about Scripture. (Cessationism is the belief that gifts of the Spirit ceased with the early apostolic church or the completion of the canon.)

Experience

Added to worldview is life experience. That is, that which has happened to me within my view of the world. As mentioned earlier, some of the effects that the Western worldview has had on our view of Christianity have been good but others have not. Like the proverbial "frog in the kettle," the unsuspecting Western church sat in the kettle of deism, and before long our experience was the same temperature as that which we were sitting in. In this case, not boiling hot, but lukewarm and void of the supernatural. Now our experience verifies what we knew all along: God doesn't do these things today.

The worldview of the Western church has produced a church that is controlled, predictable and ordered. Intellect and cognitive, objective truths are given an overemphasis as compared to emotion, the heart and actually doing the works rather than merely believing the words. We evangelize with logic and apologetics, using the four spiritual laws. Not that I am against logic and laws, but the Bible modeled a different form. When we read the book of Acts we find that virtually every occasion of salvation and church growth came directly or indirectly as a result of some tangible display of the supernatural power of God. Yet the Western church has adopted an anti-supernatural bias. We have gotten so smart in figuring out why people are sick that we have become reluctant to pray for healing. Why pray for a cold, measles or a broken limb? We know why we are sick and broken, and we'll just have to wait until we get better. Yet the fact remains that the same causes were present for the ailments of biblical days, and this did not stop the early church from praying for healing. Our experience has clouded our faith, thus impeding our ability to pray for healing.

Society Cries Out for More

In recent decades, as societies reacted to the straitjacket of a materialistic and rationalistic framework, they adopted a type of pluralism. They know the "heart has reasons that reason knows not of." With respect to habits of the heart, morality, religion and experience, Western man has

78

become pluralistic and relative. "I'm OK; you're OK." "It's only wrong if you think it's wrong." The new measurement has become subjective relativity — "my experience." On the one hand, Western society is secular and materialistic; on the other hand, it has swung back to quench the thirst of the parched inner man with experience. Hence, there has been a contradictory rise in our secular Western cultures of pseudo-Eastern religions, a belief in horoscopes, the stars, self-help philosophies and the all-embracing New Age movement.

In order to battle this anti-biblical trend, many conservative or Christian fundamentalists have reacted to this new extreme by clinging even tighter to materialistic and rationalistic assumptions. Only in their case, it is not secular materialism and secular rationalism, but a strange new concoction that I will call religious materialism and religious rationalism.

In this reactive new posture, the Bible is supposedly adhered to as "the absolute." Yet it is a Bible dispensationally edited and neutered of all that is supernaturally applicable to the present. The supernatural is relegated to some far distant past or millennial future, and the thought of God's supernatural activity being for the here and now is just too much for their materialistic and rationalistic religion to accept. Even godly experiences are viewed with suspicion, and subjective feelings are discarded as irrelevant. Some even go so far as to pit experience against the Bible as though experience were against reason. Two outspoken advocates of this are John MacArthur of Grace Community Church and Hank Hanegraaff of the Christian Research Institute.

Summary

The Western worldview, unlike the biblical worldview, assumes and interprets reality through a scientific, rational and natural grid. Therefore, Westerners find it difficult to recognize the ministry of the Spirit, demons, miracles, gifts and manifestations of the Spirit.[8] We have a Bible that teaches signs and wonders but a worldview or belief system that is rationalistic and materialistic. Because we have not believed for more, we have not stretched for more. Thus, experience continues to back up our worldview. This belief system has been foisted upon the exegetical process. The Bible tells us to pray for the sick and they will be healed (see Luke 10:9; 1 Cor. 12:9; James 5:14-15). We say, "It can't possibly mean that." Instead of the Bible meaning what it says and exegesis formulating our worldview and experience, our worldview influences our exegesis. This is a serious aberration.

In the next chapters, I challenge you to expand your worldview with me and allow God to do again what He has done before. Ask God to reveal to you, by means of His Holy Spirit and His Word, what a biblical worldview looks like. Determine not to let your limited experience be the measure of all things. The goal of Bible study is to interpret and apply the text in such a way that our experience most closely resembles the normal and normative experiences of those in the Bible. We believe that the authors of the Bible meant for the miracles and gifts of the Holy Spirit to be normal and normative. As you read the accounts of Bible experiences, I invite you to set aside a twentieth-century Western worldview and imagine for a moment that the things you will read are the way things ought to be.

The most exciting aspect of the story of the young man who wrote me that letter is that we met again. One year later our church was doing an open-air meeting in a park that sits on the busiest corner of our city. Our worship band was singing out praises to God, and I had just finished giving an evangelistic message when a young man came up to me. He asked, "Do you know who I am?"

I smiled and said, "No."

He introduced himself and then said shyly, "I'm the one who sent you that letter a year ago." He said that he and his wife had been attending our church for more than six months and had been very encouraged as a result. He apologized for writing the letter

I told him not to worry about it and introduced him to Stacey, the one who had so alarmed him the year before.

"Some of this stuff still seems a bit 'out there' to me," he admitted, "but I now know that your wife is a godly woman."

I said, "Some of your concerns may even be ours as well." We embraced, and I walked away a happy man. Our church is still his home.

6

Manifestations
of the Holy Spirit

Now there are varieties of gifts, but the same Spirit...
And there are varieties of effects, but the same God
who works all things in all persons.
2 Corinthians 12:4,6, NAS

God is above and beyond the natural world. So it is not surprising that whenever He touches this natural world, there is a supernatural reaction. Over the years, through thousands of hours of firsthand experience, I have observed the emotional, physical and spiritual responses of people to the powerful touch of God. However, as the church it is our responsibility to observe, test, discern and verify whether or not these reactions are truly from God. The acid tests are Scripture, the verifiable experiences of the persons we have interviewed and the fruit. Wherever we go, we find that people in many other locations are also experiencing the same phenomena. None of us who work in renewal claim to have absolute answers for each manifestation, nor do we claim that we can proof text them all from Scripture. But I do believe we can affirm that these phenomena and their subsequent fruit are biblical and do not contradict the intent of

Scripture.

I did not arrive at my conviction that the present-day phenomena is of the Holy Spirit from a position sympathetic to charismatic practices. As a child I grew up a third-generation Plymouth Brethren and was taught that all these sign gifts had ceased with the apostles. I believed that after the church had received the full canon of Scripture there was no need for these signs and their related experiences. After my conversion at age eighteen, I went on to become an itinerate speaker within the Plymouth Brethren movement and actively denounced all such gifts as the work of the devil. I had bought into the theory that these modern-day miraculous signs were leading up to a great end-time delusion, which would set the scene for "the man of sin to deceive many" (2 Thess. 2:3,10). I even transcribed by hand John MacArthur's (a leading cessationist teacher) sermons on "the charismatics" (before his book was out) and then fervently preached these anti-charismatic sermons whenever I could find an audience. I felt it my duty to protect everyone from these wrong charismatic teachings.

Eventually both Stacey and I enrolled in a degree program at a very conservative Baptist Bible college and seminary in Vancouver, British Columbia. It was there that I met David Ruis, and we began to encounter bona fide Holy Spirit works for which we just did not have answers. We were all forced by the evidence and further biblical study to entirely alter the positions we had previously espoused. Upon graduation we decided to plant a Baptist church that had an openness to the work of the Holy Spirit and the practice of spiritual gifts. Although we had seen little, we had come to believe that God had more in store. Shortly after planting this new church, the Holy Spirit came — in power.

Since then I have personally logged more than six thousand man hours observing phenomena such as falling, shaking, jerking, crying, laughing, prophecy and ecstatic utterance as well as many other strange and often misunderstood manifestations. As I said, I did not grow up in this, nor did I make it up. I had to be convinced of these things against my will. Since then I have been personally associated for many years with dedicated Christians who have exhibited strange but wonderful manifestations of the Holy Spirit. I have observed their chaste and godly Christian lives and found them to be some of the most spiritual people I know. We have judged or tested these so-called works of the Spirit by the strictest of methods: the Bible, personal testimonies, history, tape recordings, transcriptions, personal observations and experiences. After all these years we affirm this to be a genuine visitation of the Holy Spirit. We measure it, see it fulfilled and enjoy the fruit.

As a Baptist church we had the problem of pastoring hundreds of Baptist adults as they tested everything, held onto the good and learned not to treat prophecies with contempt (see 1 Thess. 5:20-21). Because the move of God described earlier was so dramatic and fraught with problems, many people could not handle or understand it. I was thrust into the role of becoming a sort of apologist in order to provide pastoral care for the concerned but seeking members of our congregation. The main concerns that people often asked about centered around the topic of manifestations and phenomena of the Holy Spirit. Often people ask, "Why all the manifestations and shaking? What is their purpose? Are they biblical? How do you know it's not the devil? Should I accept this stuff?" The following chapters in this section contain the basis of the biblical thought that grew in response to actual struggles concerning the phenomenal workings of the Holy Spirit.

Are Physical, Emotional and Spiritual Manifestations Biblical?

Before answering these questions we need to stop and ask, "What is actually happening?" When the Holy Spirit first fell on the gentiles the early church also had to wrestle through these types of issues. Many in the church did not think it was right. Peter's procedure was to walk the listeners through the story of what actually happened. History unfolded as follows:

> While Peter was still speaking these words, the Holy Spirit came on all who heard the message. The circumcised believers who had come with Peter were astonished that the gift of the Holy Spirit had been poured out even on the Gentiles. For they heard them speaking in tongues and praising God (Acts 10:44-46).

Peter did not even get finished with his message when God began affirming the response in the hearts of the gentiles with signs following. Upon returning back to Jerusalem, Peter was criticized by the rest of the circumcised believers for even going to the house of the uncircumcised. Peter's defense was simply to relay what actually had happened — that he had followed the leading of God and preached the gospel.

As I began to speak, the Holy Spirit came on them as he had come on us at the beginning...So if God gave them the same gift as he gave us, who believed in the Lord Jesus Christ, who was I to think that I could oppose God? (Acts 11:15-17).

In other words, this wasn't my idea. I did not initiate it; I couldn't stop it. In fact, "Who was I to think that I could oppose God?" Thankfully, the Jews in the early church had enough spiritual discernment to accept a God-initiated experience over and above their faulty hermeneutic of misinterpreted Scripture. The fact that the gentile believers had received the same gift as the Jewish brethren was enough. "When they heard this, they had no further objections and praised God, saying, 'So then, God has even granted the Gentiles repentance unto life'" (Acts 11:18).

So What Is Happening?

The following manifestations are those which we have personally witnessed countless times. We realize that not every manifestation has a particular or exact meaning. Yet after years of experience, we have observed common patterns and reactions to the Spirit of God. While many or most of these manifestations can at times have a natural or even demonic explanation, we most emphatically affirm that the Holy Spirit of God is the prime initiator of most of what we have seen in the arena of phenomena. People do not conjure up this stuff via mental suggestion, imitation or practice. Much of what we have seen cannot be accomplished through natural means. God will seize or act upon people in a similar way He acted upon Saul and the prophets in 1 Samuel 10 and 19. At other times, what we see is people reacting to the presence or moving of the Spirit, much in the same way one would react to putting a finger in an electric socket! In our church we have seen all of the following physical, emotional and spiritual manifestations.[1]

Physical Manifestations

Trembling and shaking

People will shake like a rag doll or tremble like a windblown leaf. A Bible concordance study of the terms *shake*, *shook* or *tremble* will reveal that God can cause these reactions (see Dan. 10:1-11).

Bouncing and jumping; lifted up or moved around

Some people will uncontrollably bounce up and down like a ball or jump up and down like a jackhammer. Others will be moved up or around like a puppet (see Ezek. 2:2; 3:24).

Blowing

Some people will blow and puff strongly. This action is a natural type or a picture of what is happening in the supernatural. Often this manifestation indicates that God is blowing a blessing or spiritual covering upon someone. Jesus breathed on the disciples and said to them "receive the Holy Spirit" (John 20:22).

Heat or tingling in the body

A warmth or electrical tingling will settle in a part of the body such as the hands or lips. Sometimes this seems to indicate a release of certain gifts or ministries (evangelism, healing and so on), or it's merely a sign of the presence of the Spirit. John Wesley recounts that at his conversion he felt his heart "strangely warmed." As a result of this feeling of heat, some people also perspire more intensely while the Spirit ministers to them.

Being pinned to the floor and not able to get up

We have seen and have received many reports from people who were so overwhelmed by the weight of God's presence that they had no strength to get up. Some have been pinned to the floor as if they were glued there for up to several hours (see Dan. 10:9,17).

Dancing in the Spirit

David danced with all his might before the Lord (2 Sam. 6:14). We have seen God fill people so their bodies and legs were orchestrated by the Holy Spirit to dance uncontrollably unto the Lord.

Being struck down or falling in the Spirit

We have seen hundreds of people fall down under the power of the Spirit as if hit by a tidal wave (see John 18:6; Acts 9:4; Rev. 1:17).

Twirling or running

Some twirl, spin, run, hop and do little jigs in ways that are so unusual (and amusing) that a supernatural explanation is the only valid explanation.

Bent over forward or backward

In the early days, several of our people would be bent backward or forward like an acrobat with double joints. We came to see this in our context as God calling for a time of praise for things He has already accomplished before we ask Him to do more.

Chopping and flailing

Some people will chop and flail at the air like karate fighters. Most often this manifestation indicates spiritual warfare or the breaking of bondages.

Eyelids fluttering

This is one of the most common manifestations and indicates a special presence of the Spirit. At times this manifestation becomes more intense as the person may physically have their eyes moved rapidly in their sockets — as if a restructuring or imparting was happening to their eyes. In later interviews they testified to increased prophetic sight.

"Giving birth"

Some people travail just as though they were actually giving birth or experiencing the pangs of childbirth. The pains and cramps are real and often produce groaning. Some feel that God is birthing new gifts and anointings through them (see Rom. 8:22-27; Is. 42:14; Gal. 4:19).

Emotional Manifestations

Laughing

Uncontrollable laughing that may last for hours is a phenomenon not dependent on personality type or receptivity. Even the most stoic or non-demonstrative persons have been hit with this. It is the physical demonstration of the joy of the Lord (see Ps. 126:1-3). This is the same as in earlier "laughing revivals."

Crying and weeping

When God goes deep into the emotional area, the most common response is for people to cry, weep, wail or travail. During these seasons of blessing, the gift of repentance is easily found (Rom. 2:4). Sometimes weeping is the result of a deep inner healing, and at other times it is the burden of intercession (Heb. 5:7). Occasionally this profuse weeping will suddenly turn to laughter.

Floods of joy, euphoria, boldness or worship

Any mixture of joy, euphoria, boldness, abandonment, worship and devotion might sometimes overcome a person with enthusiasm. It is interesting to note that the English word *enthusiasm* comes from a Greek word which means literally "to be filled with God."

Prophetic mime

Prophetic mime is a type of manifestation whereby the Lord enacts the word He is wanting to impart. For instance, a person will act out many characteristics, but the emphasis is on action rather than speaking. It is similar to what Agabus did in Acts 21:10 — a person acts out the message as well as speaks it.

Spiritual Manifestations

"Weighted down" by the *kavodth* (glory) of God

There are times when the presence of the Lord is so heavy that people can physically feel the weight and thickness. People will buckle under or gradually bend their heads and torsos until they fall to the floor. The Hebrew term for the glory of God is *kavodth*. It literally means the "weight or heaviness" of God. Both Ezekiel and Daniel experienced this (see 2 Chr. 5:14).

Overcome in the Spirit

This phenomenon, common for years in Pentecostal and charismatic circles, is also a normal occurrence during the present visitation. During a meeting, people are overcome by the Spirit; sometimes no one is even praying for them. We have had people tell us they were overcome by the Spirit in private at home! A lightness with feelings of euphoria and joy settle upon people. They then fall over and rest in the Spirit. Healings, fillings, visions, releases, deliverances and empowerings are common results.

Inability to talk

There are times when a speaker loses the physical ability or mental concentration to speak. This has happened to many pastors and leaders when attempting to testify or preach. The mind and spirit are still conscious and alive, but they cannot talk, sometimes for moments, hours or even days (see Ezek. 3:26; Dan. 10:15; Luke 1:22).

"Drunk in the Spirit"

Getting "drunk in the Spirit" has become a common experience. A person loses physical ability to walk and talk clearly, as if they were inebriated. The difference between alcohol and the Spirit is that with the Spirit, one's mind, emotions, spirit and will are fully alive and in touch with God and the real world. Floods of joy, laughter, devotion, worship, words of knowledge and prophecy will frequently accompany this manifestation. Some people have been drunk in the Spirit for days! "These men are not drunk as you suppose" but full of the Holy Spirit! (see Acts 2:15).

Trances

While under the power of the Spirit, some people experience a trance-like state where they are "locked into God." They will have intimate encounters that are indescribable. Both Peter and Paul experienced trances (see Acts 10:10; 11:5; 22:17).

Tongues

This gift of the Spirit is no longer predominant only in Pentecostal and charismatic circles. Those who are a part of Baptist, Presbyterian, Alliance, Mennonite, Lutheran and other Christian denominations regularly experience tongues as the Spirit gives them utterance (see Acts 2; 10; 1 Cor. 12-14).

Prophetic unctions, dreams, visions, mental pictures, words of knowledge

We regularly hear of and see prophecies, dreams, visions, mental pictures and revelatory gifts poured out on men, women, children, youth and the elderly. Joel 2 and Acts 2 are finding common fulfillment in today's visitation. Sometimes, though not always, shaking accompanies certain forms of prophecy and revelatory gifts.

Journeys

While fallen under the power of the Spirit, people are sometimes taken on a spiritual journey. It might be out of body or in the Spirit or in a dream-like state. People we have interviewed told us of fantastic journeys where God took them to heaven, a place in their past, another geographical location or an unknown place. Ezekiel, Paul and Philip reported similar experiences (Ezek. 3; Acts 8:39-40; 2 Cor. 12).

Epicenters of power

One of the most fascinating manifestations we have seen is when, in a room or sanctuary, there are certain pockets or epicenters of divine activity. When people walk into that specific area or get near it, they experience an intensity of the Spirit's work. They may laugh, shake, fall over, prophesy, receive a healing or experience any of the above manifestations. A similar example occurred with Saul, a group of prophets and Saul's men (1 Sam. 10; 19).

Another expression of this epicenter is what we call transference of power. There are occasions when power will go out from someone to empower, release, heal or stir up the gifts in others. This is similar to Jesus' experience when He said, "Someone touched me; I know that power has gone out from me" (Luke 8:46).

What Was Prayed For?

After a brief overview of the phenomena that have been happening, it is important to note that hardly any of it was actually prayed for. We did not pray, "Shake, shake," or "Fall, fall." We prayed, "Come, Holy Spirit." and this was the result. Like Peter reporting on the unexpected outpouring at the house of Cornelius, we throw up our hands and say, "Like, this wasn't my idea! I was just telling them about Jesus and suddenly, wham!"

It is also important to note that early advocates of this renewal were not trying to import phenomena but rather pray for a deeper, more Spirit-filled life. We prayed the biblical prayer of asking God to come and fill us with more of His Holy Spirit in power (see Eph. 5:18). Since then, most teaching on phenomena has been in a proactive manner to help provide pastoring for those wondering, "What is happening to us?" Today multitudes of Christians are scampering back to their Bibles to see what has happened "to them." If anything, complaints should be directed to God in the form of inquiring prayers, rather than accusing Christians to whom this has happened. It has been my observation that most of them did not ask for this, neither did they necessarily understand it initially.

7

A BIBLICAL BASIS FOR
PRESENT-DAY PHENOMENA

*But in your hearts set apart Christ as Lord. Always be
prepared to give an answer* [apologia] *to everyone
who asks you to give the reason for the hope that you have.
But do this with gentleness and respect.*
1 Peter 3:15

So what about the question, "Where do we find it in the Bible?" To
some extent, this can be a loaded question as it may be asking one of
two things: 1) Can we verify these experiences with exact Bible
verses or proof texts?; or 2) Are these experiences in accordance with
clear biblical principles? The Bible contains primary texts that tell us what
to believe and what to do — these are normative teachings. They are specific Bible verses that verify certain experiences and beliefs. However, the
Bible also contains secondary texts that describe experiences and events
that are biblical and may be repeatable but are not necessarily normative.
We do not preach these texts as something you must do to be a good
Christian. Furthermore, these secondary texts may legitimize similar activities without having an exact duplication of a given situation.

Proof Texts or Biblical Principles

For instance, Ezekiel was picked up by what looked like a hand and in visions was taken to Jerusalem (Ezek. 8:3). Numerous times he would fall face down like a dead man, only to be physically raised up or even taken away by the Spirit (Ezek. 1:28; 2:2; 3:12-14,23-24 and others). Ezekiel was even gripped by an involuntary sticking of his tongue to the roof of his mouth that rendered him unable to speak (Ezek. 3:26). While we know that these happenings were biblical and therefore may be repeatable, they are definitely not normative. Nor are they to be preached as the main and plain commandments of Scripture. Yet as descriptive passages they would probably legitimize other similar phenomena that may not look exactly like Ezekiel's experience but would still be biblical.

"Pet" Hermeneutics

Everyone interprets Scripture through a grid. How people read and understand the Bible is due largely to their denominational bias or previous training. For instance, consider Paul's comment concerning head coverings: "And every woman who prays or prophesies with her head uncovered dishonors her head — it is just as though her head were shaved" (1 Cor. 11:5). The meaning and application of this verse is interpreted very differently depending upon which group teaches it: Plymouth Brethren, Baptists or Pentecostals.

My earlier denomination, Plymouth Brethren, loved this verse. It virtually became a distinctive. They interpreted the text literally to mean "head covered," but when they came to the part on prophecy, they used a dispensational framework to render that aspect obsolete. My Pentecostal friends, on the other hand, said no to head coverings because a covering is no longer culturally relevant as a sign of authority or submission. But they gave a hearty "Amen!" to the fact that women should prophesy because that was their distinctive. Same scripture but exactly the opposite in meaning and application. Then I met the Baptists, and I found they didn't believe in head covering or prophesying. What's worse, at the end of the day, all of them believed they were right. The error is produced by faulty hermeneutical practices which support pet doctrines.

We all believe and do things that agree with Scripture but are not commanded in the New Testament. Yet we can know by inference and principle if something is biblical. For example, some people believe that we should not worship God with musical instruments since they cannot find where instruments were used in New Testament worship. In the sixteenth century, some reformers actually destroyed church organs because they were not found in the Bible. True, it is likely that no instrumental music was used in the church from the first century until the arrival of the organ. But to apply Scripture in this way is faulty. The Bible tells us to praise God with all our being and to glorify God in all that we say and do. Furthermore, the book of Psalms is replete with examples of several musical instruments used in worship. Where did the form of worship come from in the early church if not from the Old Testament? The worship orders given centuries earlier were never rescinded. Therefore, if musical instruments honored God in the Old Testament they can honor Him now.

The Bible Does Not Require Us to Proof Text Everything

John Wimber says, "God is bigger than His book." That was news to me, because I was told that He was contained in His book. I was told all that could be known of God is in the Bible. The Jews of Jesus' day had the same problem. Jesus said, "You diligently study the Scriptures because you think that by them you possess eternal life. These are the Scriptures that 'testify about me, yet you refuse to come to me to have life'" (John 5:39-40). The Scriptures are about Him, but they are not Him. It is possible to be so fixed on what we think the Word is saying and meaning that we limit who God is and what He can do.

The Bible does not require us to proof text everything. The Book says about itself: "Jesus did many other things as well. If every one of them were written down, I suppose that even the whole world would not have room for the books that would be written" (John 21:25). The whole world could not contain the experiences, reports and expansions of His teaching. Does that mean these unwritten things would be different or contradictory? No! They would just be an expansion of that which already exists. If Jesus did things that are not recorded, then there is truth that is not contained in the Bible. So to answer the question, "Are manifestations biblical?" The answer is yes. Are there specific proof texts for them? The answer is maybe yes and maybe no, depending on how one interprets the text. The following discussion will present biblical principles to verify spiritual, physical and emotional manifestations caused by the Holy Spirit.

Tongues

Tongues did not have a previous proof text, yet they were of God. An example of this is seen in the Acts 2 account of the empowering and filling of the Holy Spirit. There was an inordinate amount of phenomena and manifestations present when the Holy Spirit fell at Pentecost. One could never have anticipated all those things: the rushing wind, tongues of fire, spiritual overwhelming, the miracle of speaking in actual languages the speakers didn't previously know and appearing as though drunk in the Spirit. All of these things took place and not one of them was recorded in the Joel 2 passage.

When pressed for an explanation of the phenomena, Peter appealed to Scripture. Under the inspiration of the Holy Spirit, he says, "This is that!" Yet when we check Joel 2, we find none of "this." Peter never defended any of the phenomena. He just stated, "This is it!" Direct proof texting was not needed to show that it was biblical. And yes, a Bible-only Pharisee could say, "What do you mean this is that which was spoken by the prophet Joel? I don't read anything about a rushing wind, a manifestation of fire and this tongues thing. Where do you read that in the Bible? Even Jesus never spoke of this!" Technically the Pharisee would have been right, but spiritually he would have been dead wrong — again.

So while Joel spoke of a future empowerment, the Holy Spirit of Scripture did not deem it necessary to describe and include all that would happen. Apart from the extra privilege that Peter enjoyed in speaking inspired revelation, no believer at that time could have looked to Old Testament Scripture to verify one of the greatest biblical experiences of all church history: Pentecost! While Peter could not produce proof texts, it did not mean the event was not biblical.

What is not disallowed, is allowed.

The great theologian St. Augustine once said, "Love God and do whatever you want." What he meant was, if you really love God, you will want what He wants, and you will "obey the law without the law" (Rom. 2:14). If we apply that principle to Bible interpretation, we could say, "What is not disallowed, is allowed." That is, if something is not disallowed or contradictory to Scripture, it probably is allowed. The disciples once protested to Jesus that they "saw a man driving out demons in your name and we told him to stop, because he was not one of us." The man wasn't one of us; he didn't do it like us; it just shouldn't be allowed. "Do not stop him," Jesus said. "No one who does a miracle in my name can in the next moment say anything bad about me, for whoever is not against us is for us" (Mark 9:38-40). Jesus said that fruit produced in His name, which is not inherently against Him, is for Him!

Not adding to

It is my profound belief that we are denied the place of progressive revelation, which would be classified as going beyond or adding to the Scripture. As Bible-believing Christians it is outside of our scriptural position to add to the Bible. We do not believe in elevating teachings, creeds or dogmas to have the same binding authority of Scripture. Whatever movements in the past that have done this have inevitably come into conflict with Scripture.[1] It is outside of our arena to build authoritative "new" teachings based on personal revelation or experience. As the Vineyard position states: "No doctrine should be based on a prophetic interpretation of a particular manifestation."[2]

Not violating the main and plain

While we subscribe in the strongest of terms to this, we still believe in the biblical gift of prophecy and the existence of experiences and phenomena that are not explicitly described in the Bible. Despite the charges of some, this position is not contradictory to the above belief of *sola scriptura* — the Scripture alone. It is obvious that many things happened which weren't recorded in the Scriptures. The apostle John stated as much when he finished his gospel. The Corinthian church had prophecy in action without it needing to be the word *of* God. Paul taught that prophecies, or words that come *from* God, need not be elevated to the word *of* God as seen by the biblical gift of prophecy.

We all believe and do things that agree with Scripture but are not commanded in Scripture. We can know by inference and principle if something is biblical. Jesus and many other biblical personalities did things and had God experiences which are not written down. We cannot assume that they are untrue or contradictory simply because we do not find an exact biblical account of the experience. Recording every spiritual experience was not necessarily the purpose of the biblical writers.

Biblical Evidence Supports Various Phenomena

While it would be possible to interact with nearly every manifestation mentioned in chapter 5, space does not permit it. In an effort to be relevant we will choose the four most common and controversial manifestations. These are shaking, falling, laughing and ecstatic prophecy. All of these phenomena are documented at length in literally hundreds, if not some thousands, of books describing their historicity, the belief of participants and witnesses that these experiences were from God, and resulting spiritual fruit (see chapter 10 and bibliography). For now we will only deal with the biblical record.

Shaking

There are several places in the Bible where shaking and other physical and spiritual phenomena accompanied a visitation or the immediate presence of God. In one of the greatest visitations recorded in Bible history, God came down to deliver the Ten Commandments to Moses and "the whole mountain trembled violently." The exact account is extremely graphic.

> On the morning of the third day there was thunder and lightning, with a thick cloud over the mountain, and a very loud trumpet blast. Everyone in the camp trembled. Then Moses led the people out of the camp to meet with God, and they stood at the foot of the mountain. Mount Sinai was covered with smoke, because the Lord descended on it in fire. The smoke billowed up from it like smoke from a furnace, *the whole mountain trembled violently,* and the sound of the trumpet grew louder and louder. Then Moses spoke and the voice of God answered him (Ex. 19:16-19, emphasis added).

The New Testament account of this visitation says, "At that time *his voice shook* the earth" (Heb.12:26, emphasis added). Isaiah experienced a similar effect of the heavenly on the earthly in his visitation. "At the sound of their voices *the doorpost and thresholds shook* and the temple was filled with smoke" (Is. 6:4, emphasis added).

When God was coming to deal with the downcast prophet Elijah, who was sitting in a cave:

> The Lord said, "Go out and stand on the mountain in the presence of the Lord, for the Lord is about to pass by." Then a great and powerful wind tore the mountains apart and shattered the rocks before the Lord, but the Lord was not in the wind. After the wind

there was an earthquake, but the Lord was not in the earthquake. After the earthquake came a fire, but the Lord was not in the fire. And after the fire came a gentle whisper (1 Kin. 19:11-12).

It is interesting to note that the powerful wind, the quaking of the earth and the fire were not the Lord but preceded the actual presence of God. The metaphors of wind and fire are both examples of the Holy Spirit's work. His work is described as promising that, "Once more [He] will shake not only the earth but also the heavens" (Heb. 12:26).

At the scene of the most dramatic occasion of all of salvation history, God's presence produced the phenomena of shaking. When Jesus Christ, God's only Son, was suffering in agony on the cross, the Holy Spirit was hovering all around. The Bible says, "And when Jesus had cried out again in a loud voice, he gave up his spirit. At that moment the curtain of the temple was torn in two from top to bottom. *The earth shook and the rocks split"* (Matt. 27:50-51, emphasis added). Again this shaking was a response to the presence of God.

Finally, with the coming of the promised Holy Spirit at Pentecost:

Suddenly a sound like the blowing of a violent wind came from heaven and filled the whole house where they were sitting. They saw what seemed to be tongues of fire that separated and came to rest on each of them. All of them were filled with the Holy Spirit and began to speak in other tongues as the Spirit enabled them (Acts 2:2-4).

Notice again the phenomena of wind and fire, which is reminiscent of God's visitation to Elijah on the mount. The Bible records, "They were all filled with the Holy Spirit." The very next time the assembly was together they were filled with the Holy Spirit — this time at a prayer meeting in response to the first persecution. Again, in response to the Lord's presence, "After they prayed, the place where they were meeting was shaken. And they were all filled with the Holy Spirit and spoke the word of God boldly" (Acts 4:31).

A possible reason for shaking as a reaction to being in God's presence may be found in the work of creationist Henry M. Morris. In his scientific commentary on the book of Genesis, he made an interesting find concerning the first earthly work of God:

Now the earth was formless and empty, darkness was over the

surface of the deep, and the Spirit of God was hovering ["moved upon," KJV] over the waters (Gen. 1:2).

This activity of the Holy Spirit is called that of "moving" in the presence of the waters. The word *moved* (Hebrew *rachaph*) occurs only three times in the Old Testament, the other two being translated "shake" (Jer. 23:9) and "fluttereth" (Deut. 32), respectively. Some commentators relate the word particularly to the hovering of a mother hen over her chicks. In any case, the idea seems to be mainly that of a rapid back and forth motion.

In modern scientific terminology, the best translation would probably be "vibrated." If the universe is to be energized, there must be an Energizer. If it is to be set in motion, there must be a Prime Mover.

It is significant that the transmission of energy in the operations of the cosmos is in the form of waves — light waves, heat waves, sound waves and so forth. In fact, except for the nuclear forces which are involved in the structure of matter itself, there are only two fundamental types of forces that operate on matter — the gravitational forces and the forces of the electromagnetic spectrum. All are associated with fields of activity and with transmission by wave motion.

Waves are typically rapid back and forth movements, and they are normally produced by the vibratory motion of a wave generator of some kind. Energy cannot create itself. It is most appropriate that the first impartation of energy to the universe is described as the "vibrating" movement of the Spirit of God Himself.

There is another moving of the Spirit of God mentioned in the Bible. "For the prophecy came not in old time by the will of man: but holy men of God spake as they were moved by the Holy Ghost" (2 Pet. 1:21, KJV). Here the word *moved* is the Greek *phero,* which in fact is used in the Septuagint as the translation of "moved" in Genesis 1:2. As the Holy Spirit energized the primeval universe, to bring form and life to God's creation, so He later empowered God's prophets, to bring beauty and spiritual life to His new creation, through the energizing Word which they inscripturated.[3]

Whether the word *moved* (Hebrew *rachaph*) can actually be interpreted as "vibrated" is not the point. Rather it is the understanding of how energy is transmitted and released that interests me. Shaking may simply be a response to power. The biblical data, while not being a one-to-one correlation, would support the position that things can be physically shaken in response to the presence of God. Whether the Spirit moved (*phero*) upon inanimate objects or moved upon holy men of God to speak the word of prophecy, it is consistent with the record to say that this experience is biblical. We will discuss later the whys and wherefores, and whether or not the work of unholy spirits can produce similar manifestations. It is sufficient for now to state that shaking is biblical in that it is in the Bible and that God has initiated it.

It cannot be proven that all shaking is induced by the devil. In cases of Christians being moved upon and shaken, our observation has simply been that the phenomena of shaking is the physical response of our bodies to the mighty filling power of the Holy Spirit. It is true that in some cases we have witnessed shaking that was obviously in response to unholy or demonic spirits. But for the initiated the demonic counterfeit is easily discernible and is usually dealt with quickly. For some this may be unnerving, but it is only logical that if people or things can be impacted and moved by the Holy Spirit, it also stands to reason that things or people can be moved by spirits who are unholy. The reality that Spirit power may cause a response of manifestations to both things and people is biblical.

Ecstatic prophecy

No doubt one of the most graphic examples of God moving on a human being is the scriptural description of Saul and his soldiers. The first encounter is seen in 1 Samuel 10:1-12 where Samuel, directed by God, anoints Saul as the first king of Israel by pouring the anointing oil upon his head. The heavenly anointing is prophesied to come upon Saul soon after.

> As you approach the town, you will meet a procession of prophets coming down from the high place with lyres, tambourines, flutes and harps being played before them, and they will be prophesying. *The Spirit of the Lord will come upon you in power, and you will prophesy with them; and you will be changed into a different person.* Once these signs are fulfilled, do whatever your hand finds to do, for God is with you (1 Sam. 10:5-7, italics added).

Many Bible scholars have not known what to make of this roving, worshiping band of prophets. They seem to have come out of nowhere and yet the people of their day knew they were a distinct company and that the Spirit of God was in their midst (the reference to it ran for generations; see 1 Sam. 10:11-12; 19:20-24). The question by all the onlookers, "Who is their father?" implies a generational thing that had been passed down from father to son (1 Sam. 10:11; Amos 7:14). Therefore, it seems a spiritual structure had existed for generations. Even in the days of Elijah and Elisha and beyond, large bands of prophets were still functioning together (see 1 Kin. 20:35; 2 Kin. 2:1-15; 4:1,38; 5:22; 6:1; 9:1; Amos 7:14).

The description of the encounter of the Lord coming upon Saul in power, and later in judgment power, leaves no doubt that there was more going on than mere words (1 Sam. 19:23-24). "When all those who had formerly known him saw him prophesying with the prophets, they asked each other, 'What is this that has happened to the son of Kish?'" (1 Sam. 10:11). David Aune agrees and points out:

> The verbs *hitnabbe* and *nibba* in 1 Samuel 10:5-6;10; 19:20-21,23, usually translated "prophesy," should probably be rendered "rave." The verb *hb* takes on the following meanings in chronological order: 1) to rave; 2) to proclaim while raving; and 3) to proclaim.[4]

John White, a well-known evangelical author and speaker, says of this text:

> The passage seems to focus on the awesome power of the Spirit, which causes Saul to do something he has never done before, and what probably astonishes Saul as much as people who observed him. His acquaintances are watching and their surprise is clearly caused as much by what they saw (10:11) as by what they heard. It seems likely that the Spirit's power produced discernible (possibly ecstatic) changes in the prophets, changes the people observing Saul were familiar with. The effects of the Spirit's power evidently lasted for some time (10:13).[5]

God empowers Saul and Saul's men to prophesy

The second account which took place years later leaves no doubt as to the ecstatic nature of the seizing by the Spirit of God (see 1 Sam. 19:18-24). Even the scant picture contained in a few verses is very graphic. Saul sends a battalion of tough soldiers to capture David. A reasoned guess may put the number at about fifty men. One thing was obvious: They were certainly not willing vessels on their way to a renewal meeting.

> When they saw a group of prophets prophesying, with Samuel standing there as their leader, the Spirit of God came upon Saul's men and they also prophesied. Saul was told about it, and he sent more men, and they prophesied too. Saul sent men a third time, and they also prophesied (1 Sam. 19:20-21).

Our imaginations can just picture the Spirit of God leaping from the midst of these prophets and landing on the heads of these tough soldiers causing *them* to prophesy in wonderment. It is obvious that this experience happened against their will. They didn't have a choice. After Saul was told about it, he sent more men and they prophesied, too. Saul sent men a third time. Again the same result: They also prophesied. This is an example of an epicenter of spiritual power and anointing that others walked into and received spiritual blessing.

> Finally, [it says of Saul] he himself left for Ramah...And he asked, "Where are Samuel and David?" So Saul went to Naioth at Ramah. But the Spirit of God came even upon him, and he walked along prophesying until he came to Naioth. He stripped off his robes and also prophesied in Samuel's presence. He lay that way all that day and night (1 Sam. 19:22-24).

The King James Version says, "He lay down naked all that day and all that night." Coupled as it is in the same story, it is likely that the action of Saul ripping off his clothes and being stuck like a bug on the ground prophesying for long durations is the same type of involuntary prophesying that happened to the three groups of soldiers. This was not a penitent Saul. No, this was an unrepentant man who was seized against his will and taken over in body, soul and spirit. An ecstatic condition would better suit the context than a willing vessel. It is uncertain if this condition included shaking ecstatic utterances as was the case in historical revival settings as well as present-day examples. But the possibility cannot be ruled out. Over the course of his life, Saul had entered the spiritual epicenter of the company of prophets and ended up becoming like them. God still has the right to initiate what would seem to us to be the most outlandish spiritual experiences. We would do well to remember, *God is God, and we're not!*

Falling

The most common manifestation by far is that of falling or being over-whelmed by the Spirit. For years Pentecostals have called the experience "being slain in the Spirit." But far from being an exclusively Pentecostal experience, Christians from every tradition have written extensively about this phenomena for centuries.[6]

The fact that this manifestation is biblical is well supported by texts which describe everything from deep sleeps, an inability to stand in the glory of God and falling at His feet like a dead man (Gen. 15:12; 2 Chr. 5:14; 7:2; Rev. 1:17). All the accounts are similar in that the believer is incapacitated in some way. They differ in particulars with some not being able to stand (John 18:6; Acts 9:4); others going into trance-like states (Num. 24:4); some into a deep sleep (Dan. 10:9); while others are actually teleported to wherever the Spirit willed (Ezek. 3:14; 8:3; 11:24).

Daniel in Babylon is not only a classic example of falling, but also of whatever else may be happening while the worshiper is overwhelmed.

> I, Daniel, was the only one who saw the vision; the men with me did not see it, but such terror overwhelmed them that they fled and hid themselves. So I was left alone, gazing at this great vision; I had no strength left, my face turned deathly pale and I was helpless. Then I heard him speaking, and as I listened to him, *I fell into a deep sleep, my face to the ground.*
>
> A hand touched me and set me trembling on my hands and knees. He said, "Daniel, you who are highly esteemed, consider carefully the words I am about to speak to you, and *stand up,* for I have now been sent to you." And when he said this to me, I stood up trembling.
>
> Then he continued, "Do not be afraid...Now I have come to explain to you what will happen to your people in the future, for the vision concerns a time yet to come."
>
> While he was saying this to me, I bowed with my face toward the ground and was speechless. Then one who looked like a man touched my lips, and I opened my mouth and began to speak. I said to the one standing before me, "I am overcome with anguish because of the vision, my lord, and I am helpless. How can I, your servant, talk with you, my lord? My strength is gone and I can hardly breathe."
>
> Again the one who looked like a man touched me and gave

me strength. "Do not be afraid, O man highly esteemed," he said. "Peace! Be strong now; be strong."

When he spoke to me, I was strengthened and said, "Speak, my lord, since you have given me strength" (Dan. 10:7-19, italics added).

Daniel's experience is incredible. He doesn't even record that he fell; only that he had no strength and was overcome by fear and helplessness. Daniel could hear and was cognizant of his state. He was aware that he was "in a deep sleep" with his "face to the ground." He was physically helped to his hands and knees by the visible theophany. Next Daniel stood in obedience to the command and bowed to the ground in a speechless state. He complained that he was overcome with anguish because of the weight of the *kavodth* (glory) of God. It so depleted his strength that Daniel could hardly breathe. We could say that falling was the least of his concerns. Daniel's strength and speech finally returned after a physical touch from "the one who looked like a man."

Whole crowds could be affected like this either negatively or positively. An example of this is evidenced from the great temple dedication of Solomon. The celebration was glorious. Elders, chiefs of tribes, priests, musicians — they were all there.

The trumpeters and singers joined in unison, as with one voice, to give praise and thanks to the Lord. Accompanied by trumpets, cymbals and other instruments, they raised their voices in praise to the Lord and sang: "He is good; his love endures forever." Then the temple of the Lord was filled with a cloud, and the priests could not perform their service because of the cloud, for the glory of the Lord filled the temple of God (2 Chr. 5:13-14).

These men had prepared for months for this occasion. They had a service to perform which would have been the highlight of their lives. Then, all at once, none of them could perform their services. They were incapacitated. Later when Solomon finished dedicating the temple with prayer, "fire came down from heaven and consumed the burnt offering and the sacrifices, and the glory of the Lord filled the temple. The priests could not enter the temple of the Lord because the glory of the Lord filled it" (2 Chr. 7:1-2). For the second time in one day, no one could function in the expected because the unexpected had taken its place.

Laughing in the Spirit

The more spectacular manifestation of hundreds of people laughing in church has caused chagrin. Why would people laugh in church? It doesn't appear reverent. Shouldn't there be tears not belly laughs? We must say no, not exclusively. Joy should also be a natural response in church due to the filling of the Holy Spirit. "For the kingdom of God is...righteousness, peace and joy in the Holy Spirit" (Rom. 14:17). Indeed the fruit of the Spirit is love, joy, peace and so on. I often ask people, "What did you think joy would look like? Why does it seem so odd to see joy expressed with laughter?" After all, the two do go together.

One of the Psalms describes the time when the Lord brought back the captives to Zion: "We were like men who dreamed. Our mouths were filled with laughter, our tongues with songs of joy. Then it was said among the nations, 'The Lord has done great things for them.' The Lord has done great things for us, and we are filled with joy" (Ps. 126:1-3).

Contrary to what some might say, laughter belongs with joy. Joy is not merely a deep state of contentment. The captives jumped and skipped; their mouths were filled with laughter and joy. Laughter and joy do go together and should go together in church.

In summary, without forcing texts to say what they were not meant to say, biblical data is so varied and encompassing that there is not much that could happen that cannot be attributed to God. Space only allows for the scantiest cataloguing of the supernatural workings of God. There is still so much more that could be said: a talking animal (Num. 22:28); walking on water (Matt. 14:29); riding with angels (2 Kin. 2:11); bones that raise the dead (2 Kin. 13:21); wrestling with theophanies (Gen. 32:28); and even visiting the third heaven to receive visions of paradise (2 Cor. 12:2-3).

The words of the Teacher, son of David, said it right: "Is there anything of which one can say, 'Look! This is something new'? It was here already, long ago; it was here before our time" (Eccl. 1:10). The spiritual experiences of men and women in the Bible are so fantastic that they boggle the mind. Far from the present phenomena being questioned as to whether it is biblical, would to God it went deeper so as to be even more like the Bible. Truly we have only experienced water up to our ankles. We are really praying for water deep enough to swim in — a river that no one can cross (see Ezek. 47:3,5).

Conclusion

To answer the question as to whether spiritual, physical and emotional manifestations are biblical, we can say yes on all counts. In and of themselves they are not evil or antagonistic to biblical teachings or principles. In and of themselves they could be called natural, the response of finite human beings to the presence of an infinitely powerful God. Neither are we compelled to proof text each and every phenomenal manifestation since they are not considered to be part of the main and plain of Scripture and therefore may have been present from time to time, without being recorded. The parameters and application of Scripture would far more allow for them than disallow them. There is no reason to assume manifestations are contradictory to the Bible, but rather they are every bit in line with the phenomenal encounters of God throughout history.

8

HOLY SPIRIT APOLOGETICS

Do not put out the Spirit's fire; do not treat prophecies
with contempt. Test everything. Hold on to the good.
1 Thessalonians 5:19-21

The advertisement said, "Don't be fooled by the counterfeit revival, come to..." The name of a prominent contemporary denomination was given as the place to find the "true teaching and true move of the Holy Spirit." Sadly, there is scarcely ever a bona fide move of the Holy Spirit wherein adherents of the previous move of the Spirit did not label the next as being the move of the devil.

This has always been so, even in Jesus' day. In fact, Jesus said of Jerusalem that she "killed the prophets and those sent to her," all the while building monuments to the righteous persons she had previously killed in her streets. Jesus was not impressed with the homage attributed to those in the past. On the contrary, He pointedly declared, "You testify against yourselves that you are the descendants of those who murdered the prophets" (Matt. 23:31). The history of revivals is a history of man quenching what

God Himself had initiated. In the 1740s the revival under Jonathan Edwards had its opponent, Charles Chauncy, who decided to make it his calling in life to save the colonists from the outbursts of enthusiasm related to the Great Awakening. In 1743 Chauncy published *Seasonable Thoughts on the State of Religion in New England,* which was a compendium of every abuse, mistake and exaggerated event he could find.[1] At the time Chauncy was very successful in not only opposing the revival, but also in actually stamping it out.[2] Today, however, Chauncy is not remembered as the great hero who saved the colonists from outbursts of enthusiasm. His only claim to fame is that he was the chief antagonist who opposed a true move of the Spirit. The tragedy of his life is that he became one of the founding theologians of Unitarianism, the American deistic cult.[3] He opposed the truth and became a cultist.

Evan Roberts had his opposition: Peter Price. At the height of the Welsh Revival, Reverend Price published a biting letter in the *Cardiff Papers.* The gist of the attack was that there were two revival movements going on in Wales: the real and the sham. Price maintained that his church had experienced a true revival, with hundreds of conversions. But the revival under Evan Roberts was "a sham revival, a mockery, a blasphemous travesty of the real thing."[4] Price went on to belittle Roberts' prophetic ministry by asking if the lay preacher thought himself the fourth person of the godhead. He denounced Roberts as possessing inferior intellectual and spiritual powers. And finally, Price denounced the "mock revival" as "exhibition," "froth," "vain trumpery," "false fire" and "bogus" performance.[5] All this in the face of seventy thousand converts in two months, which was directly credited to the work springing from the fires ignited by Evan Roberts.[6]

Today Peter Price is known only for his blatant lack of discernment. Like Korah and Dathan who opposed Moses, Chauncy and Price are infamous for what they were wrongly against. Yet in their day, even though they were wrong, their words had weight. The fact that these men obstructed and quenched the move of the Spirit is example enough that today's attacks should not go unchecked. Left to themselves, they stumble the sincere, smear the righteous and divide the body of Christ.

Modern-Day Accusers of the Brethren

A modern-day example of selective editing and unreasonable accusation against some true moves of the Holy Spirit is found in the book by John F. MacArthur Jr., *Reckless Faith,* subtitled, "When the Church Loses

Its Will to Discern." In the subsection entitled "Feeling Good, and Thinking Nothing," MacArthur goes on a diatribe about how the laughing revival of 1994 is a classic example of "feeling good and thinking nothing" and "may in fact be the most profound religious experience pure mysticism can produce."[7] MacArthur alludes to certain selected quotations from the events of the current renewal and from the Toronto Airport Christian Fellowship and Randy Clark. The conclusion is then made that renewalists are people who are "feeling good and thinking nothing." He writes:

> Scripture never indicates that the Holy Spirit wants us to close our minds to objective truth and blindly accept sensational phenomena as proof that He is at work. Quite the opposite is true. We are commanded to examine such things with extreme care. To fail to do so is the essence of reckless faith.[8]

This self-appointed judgment is a broad generalization made about good Christian people, and it simply is not true. Does MacArthur really believe that the thousands of Christians from every denomination, whether they be scholars, pastors or lay people who are presently involved in this current renewal, are "closing their minds to objective truth and blindly accepting sensational phenomena"? Does the discernment of the participants count for nothing? I believe such people would resent being lumped together as those who are "feeling good and thinking nothing." They would resent the assumption that they are not "examining such things with extreme care." The renewal has impacted dozens of denominations — Anglican, Presbyterian, Baptist, Vineyard, Pentecostal — and has impacted every strata of these denominations from bishop to layperson. Therefore, MacArthur is making gross generalizations about a very diverse group of people.

The problem is that MacArthur and others like him are looking through the thick lenses of his own worldview and experience. This can blind him to the fact that he is clearly misrepresenting the oft-repeated words of those preaching, writing and facilitating this renewal. Is it because he has a theological ax to grind? In the section entitled "Quenching the Spirit," MacArthur writes:

> Defenders of phenomena such as "holy laughter" frequently admonish critics that they are in danger of grieving, quenching, or worst of all, blaspheming the Holy Spirit...Notice, however, that all the stern warnings against quenching the Spirit constitute

a very obvious circular argument. They (i.e., the defenders of phenomena) assume phenomena are the work of the Holy Spirit.[9]

Wrong! From the very beginning both I and my associates have stated repeatedly (in context) that phenomena is not necessarily the work of the Holy Spirit. John Wimber, representing the Vineyard movement, wrote in July 1994: "Neither I nor the Bible equate phenomena such as falling, shaking, crying out, laughing or making animal noises as an experience with God. However, you can have an experience with God that 'may' result in some of those responses. So when I pray for someone I don't say, 'shake' 'fall' or 'roar.' I've never prayed for anybody to do anything except get closer to God, get filled with the Spirit, get touched by God, get blessed, come into greater belief — things that are clearly defined in Scripture."[10]

MacArthur also writes:

> This is the essence of the argument: if things happen we cannot explain or find a basis for in Scripture, we dare not question or challenge them. Such phenomena are *de facto* proof that the Holy Spirit is working. Thus sheer mysticism is equated with the moving of the Holy Spirit.[11]

Wrong again. Wimber has stated from the beginning that just because something happens does not mean that it is God. He writes, "So I discourage trying to pry an explanation out of the Bible for the more exotic, and extra-biblical experience of some. You won't find any scripture that says 'pogo your way to Jesus.'" Randy Clark, John Arnott, Ken Gott and other leaders at renewal centers would say the same thing.

MacArthur finishes the paragraph by stating that: "Any discerning souls who attempt to 'examine everything carefully' in accordance with 1 Thessalonians 5:21 are warned that they are sinning against the Holy Spirit."

Wrong for the third time in one paragraph! John Wimber, John Arnott and many other pastors and leaders for that matter, do not assume that "the things we cannot explain are not to be questioned" or that "they are automatically the work of the Holy Spirit." Neither do we discourage people from "examining everything carefully." On the contrary, Wimber writes:

> We have the challenge of evaluating something that we are participating in as well as observing. Nevertheless, we assess this from both biblical criteria and from an objective understanding

of our experience. That doesn't mean experience carries the same weight as the Word of God...And we can't rule out the possibility of demonic activity either, or else why do we read in the epistles, "Test everything. Hold on to the good" (1 Thess. 5:21)? So someone may say, "Oh, that's the flesh" or "That's a demon" or "That's just people acting up" or "That's God." All those answers might be accurate at any given time. Our role, as pastoral leaders, is to exercise discernment and bring correction when it's needed.[12]

Why bring this up? Because it is precisely this type of exaggeration and misinformation by so-called authorities that can quench the Spirit and scare away Christians who deeply desire a closer walk with Jesus. The truth is that MacArthur and others like him are guilty of their own circular reasoning but they can't even see it. Emotion and experience (which MacArthur takes the liberty of labeling "mysticism") are, according to him, "antithetical to discernment, objective verification, and sound doctrine."[13] His presupposition is that God no longer inspires prophecy, tongues, gifts of healing or various revival phenomena such as falling, shaking, laughing, crying, personal visitations and the like. Because, by his own belief system, God no longer initiates these things, yet since they are happening, it is *de facto* proof that these things are either demonic or at best psychosomatic. He will not even objectively look at the facts and consider that this could be God.

What if MacArthur and other critics are wrong in their presuppositions and conclusions? What if he and the others are so bent on proving their own bias that they misinterpret the Scriptures just like they misread, misinterpret and misrepresent those involved in the current renewal? What if the millions of born-again, Bible-believing, rationally thinking Christians, who do believe that God is in much of what is taking place in this present renewal are not all psychosomatic or demonized? Thus, how we interpret and apply the Bible is of critical importance.

Why This Is God and Not the Devil

The real issue is not whether these experiences happen and whether God can do them. A cursory reading of the Bible will verify both. The crux of the issue is whether the source of each individual experience is God, the flesh or the devil. People have always misconstrued the work of God for the work of the devil. Even Jesus Christ, the very Son of God, was

110

accused of doing His work by the power of the devil. "Some of them said, 'By Beelzebub, the prince of demons, he is driving out demons'" (Luke 11:15). The gospel of John records that people accused Jesus of being "demon-possessed" and "raving mad" (John 7:20; 9:48,52; 10:19).

Jesus was foretelling the future when He said, "If the head of the house has been called Beelzebub, how much more the members of his household" (Matt. 10:25). It is true that every renewal or revival should expect — and will receive — the very same treatment Jesus got from those who thought they were doing God a favor by being valiant for truth. I know some individuals who have said, "This does not feel like God to me; therefore, it must be the work of the devil. Just because someone says those words does not mean that the manifestation actually is of the devil. Similarly just because someone cries foul does not mean that an injustice has occurred. It's the umpire who decides, not the overzealous fans.

How do we test everything so that we can "hold on to the good? The three main tests are:

- The doctrinal test
- The fruit that the tree of renewal is producing
- The corporate witness of church history

In the rest of this chapter I will describe the doctrinal test. Chapter 9 describes the fruit test, and chapter 10 presents the historical perspective.

The Doctrinal Test

Years ago when God first poured out His Spirit on us, I would relay our testimony to other groups. They would wince and say, "Really? That really happened to you? Ooh, uh, well...did you test the spirits?" As if to say, "Are you sure that was really God? Did you test it to make sure?" The answer was an obvious, "Of course we did!" As conservative evangelicals we were so freaked out that we prayed every protection prayer and did every test we knew of.

But what does it mean to test the spirits? (1 John 4:1-3; 1 Cor. 12:1-3). To be sure, accusations of "false prophets," "demon-possessed" and "New Age" are bantered about continually. In fact, because of Satan's great propensity to imitate the real thing, Christians are warned to "believe not every spirit," but to be careful because:

The coming of the lawless one will be in accordance with the work of Satan displayed in all kinds of counterfeit miracles, signs and wonders, and in every sort of evil that *deceives* those who are perishing...For this reason God sends them *a powerful delusion so that they will believe the lie* (2 Thess. 2:9-11, italics added).

This vigilance has, at times, turned into an unreal paranoia about everything that is called supernatural. The testing of spirits described in the Bible has nothing to do with what a manifestation looks like or whether someone missed a prophecy or prayed for someone that did not get healed. It does not depend on how we feel or if something happens which may or may not have a biblical precedent. Rather, it has everything to do with doctrine and its resulting practice!

The biblical injunction to test the spirits was given by the apostle John in order to help Christians really know "that He lives in us" and that the Spirit inspiring the message is from God. He writes:

And this is his command: to *believe* in the name of his Son, Jesus Christ, and to *love one another* as he commanded us. Those who obey his commands live in him, and he in them. And this is how we know that he lives in us: We know it by the Spirit he gave us (1 John 3:23-24, italics added).

The context is orthodox Christianity. John says we can know that God lives in us by what we believe — concerning the person of His Son, Jesus Christ — and how we behave — obeying His commandments, namely, loving one another. The test to measure how we can be sure that we have the genuine article is *doctrine* and its spiritual outworking of fruit — *behavior.*

Dear friends, do not believe every spirit, but test the spirits to see whether they are from God, because many false prophets have gone out into the world. This is how you can recognize the Spirit of God: Every spirit that acknowledges that Jesus Christ has come in the flesh is from God, but every spirit that does not acknowledge Jesus is not from God. This is the spirit of the antichrist, which you have heard is coming and even now is already in the world...They are from the world and therefore speak from the viewpoint of the world, and the world listens to them. We are from God, and whoever knows God listens to us; but whoever is not from God does not listen to us. This is how we recognize the Spirit of truth and the spirit of falsehood (1 John 4:1-6).

John says that the test of spirits is what they say of Christ. Obviously more is meant than a superficial affirmation that "Jesus Christ has come in the flesh." It is all that this implies. Like Peter's great confession, "You are the Christ, the Son of the living God" (Matt. 16:16). The rock of Peter's confession was that this man Jesus was the Christ, the anointed One, the Messiah, the long-awaited-for Representative of God. Jesus is the Christ, the Son of the living God. To affirm that "Jesus Christ has come in the flesh" is not merely a trite verbal jingle. It is acknowledging the "we" of the apostolic authority and the receiving or "listening to" of their message (see 1 John 4.6; Eph. 2:20).

Paul's entire treatise on spiritual gifts and the manifestations of the Spirit begins with the Christological test. Paul writes to the Corinthian believers and says, "You know that when you were pagans, somehow or other you were influenced and led astray to dumb idols" (1 Cor. 12:2). It is a well-known fact that when they were outside of Christ and participated in pagan religions or cults, their tongues, prophecy and miracles were done by the power of demons (see 1 Cor. 10:20).[14] Like John, Paul offers a test of the source and message of the spirit behind the gifts and manifestations they were experiencing.

> Therefore I tell you that no one who is speaking by the Spirit of God says, "Jesus be cursed," and no one can say, "Jesus is Lord," except by the Holy Spirit (1 Cor. 12:3).

Again the test of the spirits was Christology; that is, what do you confess about Christ? Those who confess an orthodox "Jesus is Lord" faith, backed up with the life that lordship demands, do so by the impetus of the Holy Spirit. The revelations and manifestations from people such as Joseph Smith, Mother Ann Lee or Muhammad can be measured and tested by their source — What do they say about Christ? No doubt an even fuller set of tests could actually be employed; that of the apostles' doctrine (see Acts 2:42). This would include, as MacArthur so vigorously requests, "the fundamentals of the faith which are all summed up in the person and work of Christ."[15]

So it's all about doctrine and practice. It's not about the strangeness of manifestations or the mishandling of gifts, even though the Bible does describe strange manifestations and does lay out guidelines for gifts used improperly. No, a false prophet or a false teacher is measured by what they confess about the person of Jesus Christ — His lordship, teaching and second coming. What is believed and confessed about Jesus is what determines which spirit has legal access to move in and produce a given work.

Can Born-Again Christians Really Be False Prophets?

I am well aware of the accusations made by Hank Hanegraaff, MacArthur and others that the Toronto Blessing and subsequent worldwide renewal is actually a counterfeit revival led by false prophets who employ occultic measures.[16] These are very serious accusations. For weight they cite the various warning texts mentioned earlier (for example, see 2 Thess. 2:9-11; 2 Tim. 4:3-4; 2 Peter 2:1-2; Jude 3-4; 17). Their harsh denunciations of these gifts and manifestations are set in a context of "contending earnestly for the faith." They claim that the faith is in danger of being corrupted or perverted by so-called false teachers and false prophets.

As proof of their assertions that those involved in these manifestations of the Spirit are being fueled by the devil, critics will cite Matthew 7:15-23, where Jesus said:

> Watch out for false prophets. They come to you in sheep's clothing, but inwardly they are ferocious wolves. By their fruit you will recognize them. Do people pick grapes from thornbushes, or figs from thistles? Likewise every good tree bears good fruit, but a bad tree bears bad fruit. A good tree cannot bear bad fruit, and a bad tree cannot bear good fruit. Every tree that does not bear good fruit is cut down and thrown into the fire. Thus, by their fruit you will recognize them.
>
> Not everyone who says to me, 'Lord, Lord,' will enter the kingdom of heaven, but only he who does the will of my Father who is in heaven. Many will say to me on that day, 'Lord, Lord, did we not prophesy in your name, and in your name drive out demons and perform many miracles?' Then I will tell them plainly, 'I never knew you. Away from me, you evildoers!' (Matt. 7:15-23).

The application is direct. Watch out for false prophets; they look real but they are not. As proof, look at their fruit. The person who believes this is the work of the devil will cite a number of bizarre examples that are not typical of the whole. But examples of bad fruit can be found in every church of every persuasion. It proves nothing but a need for ongoing teaching and growing in maturity. It is the good fruit that is the issue. To dramatically demonstrate that this renewal work is in a league with the devil, Matthew 7:22 will be quoted to prove that these false teachers can prophesy, drive out demons and perform miracles and still not know the Father. Hank Hanegraaff described a renewal meeting he attended in Anaheim:

> I never thought I would live to see what is now happening,
> "awful, devilish manifestations" have appeared in God's sanctu-
> ary. Things that I have seen for years in the cults and occult — but
> I never thought they would appear among God's people. We are
> being sensitized to the occult and desensitized to God's Word.[17]

He goes on to say that Hindu and other pagan religions can do the
same works, and he compares the renewalists to shamans. At face value
this can be very disconcerting to the casual listener. But as the text is
unpackaged and the context studied, we see that to apply the text the way
Hanegraaff and others have done violates the very intent of the text.

Jesus was warning about non-Christian, false believers. The message
commonly known as the Sermon on the Mount was the Magna Carta of
the kingdom. It contrasted true saving faith with the false Jewish religious
system as it had become in that day. Matthew 7:17-23 is set within the
greater context and addresses their false religious system which was producing death (see Matt. 23:15,27). A complete reading of Matthew 23 cat-
alogues the bad fruit Jesus was referring to.[18] Jesus is saying that those
people even do spiritual works in His name, and they were still false —
that is, not possess true saving faith. But the key is, "Then I will tell them
plainly, 'I never knew you. Away from me, you evildoers!'" They were not
going to heaven; they were going to hell. Jesus had just finished saying
that these people were on the road to destruction, that they would be cast
into the fire and that unless they changed and built their (religious) houses
on the rock, they would crash (see Matt. 7:13,19,25.)

A further example of how Jesus viewed false prophets is found in
another oft-cited "beware text."

> For false christs and false prophets will appear and perform
> great signs and miracles to deceive even the elect — if that
> were possible (Matt. 24:24).

How can "the elect" (we who are Christians) be false prophets who, if
it were possible, would deceive the very elect. No, false prophets are:

> blemishes at your love feasts...shepherds who feed only them-
> selves. They are clouds without rain, blown along by the wind;
> autumn trees, without fruit and uprooted — twice dead. They are
> wild waves of the sea, foaming up their shame; wandering stars, for
> whom blackest darkness has been reserved forever (Jude 12-13).

They are going to hell, and as such are not the elect. When the definition is spelled out so boldly most critics who throw around these terms would not stand behind their own pronouncement. It is one thing to "eagerly desire...the gift of prophecy" and miss it (see 1 Cor. 14:1). That is non-prophecy. But that does not make one a New Testament false prophet. In Matthew 7 the true test is doctrine. What did the Jews believe that saved them? Was it their good works and observance of the law, or was it Christ? It is obvious this text cannot be applied to those involved in and leading the renewal because we are saved. The Father does know us.

Do these so-called spiritual watchdogs really believe Jesus will say to us on that day, "Depart from Me, you who practice lawlessness" (Matt. 7:23, NAS)? It is worth noting that most people who stumble over the manifestations or cause others to stumble scarcely ever ask, "What do you believe?" Hanegraaff has not asked, "What do you say about Christ? Whose Son is He?" It must be known that the leading individuals and churches in this movement have beliefs concerning Christ and the fundamental doctrines that are thoroughly orthodox and evangelical. The true spiritual fruit that results from sound doctrine is also present.

Instead of questioning what we are professing concerning the historical, orthodox doctrines of the message and person of Jesus Christ, there is a continual preoccupation with how these gifts and manifestations have been observed in the cults and occult. (It is rarely mentioned that the same manifestations have also been observed in previous revivals.) Just because the false prophets referred to in Matthew 7:15-23 did many wonderful works that were demonic in origin does not mean that the same genuine supernatural works were not also done by the true disciples. The fact that the cults and occult appear to have similar gifts (such as healing and prophecy) and manifestations taking place in their meetings proves nothing but the obvious: Satan is an imitator of the genuine. Someone once told me that counterfeiters only imitate the real thing, or it wouldn't sell. The onus on the church is to test the spirits, not reject the Spirit.

The Real Danger: Judging, Stumbling and Division

The real danger is not something so covert as an end-time delusion with those who appear the most zealous being the most dangerous. No, the real danger is much more obvious. It is a violation of the simple commands against judging falsely, stumbling the little ones and dividing the body of Christ (see John 7:24; Luke 17:1-2; John 17:22; Prov. 6:19). A particularly disturbing example of just one of a continuous chorus of false accusations took place at a Let the Fire Fall conference at the Anaheim Vineyard in July 1994. During one of the morning sessions Lance Pitluck, pastor of the New York Vineyard Church, was describing in detail the blessing he had received at the Toronto meetings. After he returned home the refreshing broke out powerfully in his own church. Salvations increased; apathetic believers became surprisingly zealous. The gifts of the Spirit were revived, and healings and deliverances were once again happening. Of course, the accompanying manifestations described in earlier chapters came with the package, causing some to say, "This is the work of the devil!"

While preaching to a supportive crowd at the conference, Lance said in a facetious, joking way, "Well, if that is the devil, let him do more of it!" He immediately realized it was a poor way to make a point and said, "Oh, you know what I mean." Everyone sort of laughed at the absurd idea of so much good fruit being produced and the devil getting credit for it. Lance said playfully to a friend in the sound booth, "You had better strike that from the tape." To his horror and disappointment, Hanegraaff, using the Christian Research Institute platform, got hold of this very tape and began playing just the one line, "Well, if this is the devil, let him do more of it" over and over on his radio program. Hanegraaff did not explain the context, nor did he play the retraction. In essence, he took half a statement to make a righteous man look as if he were saying something which in fact he did not mean. Even after being confronted with this practice, Hanegraaff would not own up to it and continued playing that statement out of context on the radio.

Because the renewalists are truly born-again, Bible-believing Christians and not false prophets, the opponents of renewal have actually turned their guns on the bride of Christ. The stumbling of sincere believers, who are scared away from seeking more of God is shameful. Not unlike the persecuting spirit of the Pharisees, such antagonists have brought disruption to the prayer of Jesus, who asked "that they may be one just as we [the Father and the Son] are one" (John 17:22). Yes, we need to test or examine everything carefully, but we also need to "hold on to the good" (1 Thess. 5:21). In the words of Jesus, "Stop judging by mere appearances, and make a right judgment" (John 7:24).

9

You Will Know
Them by Their Fruit

*A good tree cannot bear bad fruit, and a bad tree cannot
bear good fruit...Thus, by their fruit you will recognize them.*
Matthew 7:18,20

It was 11:30 on a Sunday night, and we were just winding up what had
been an incredible dedication weekend for our new church facilities.
We had believed that God would visit us dramatically during the dedication, and He did. The weekend was glorious! There was, however, a visiting Vineyard pastor sitting off to one side of the sanctuary. I went up to
greet him, obviously excited about the weekend. We started talking. Then
out of the blue he looked at me and said, "You're really into this stuff
aren't you?"

I was taken back. *What an odd question,* I thought. "Yeah," I answered,
"I am!" He asked again, "Why are you so into this?" He was not trying to
be negative, yet his query revealed there was more under the surface. It
hinted at his own disappointment, his own inability to see "this stuff" take
place to any degree in his own church. Besides, he was a no-nonsense man

with a heart as big as the outdoors. He would give the shirt off his back and lived it daily, but all "this stuff"? We talked further, but after he left, the question stayed with me for days. "Why are you so into this? What good is it?"

Similarly, after the initial surprise of attending a renewal meeting simmers down, many people ask the legitimate question, "What's the fruit?" So they fell, shook, laughed or cried. But after the meeting was over, then what? What good did it do? As the question asked by my pastor friend rolled over and over in my mind, I went aside and scribbled down eighteen pages of what good I felt this did. A basic answer began to take shape. I found out that "the good," is what our Christian walk is all about — spiritual fruit. That question was the beginning of this book.

What Is Our Christian Walk All About?

If I were to go to any Bible-believing church and ask the same question about all their programs and activities that my friend asked me, what would the answer be? If I said, "I notice people go to church here. What good is that? People read the Bible a lot here. What good is that? Why does everyone seem to put a value on singing to God? What good is that?" The answers, of course, are: it's good to come to church, read the Bible and sing to God because you are built up in the faith; you are taught, and you learn to love God more. If we were to line up one hundred pastors and ask them what they were trying to accomplish by pouring their lives into leading churches of people, we would hear a variety of answers. But in the end it would all boil down to simply discipling people to do God's will.

According to Jesus, the bottom line is this: "Love the Lord your God with all your heart and with all your soul and with all your strength and with all your mind; and, 'Love your neighbor as yourself' (Luke 10:27). He also taught His disciples a prayer that begins with: "Our Father in heaven, hallowed be your name, your kingdom come, your will be done on earth as it is in heaven" (Matt 6:9-10). Furthermore, He implored: "Seek first the kingdom of God and his righteousness, and all these things will be added unto you" (Matt. 6:33). Christianity is about loving God and others while working to fulfill His will on earth. It is this fulfilling of the will of God that is called spiritual fruit.

In the previous chapter we determined that a biblical process of testing the spirits had to do with our words and works. What do we say about Christ, and what are the fruits we produce in His name? The Matthew 7:15-23 passage is set within a larger context of works produced out of a

119

religious system but devoid of a personal saving faith. Jesus said He would tell them plainly, "I never knew you. Away from me, you evildoers!" (Matt. 7:23). This text cannot be used as proof against *authentic believers* who are doing the works of prophecy, miracles and demon expulsion. It cannot be inferred that these works are nothing more than demonically inspired false signs. No, Jesus was speaking to a people who were doing works devoid of a saving relationship. But once the doctrinal issue has been settled, the text does have application in defining what works do accompany true disciples. A good tree still bears good fruit (Matt. 7:17), and true sheep are still recognized by the works which flow out of their confession.

Thus, the second criteria for testing the spirits is good works or spiritual fruit produced by the Holy Spirit in the life of a true believer who prays to the Father for the glory of the Son. It is my firm conviction that there is no biblical leg to stand on when it comes to labeling truly spiritual fruit as the deception of the devil when the persons praying and receiving these works are real Christians seeking to build Christ's kingdom.

Aspects of God's Revealed Will

So what is the spiritual fruit that determines whether a tree is good or bad and whether the spirit behind these deeds is holy or unholy? As mentioned earlier, it is the discipling of people to do God's will that defines spiritual fruit (see Matt. 28:19-20; John 15:8,14-16; 1 John 5:2-3). While we could highlight many aspects of God's will, we will limit ourselves to a few very basic and obvious texts. Then, if the works of the renewal and those involved in it are facilitating God's revealed will, we can safely conclude that the second criteria for testing the spirits has been met, and passed with positive results.

God's will is that you be saved.

This is good, and pleases God our Savior, who wants all men to
be saved and to come to a knowledge of the truth (1 Tim. 2:3-4).

If "this stuff" results in people coming to salvation in Christ, then the question, "What good is it?" has already been answered. One of the earlier criticisms of both the laughing revival and the Toronto Blessing is that it was all laughter and no tears. People asked, "Where are the tears? Where is the repentance? Where are the conversions?" The Pharisees asked Jesus

120

a similar question, "Why don't Your disciples fast?" Obviously there are times and seasons for both laughter and tears, for feasting and fasting. We see the bud before the flower and the fruit. It is wrong to look at a fruit tree and curse it because it is full of buds but no fruit. We must let it grow and ripen, and there will be fruit soon enough. Conversions are in fact becoming a prominent part of the present renewal. By the end of its second year or renewal, the Toronto Airport Christian Fellowship saw ten thousand conversions and rededications. By the eighteen-month mark they were seeing an average of more than one hundred people every week coming to Christ. And that from a church that just two years before had only 350 attendees.[1]

The Tabernacle in Melbourne, Florida, a renewal center which was a direct spin-off of the Toronto Blessing, saw more than one thousand conversions and rededications in eight months. Fred Grewe, the administrator of the Melbourne renewal meetings, said with tears in his eyes, "I personally have led more than one hundred people to Christ in the last six months. That is more than I saw receive Christ in the last ten years of my Christian life."

The later Pensacola Outpouring, which is directly traceable to activities in Toronto, saw twenty thousand conversions and rededications in just twelve months. In fact, what they call the turning point of the revival was a shaking prophecy delivered by a newly dedicated nineteen-year-old girl. This is incredible fruit.

Ron Allen, the Vineyard overseer mentioned in chapter 1, has been leading people to Jesus ever since his introduction to the renewal. He also told me with fire in his eyes, "I have never been so empowered to preach and lead people to Christ as I am now." His church led more than six hundred people to Christ within the first six months after Ron was touched by God at the Toronto meetings.

I heard one young man named Luke testify at renewal meetings in Pasadena, California. They asked him what had happened to him at the meetings. He said he had come to the meeting and then went up for prayer after the altar call. Suddenly, he said, the Holy Spirit came upon him and he began to shake violently. The interviewer, seeking for a little more substantive answer, pressed the man further. "Well, what happened to you on the inside?" Luke replied, "Oh, I gave my life to Jesus Christ!" It wasn't until then we all realized the young man was not even a believer when he was mightily moved upon by the Spirit of God. He had no trouble understanding what "this stuff" was about and who he should believe in.

When the Holy Spirit first moved in power at our church, hundreds of people came to Christ and were baptized. To those who ask, "Where are the conversions?" I can only say, "Open your eyes and look. They are everywhere!"

God's will is that you be sanctified.

> For this is the will of God, even your sanctification, that ye should abstain from fornication (1 Thess. 4:3, KJV).

> May God himself, the God of peace, sanctify you through and through. May your whole spirit, soul and body be kept blameless at the coming of our Lord Jesus Christ (1 Thess. 5:23).

If this "stuff" helps people become more holy and be set aside for God's purposes, then this is what we are all about. I already described how the Holy Spirit was mightily poured out on us when we were still a Baptist church. One of the results of this was that nearby Christian college students began cleaning up their personal lives. Some confessed of immorality and had to be expelled for a time, but the conviction accompanying that outpouring was very heavy. Many testified to a new sensitivity to sin that would not let them even walk a city street without feeling an awful burden of holiness on their spirits.

Often the gifts of prophecy and word of knowledge were used to expose sin and convict or bring about a holy fear of the Lord. On one occasion, when shaking prophecy was just breaking out in our church, I was explaining to a house group how God often speaks words of edification and comfort and how they were not to be afraid but expectant. Suddenly the spirit of prophecy come on Stacey, and she spoke in a very strong voice to a young gal, "Be not deceived; God is not mocked. If you sow to the flesh corruption, you will reap of the flesh corruption."

The young girl burst into tears, wailing out, "I didn't know what to do." Then she said, "He caught me; He caught me. I didn't think it would matter, but He caught me." Without my knowing it, this girl had begun going to nightclubs and was on the verge of jettisoning her faith. She instantly confessed and repented of her cold heart. Within months she was in full-time missions and has served God ever since. This has been the continual spiritual fruit of this renewal.

God's will is that you love Him and others.

> Jesus replied: "'Love the Lord your God with all your heart and
> with all your soul and with all your mind.' This is the first and
> greatest commandment. And the second is like it: 'Love your
> neighbor as yourself'" (Matt. 22:37-39).

Most people touched by the Spirit end up loving God and others more.
We have seen business partners who have had very strained relationships
cry and pray for one another after breaking down their walls of hostility.
We have seen marriages saved, youths get turned on for Jesus and prodi-
gals come back to church.

Eleanor Mumford, who left Toronto and returned home to London with
an overflowing, contagious love for God, said that the mere expressing of
it was like lighting a match to a haystack. A burning love for God was the
immediate impartation passed on to hundreds during Eleanor's first Sunday back at Holy Trinity Brompton Church. It is worth noting that such
results had not been evident in their church in the years preceding the
Toronto Blessing. The number of testimonies climbs by the thousands.
People who go to the renewal meetings testify to an increase of the spiritual fruit of love for God and others.

God's will is to destroy the works of the devil.

> The reason the Son of God appeared was to destroy the devil's
> work (1 John 3:8).

One of the most interesting things that happened after the spirit of
prophecy fell on our church was that immediately scores of people were
set free from demonization. When God visits in a close way, it is like shining a floodlight on a bunch of pheasants in a bush. Demon expulsion is the
result. In Jesus' first public teaching visit to Capernaum, a demon manifested right in the meeting (Mark 1:21-26). There are similar testimonies
today. Everywhere the renewal goes the power of the devil is destroyed.

Healing is also an aspect of Jesus' delegated authority over the realm
of the devil. A couple of months after my friend had asked, "What good is
all this stuff?" Kathleen, a young woman on our worship team, testified to
being healed of dyslexia. She had suffered her entire life with this humili-
ating condition that caused reading to be an unpleasant ordeal. During a
ministry time Kathleen came forward for prayer about another matter. She
soon found herself on the floor, resting in the Spirit. Donna, a fellow wor-

ship team member, came over and felt impressed to pray for Kathleen's eyes. Another close friend who was watching encouraged this prayer and said, "Kathleen has dyslexia." Donna took off Kathleen's glasses and asked if she could put spit on her eyes. Kathleen agreed, and she prayed for healing.

As they continued to pray Kathleen began to laugh uncontrollably. She rolled and laughed for over half an hour. When Kathleen finally got up, Donna said, "You should try to read now." Kathleen then realized she had been healed of dyslexia. She told me six months later, "For the first time since I was saved I look forward to daily reading the Word. I'm finally able to understand what I read, and I'm not frustrated. Truly He is the Lord who heals."

As the Holy Spirit releases people from demonic bondage or oppression, heals others from diseases and frees still others from compulsive addictions, I am fully confident in saying that the will of God is being fulfilled. He may do this with or without phenomena and manifestations.

God's will is that you be filled with His Spirit.

> Therefore do not be foolish, but understand what the Lord's will is. Do not get drunk on wine, which leads to debauchery. Instead, be filled with the Spirit (Eph. 5:17-18).

To be filled with the Spirit means you have the Holy Spirit directing and empowering your life to the point that He influences every part of you. To be full of the Spirit means He is the influence and power that enables your walk and witness. But what are the results of being filled with the Spirit?

> But the fruit of the Spirit is love, joy, peace, patience, kindness, goodness, faithfulness, gentleness and self-control. Against such things there is no law (Gal. 5:22).

If you were a tree and the Holy Spirit rained on you, the fruit growing on your branches would be character and godly emotions, namely, love, joy, peace, patience, kindness, goodness, faithfulness, gentleness and self-control. One night during our twenty-one days of prayer, fasting and renewal meetings, about four hundred youth showed up. Marc Dupont had been preaching, and we were moving into ministry time when he pointed to a young girl and said, "The joy of the Lord is on you." Suddenly she began to laugh with the joy of the Lord. It spread to other young people. Before long it was like a great pool of joy, and most people who came over to the area were overcome with joy manifested by laughter. This went on and on.

Finally at about one o'clock in the morning the parents were trying to get their teenage kids to go home from church. This girl laughed all the way home. She laughed in her bed. She woke herself up from sleep laughing. She laughed as she went to her Christian school the next day. Soon it began to spread to the other students. As the laughter spread, they joyfully shut the school down for the rest of the day and moved into ministry time. This girl laughed for virtually twenty-seven hours straight. She testified of being overcome by the joy of the Lord.

All of the fruits of the Holy Spirit can be acted out in a tangible way, and we are seeing that happen. If the Holy Spirit touches somebody and that person shows with both words and deeds that he or she has more fruit and character than before, then we say that it is good. This fulfills God's will.

> If you then, though you are evil, know how to give good gifts to your children, how much more will your Father in heaven give the Holy Spirit to those who ask him! (Luke 11:13).

> Now to each one the *manifestation of the Spirit is given for the common good.* To one there is given through the Spirit the message of wisdom, to another the message of knowledge by means of the same Spirit, to another faith by the same Spirit, to another gifts of healing by that one Spirit, to another miraculous powers, to another prophecy, to another the ability to distinguish between spirits, to another the ability to speak in different kinds of tongues, and to still another the interpretation of tongues. All these are the work of one and the same Spirit, and he gives them to each man, just as he determines (1 Cor. 12:7-11, italics added).

Paul says that the manifestation or visible representation of the Spirit is "for the common good." The outward demonstration of this common good is gifts. When the Spirit fills people, spiritual gifts flow out. One of the amazing correlations between the experience of our church and thousands of other churches is the mighty outpouring of the gifts of the spirit. Everything described above in the Corinthian passage is beginning to happen. This is especially true with respect to the revelatory gifts. Just like in Acts 2, believers are prayed for; in some cases various phenomena are evident, and then they prophesy. Or they are suddenly endowed with words of knowledge about others that they did not know before. Some become filled with incredible faith.

While we were still conservative Baptists, ordinary people in our church were prayed for and in a single night, in a single moment, many received an impartation for prophecy. This ability was given at a point in time and never went away. Now several years later, they still prophesy and people continue to be blessed. Paul goes on to describe it this way: "If an unbeliever comes into your group, and somebody prophesies, revealing the secrets of their hearts, they will fall on their faces to the ground and declare 'truly God is among you!'" (1 Cor. 14:24-25). This is power evangelism. This is the type of thing that is actually happening. If prophecy brings an awe for God and provokes people into the kingdom, then there is much good with "this stuff."

> I no longer call you servants, because a servant does not know his master's business. Instead, I have called you friends, for everything that I learned from my Father I have made known to you. You did not choose me, but I chose you to go and bear fruit — fruit that will last (John 15:15-16).

When people are full of the Holy Spirit, He produces the things described above. These things are spiritual fruit. One of the common trademarks of renewal services around the world has been the request for testimony. In place after place I continue to hear testimonies of fruitfulness. The bitter begin to love. The depressed find joy. The addicted are freed. The fearful receive boldness to be witnesses. The coldhearted leap with worship. And the faithless find faith. Simply put, the bad become good. It is important to note these fillings are not one-time events, but are part of an ongoing repeatable process. When Christians do the will of God, anointed by the Holy Spirit, the power of the devil is overcome. The marks of true spirituality become evident, and good fruit will inevitably take place. The test of a genuine work of the Holy Spirit is fruitfulness.

Good and Perfect Gifts

I have set forth that fruit (as demonstrated in the words and the works) is one of the ways we test the spirits associated with the phenomena in this work of God. Still some people continue to believe that the devil is the author of many good and perfect gifts (see James 1:17) in order to deceive us and get us filled with him. Strange as it may be, this has always been the case. Jesus continually faced the same accusations in His ministry, not because of His good fruit, but simply because of the visible power. Luke records an example of this.

> Jesus was driving out a demon that was mute. When the demon left, the man who had been dumb spoke, and the crowd was amazed. But some of them said, "By Beelzebub, the prince of demons, he is driving out demons." Others tested him by asking for a sign from heaven. Jesus knew their thoughts and said to them: "Any kingdom divided against itself will be ruined, and a house divided against itself will fall. If Satan is divided against himself, how can his kingdom stand? I say this because you claim that I drive out demons by Beelzebub. Now if I drive out demons by Beelzebub, by whom do your followers drive them out? So then, they will be your judges. But if I drive out demons by the finger of God, then the kingdom of God has come to you" (Luke 11:14-20).

This passage elaborates a few important issues related to the source behind the controversial phenomena. The first point is that if Satan is doing God's work through God's people then his house is divided and his kingdom cannot stand. The fruit produced by Christians who pray for people is salvation, healing, deliverance, joy and gifts of the Holy Spirit. Jesus taught that it was ludicrous to attribute these good works to the devil. Even if the Jews did not believe Jesus' doctrine was orthodox, Jesus appealed to works as a self-authenticating apologetic. He said, "Believe me that I am in the Father, and the Father in me: or else believe me for the very works' sake" (John 14:11, KJV). We need more faith in God's ability to lead us than fear of Satan's power to deceive us.

The second major inconsistency that Jesus pointed out to His critics was their own rule or standard of measuring. "Now if I drive out demons by Beelzebub, by whom do your followers drive them out?" In effect Jesus was saying, "If the devil is answering My prayers then who is answering yours? If you accuse Me of exorcism by the power of Beelzebub, where do you get your power?" I have often found this question to cause a real jarring in the mental gears of would-be heresy hunters. From time to time people tell me, "I believe the stuff that is taking place here is of the devil."

Even after I point out that many have been saved, imparted with gifts, blessed and so on, they are still adamant that this cannot not be the work of God. The main reason is because of the accompanying phenomena which they believe is beyond what God would do.

I have on occasion asked these simple questions: "Do you pray for people to get saved? Do you pray for people to be imparted with gifts of the Holy Spirit? Do you pray for people to get blessed?" Invariably they will say yes. Then I ask, "Did they get saved, filled and blessed?" The answer is usually, "Yes, some of them." Then I ask, "How do you know that the devil did not get them saved and do all those wonderful things for your prayer recipient?" They often answer by simply saying, "That's ridiculous. He can't do that!" I say, "How do you know?" At this they usually sputter and say, "He just cannot and would not do this." Of course the natural consequence of such a belief system would produce such paranoia that we could never really be sure who was answering our prayers — God or the devil.

Finally I ask, "If you know the devil can't answer your prayers to get people saved and filled and blessed, why do you assume he has legal access to answer my prayers when I'm just as saved as you and asking for the same things as you? The only difference is our answers are sometimes accompanied by phenomena and manifestations, not of our own initiation." To this there is no reply. Jesus said, "Now if I drive out demons by Beelzebub, by whom do your followers drive them out?"

In the verses directly preceding the passage on the Beelzebub controversy, Jesus assured His disciples that the heavenly Father is capable of making sure they do not get an evil gift in place of the work and filling of the Holy Spirit when they ask for things from His hand.

> Which of you fathers, if your son asks for a fish, will give him a snake instead? Or if he asks for an egg, will give him a scorpion? If you then, though you are evil, know how to give good gifts to your children, how much more will your Father in heaven give the Holy Spirit to those who ask him! (Luke 11:11-13).

God can take care of us. John Arnott recently told me an encouraging story. He met an Indian pastor named John Babu who asked Arnott to come and speak at his churches in Madras, India. Babu's testimony is most interesting. Years ago he was dying of a liver disease, and there did not appear to be any hope left. As a Hindu, John went to the Hindu temple to seek help from the many thousands of gods in which they believe. But nothing had been working. Finally in desperation he looked up and prayed piteously, "Surely there is one of you up there who can help me. Please heal me, and I will serve you forever." His reasoning was like the Athenians who had an altar with the inscription, "To the unknown God." Afraid of missing a deity, John invited any god to answer his prayer for healing.

In an instant Jesus appeared to him in the midst of the Hindu temple and said, "I am the way, the truth and the life." Lovingly Jesus reached out and touched his body. Immediately John was healed. In gratitude and worship, John became a follower of Jesus Christ. He has since gone out and started more than five hundred churches. Today we have Christians telling other Christians to be careful when praying at the altar for the filling of the Holy Spirit. "You never know which spirit will fill you or answer your prayer," they warn. We need to have more faith in God's ability to lead us than fear of Satan's power to deceive us, especially when our prayers are directed to the one true God!

Getting God's Work Done a Different Way

Jesus' disciples encountered a situation when someone was doing Jesus' work in a way they were not accustomed to. This man was not with their group; he was not doing it their way. Jesus' response was enlightening.

> "Teacher," said John, "we saw a man driving out demons in your name and we told him to stop, because he was not one of us." "Do not stop him," Jesus said. "No one who does a miracle in my name can in the next moment say anything bad about me, for whoever is not against us is for us. I tell you the truth, anyone who gives you a cup of water in my name because you belong to Christ will certainly not lose his reward" (Mark 9:38-41).

In essence Jesus was saying, "Leave them alone. If they are actually true followers of Mine and are truly doing wonderful works in My name, they can't in the next moment say something bad about Me." The doctrinal test says that those who are actually true Christians and seeing real fruit produced in His name are to be left alone because we who are not against Him are for Him. Doctrine and spiritual fruit are the criteria for testing the spirits, not prophecy, manifestations or corporate sameness.

10

THE CORPORATE WITNESS
OF CHURCH HISTORY

By faith Abel offered God a better sacrifice than Cain did.
By faith he was commended as a righteous man, when God
spoke well of his offerings. And by faith he still speaks,
even though he is dead.
Hebrews 11:4

The heroes of the hall of faith recorded in Hebrews 11 were all commended for the way their faith moved them to action. The result was a testimony. The first example of faith mentioned was that of Abel, the second child of Adam. The writer to the Hebrews credits Abel with still speaking even though he is dead. In other words his testimony had significance thousands of years later. In a real way the testimonies of all those who have died in Christ still speak today. Their testimonies form the ongoing salvation history of God.

The speech of the Christian dead, or those who sleep in Jesus, is the final major test and affirmation of whether or not the phenomena and manifestations of the Holy Spirit as demonstrated today are from God. The line of reasoning is simple. In previous chapters we have described the various activities God has been initiating among His people. Then we showed how they are generally consistent with biblical intent, although it does not appear to be the purpose of the writers of Scripture to describe everything God can or does do in His people. We noted the spiritual source can be tested by doctrine (what is confessed about Christ) and fruit (what is produced for Christ). The final test is the corporate voice of church history. The same "stuff" has happened in the lives of godly people in other ages and other places. If the corporate testimony of church history is congruent with the present testimonies, then we are safe in affirming that "the Lord has done this, and it is marvelous in our eyes" (Matt. 21:42).

A couple of things need to be mentioned at this point. The first is that we should not expect various phenomena to occur at every place at every time. The fact they occur at all is testimony enough. For instance, Israel was in bondage under Egypt for four hundred years, and during that time they waited for a visitation of God. Maybe whole generations came and went with no words from heaven. On the other hand, from the time of Samuel to Elisha there is evidence of prophetic activity and the phenomena of God which appeared to happen on a regular basis within a prophetic community.

It is not the regularity that authenticates an issue, but the fact that it happens at all. A thousand testimonies from people who doubt that God heals are silenced with just a couple of authentic, documented healings.[1] Two or three exceptions to the rule prove that it is not a rule. Smatterings of accounts are accounts enough. Yet with respect to phenomena, as church archives are researched and historical data produced, we are finding such an abundance of accounts that one hardly knows where to begin.

Second, it is interesting to note that historical accounts of manifestations are evidenced during what we now know were heightened times of God's salvation work. Testimonies abound to confirm that most of the phenomena listed in chapter 6 took place during the first and second Great Awakenings; during the Welsh and Azusa Street revivals as well as during many other recognized moves of the Spirit. The regularity of phenomena linked to revivals led Dr. John White, in his timely book, *When the Spirit Comes With Power*, to conclude: 1) manifestations of the Spirit are an evidence of a heightened move of God; and 2) another major revival could be on the way.[2] This is most interesting considering that White's conclusion was stated just years before the worldwide renewal of 1994.

The sheer weight of material to extract from original sources is overwhelming, and many books could be written just summarizing the material. Please do not think this brief exposé of examples has exhausted the supply.[3] It is only due to page restraints that I include so little. My goal is merely to provide a few examples of various types of manifestations. Please remember that for every example provided there are scores left on the table.[4]

The Corporate Witness of Church

Vibia Perpetua and Felicitas: Carthage, North Africa (circa. A.D. 202–203)

The Passion of Perpetua and Felicitas is one of the earliest and most influential accounts of martyrs. It describes the events leading up to and including the executions of several Christians, including Perpetua and her slave girl Felicitas. What makes this account so important is that it contains some startling reports of visions and prophecies that came to pass and made their way into recorded church history. Tertullian, a church father and presbyter in Carthage during the time of this persecution, was greatly impacted by Perpetua's visions and martyrdom. He made a legitimate place for such phenomena in the church of his day, which impacted the church for hundreds of years.[5]

Perpetua's first vision came while in prison after her brother had suggested she ask God for insight about how to pray and what to expect in her upcoming trial. She believed she was one "who could speak with the Lord whose great blessings [she] had come to experience."[6] She asked her brother to wait until the next day so that she could pray. That night the vision came. "Perpetua was awakened or aroused from a dream or trancelike state with full recollection of what had transpired in the vision, and it has been preserved in writing."[7] Her brother visited her the next day, and she related the vision. They both "realized that we would have to suffer." Perpetua gave up any hope for escape or acquittal, and both she and her brother expected her to receive the death penalty. Perpetua received other visions as well which strengthened her and her companions during the time leading up to her final suffering. Shortly thereafter she and her slave girl faced wild beasts in the arena and were torn apart for their confessions of Christ.

Saint Birgitta of Sweden, mystic and founder of the Bridgettine Order (1303-1373)

One of the most erudite female saints of the medieval church was Bridget, who was a voice of reform and correction within the Roman Catholic Church. Married at age thirteen, she became the mother of eight children and the founder of a new religious order. She is considered perhaps the finest Scandinavian writer of her time. She described how the Lord would move upon her and inspire striking visions.

> O sweetest God, strange it is what Thou dost to me! For Thou dost put my body to sleep, and my soul Thou awakenest to see and hear and feel the things of the spirit. When it pleaseth Thee, Thou dost send my body to sleep, not with bodily sleep, but with the rest of the spirit, and my soul Thou dost awaken as though from a trance to see and hear and feel with powers of the spirit.[8]

Saint Teresa of Avila, Spanish Carmelite reformer (1515-1582)

At the same time as the Catholic monk Martin Luther was reforming Germany and lawyer John Calvin was reforming France and Geneva, another saint was reforming within a region where it was most dangerous to do so. During the Spanish Inquisition, St. Teresa of Jesus established sixteen nunneries of her order and fourteen convents of Barefoot Carmelites. She worked tirelessly among the poor and needy and was as tough as a sea captain. Though plagued by chronic ailments and near-death sickness, her vigorous personality comes through in statements like these:

> Rest, rest indeed! I need no rest; what I need is crosses...If thou wilt [prove me] by means of trials, give me strength and let them come...Strive like strong men until you die in the attempt, for you are here for nothing else than to strive.[9]

Today, despite her heroic reforms and good works, St. Teresa is most remembered for her deep life of prayer and devotion and the incredible spiritual phenomena that happened in and around her on a regular basis. The following is just one paragraph out of a four-hundred-page autobiography teeming with spiritual accounts.

> While seeking God in this way, the soul becomes conscious that it is fainting almost completely away, in a kind of swoon, with an exceeding great and sweet delight. It gradually ceased to breathe and all its bodily strength begins to fail it...He can apprehend nothing with the senses, which only hinders his soul's joy and thus harm rather than help him. It is futile for him to attempt to speak: his mind cannot form a single word, nor, if it could, would he have the strength to pronounce it. For in this

condition all outward strength vanishes, while the strength of the soul increases so that it may the better have the fruition of bliss. This prayer, for however long it may last, does no harm; at least it has never done any to me...What harm can possibly be done by so great a blessing? The outward effects are so noteworthy that there can be no doubt some great thing has taken place: we experience a loss of strength but the experience is one of such delight that afterwards our strength grows greater.[10]

The French Calvinist Huguenots (formally organized in 1559)

The prophecies given by the Huguenots were well documented by both believers and detractors. This is an account recorded in an 1895 book by Henry Baird.

Respecting the physical manifestations, there is little discrepancy between the accounts of friend and foe. The persons affected were men and women, the old and the young. Very many were children, boys and girls of nine or ten years of age. They were sprung from the people — their enemies said, from the dregs of the people — ignorant and uncultured; for the most part unable to read or write...

Such persons would suddenly fall backward, and, while extended at full length on the ground, undergo strange and apparently involuntary contortions; their chests would seem to heave, their stomachs to inflate. On coming gradually out of this condition, they appeared instantly to regain the power of speech. Beginning often in a voice interrupted by sobs, they soon poured forth a torrent of words — cries for mercy, calls to repentance, exhortations to the bystanders to cease frequenting the mass, denunciations of the church of Rome, prophecies of coming judgment. From the mouths of those that were little more than babes came texts of Scripture, and discourse in good and intelligible French, such as they never used in their conscious hours. When the trance ceased, they declared that they remembered nothing of what had occurred, or of what they had said. In rare cases they retained a general and vague impression, but nothing more. There was no appearance of deceit or collusion, and no indication that in uttering their predictions respecting coming events they had any thought of prudence, or doubt as to the truth of what they had foretold.

Brueys, their most inveterate opponent, is no less positive on this point than are the witnesses who are most favourable to them. "These poor madmen," he said, "believed that they were indeed inspired by the Holy Ghost. They prophesied without any (ulterior) design, without evil intent, and with so little reserve, that they always boldly marked the day, the place and persons of whom they spoke their predictions."[11]

The Revivals in England

John Wesley, English Methodist revivalist (1703-1971)

Probably the most well-known of all revival preachers is John Wesley. Wesley, a brilliant Oxford fellow and lecturer was converted at thirty-five and went on to become the founder of the Methodist movement. John Wesley experienced almost all the same phenomena in his meetings that are taking place today.[12]

In April 1739 Wesley preached at Newgate Prison in Bristol. Wesley records that as he was preaching:

> One, and another, and another sunk to the earth: they dropped on every side as thunderstruck. One of them cried aloud. We besought God on her behalf and He turned her heaviness into joy. A second being in the same agony, we called upon God for her also; and He spoke peace unto her soul...[13]

The next day a doctor who suspected trickery or fraud accompanied Wesley to the prison to see for himself. He closely observed a woman who:

> broke out into strong cries and tears. He went and stood close to her, and observed every symptom, till great drops of sweat ran down her face, and all her bones shook. He then knew not what to think, being clearly convinced it was not fraud, nor yet any natural disorder. But when both soul and body were healed in a moment, he acknowledged the finger of God.[14]

Wesley notes,

> Many more were brought to the berth. All were in floods of tears, cried, prayed, roared aloud, all of them lying on the ground.[15]

> When I began to pray, the flame broke out. Many cried aloud, many sank to the ground, many trembled exceedingly.[16]

Throughout his life Wesley witnessed such incredible revival phenomena that even though his preaching was the tool God used, he was continually amazed. In an entry in his journal recorded on July 29, 1759, Wesley records a number of examples that occurred while preaching.

> Several fell to the ground, some of whom seemed dead, others in the agonies of death, the violence of their bodily convulsions exceeding all description...A child, seven years old, sees many visions and astonishes the neighbors with her innocent awful manner of declaring them.

Describing the same meeting Wesley detailed how the power of God then moved out into the churchyard. The people were affected in ways that were beyond what he could describe. One man was "wounded by the Lord" while others tried to hold him up.

> His own shaking exceeded that of a cloth in the wind. It seemed as if the Lord came upon him like a giant, taking him by the neck and shaking all his bones in pieces...Another roared and screamed...Some continued long as if they were dead, but with a calm sweetness in their looks. I saw one who lay two or three hours in the open air, and, being then carried into the house, continued insensible another hour, as if actually dead. The first sign of life she showed was a rapture of praise intermixed with a small, joyous laughter...

Four days later:

> While I prayed with them many crowded into the house, some of whom burst into a strange, involuntary laughter, so that my voice could scarce be heard, and when I strove to speak louder a sudden hoarseness seized me. Then the laughter increased...

A week later Wesley wrote:

> I have generally observed more or less of these outward symptoms to attend the beginning of a general work of God. So it

was in New England, Scotland, Holland, Ireland, and many parts of England...[17]

George Fox and the Quakers (1640-present)

George Fox and the Quakers had a tremendous influence for righteousness during his own time and afterward. Their nickname Quakers was due to the phenomena of quaking, trembling and shaking that accompanied their ministry. Often they would be seized by this unction and would then prophesy in this state with great presence of the Lord attending it. Thousands were converted.

> In the year 1648, as I was sitting in a friend's house in Nottinghamshire (for by this time the power of God had opened the hearts of some to receive the word of life and reconciliation), I saw there was a great crack to go throughout the earth, and a great smoke to go as the crack went; and that after the crack there should be a great shaking: this was the earth in people's hearts, which was to be shaken before the seed of God was raised out of the earth. And it was so: for the Lord's power began to shake them and great meetings we begun to have, and mighty power and work of God there was amongst the people, to the astonishment of both people and priests.[18]

> Being set at liberty, I went to the inn where Captain Drury at first lodged me. This captain, though he sometimes carried it fairly, was an enemy to me and to the Truth, and opposed it. When professors came to me, while I was under his custody, and he was by, he would scoff at trembling, and call us Quakers, as the Independents and Presbyterians had nicknamed us before. But afterwards he came and told me that, as he was lying on his bed to rest himself in the daytime, a sudden trembling seized on him; that his joints knocked together, and his body shook so that he could not rise from his bed. He was so shaken that he had not strength enough left to rise. But he felt the power of the Lord was upon him; and he tumbled off his bed, and cried to the Lord, and said he would never speak more against the Quakers, such as trembled at the word of God.[19]

The Revivals in America

Jonathan Edwards, New England theologian/pastor (1703–1758)

Seminarian professor Richard Lovelace believes "Jonathan Edwards may well be the greatest American theologian and philosopher — and perhaps also the greatest mind — that America has yet produced." Edwards had firsthand experience with the manifestations of the Holy Spirit and became the chief spokesperson for the work of revival, trying to bridge the difficult chasm of emotional excess and freedom of the Spirit as evidenced with phenomena. Edwards' wife, Sarah, a mother of eleven children, experienced her own major visitation from God and was incapacitated for seventeen days. Edwards supported and blessed the graces of God in both his wife and others.

> It was a very frequent thing to see a house full of outcries, faintings, convulsions, and such like, both with distress, and also with admiration and joy. It was not the manner here to hold meetings all night, as in some places, nor was it common to continue them till very late in the night; but it was pretty often so, that there were some that were so affected, and their bodies so overcome, that they could not go home, but were obliged to stay all night where they were...and there were some instances of persons lying in a sort of trance, remaining perhaps for a whole twenty-four hours motionless, and with their senses locked up; but in the meantime under strong imaginations, as though they went to heaven and had there a vision of glorious and delightful objects. But when the people were raised to this height, Satan took the advantage, and his interposition, in many instances, soon became very apparent: and a great deal of caution and pains were found necessary to keep the people, many of them, from running wild.[22]

George Whitefield, English Methodist revivalist (1714–1770)

George Whitefield was a contemporary of Wesley and Edwards and a personal friend of Benjamin Franklin. He preached at least eighteen thousand times to perhaps ten million hearers and also witnessed the same phenomena and manifestations of revival.[23] Wesley at first chided Whitefield for not stopping the outward symptoms that were breaking out in his meetings. Later Wesley was to find out that it was God, and He was not to be stopped. The accounts of Whitefield are detailed in his journals and are similar to those described by Wesley and Edwards.

Camp meeting with Barton Stone at Cane Ridge, Kentucky (1801)

The following account is by the Reverend Moses Hodge who witnessed the Cane Ridge meeting.

> The careless fall down, cry out, tremble, and not infrequently are affected with convulsive twitchings...Nothing that imagination can paint, can make a stronger impression upon the mind, than one of those scenes. Sinners dropping down on every hand, shrieking, groaning, crying for mercy, convulsed; professors praying, agonizing, fainting, falling down in distress for sinners or in raptures of joy![24]

The following account is by James B. Finley, who witnessed the same meeting.

> The noise was like a roar of Niagara. The vast sea of human beings seemed to be agitated as if by a storm...some of the people were singing, others praying, some crying for mercy in the most piteous accents, while others were shouting most vociferously. While witnessing these scenes, a peculiarly strange sensation such as I had never felt before came over me. My heart beat tumultuously, my knees trembled, my lips quivered and I felt as though I must fall to the ground. A strange supernatural power seemed to pervade the entire mass of mind there collected...I stepped up on a log where I could have a better view of the surging sea of humanity. The scene that then presented itself to my mind was indescribable. At one time I saw at least five hundred swept down in a moment as if a battery of a thousand guns had been opened upon them and then immediately followed by shrieks and shouts that rent the very heavens.[25]

Peter Cartwright, Methodist frontier circuit-rider (1785–1872)

The following is his account of "the jerks" at an early Kentucky camp meeting.

> No matter whether they were saints or sinners, they would be taken under a warm song or sermon, and seized with a convulsive jerking all over, which they could not by any possibility avoid,

and the more they resisted the more they jerked. If they would not strive against it and pray in good earnest, the jerking would usually abate...To see these proud young gentlemen and young ladies, dressed in their silks, jewelry, and prunella, from top to toe, take the jerks, would often excite my laughter. The first jerk or so, you would see their fine bonnets, caps, and combs fly; and so sudden would be the jerking of the head that their long loose hair would crack almost as loud as a waggoner's whip...[26]

Charles Finney: Revivals at Evan's Mills and De Kalb, New York (1825)

Charles Grandison Finney is considered one of America's greatest revivalists. He is often credited with directly or indirectly being the instrument that brought about half a million conversions from 1825 to 1875.[27] Finney also witnessed the same phenomena as we are witnessing today, and in his own memoirs described a personal experience where he "literally bellowed out the unutterable gushings" of his heart, as he was (what he calls) "baptized in the Spirit." Richard Riss says of this experience:

> That he was in all probability describing what John Wesley described in several places as 'roaring' at his meetings...It is also of interest that, when one of the elders of his church arrived, the power of the Spirit came on him in the form of 'spasmodic laughter.' It seemed as if it was impossible for him to keep from laughing from the very bottom of his heart.[28]

The following revival account describes the phenomena of speechlessness.

> As the people withdrew I observed a woman in one part of the house being supported in the arms of some of her friends, and I went to see what was the matter, supposing that she was in a fainting spell. I soon found out that she was not fainting but that she could not speak...I advised the women to take her home and pray with her to see what the Lord would do. They informed me that she was Miss G—, sister of the well-known missionary, and that she was a member of the church in good standing...After lying in a speechless state about sixteen hours, Miss G—'s mouth was opened, and a new song was given her. She was taken from the horrible pit of miry clay, her feet were set upon a rock, and many saw it and feared.[29]

Frank Bartleman and the Azusa Street Revival (1906)

The following is an eyewitness account by a journalist of the Azusa Street Revival in Los Angeles, which gave birth to the modern Pentecostal movement.

> Someone might be speaking, suddenly the Spirit would fall upon the congregation. God himself would give an altar call. Men would fall all over the house, like the slain in battle, or rush for the altar en masse, to seek God. The scene often resembled a forest of fallen trees. Such a scene cannot be imitated...The whole place was steeped in prayer. God was in His holy temple. It was for man to keep silent. The shekinah glory rested there.[30]

The accounts of Azusa Street Revival contain descriptions of every kind of manifestation taking place today, including shaking, speechlessness, motionlessness, being enraptured, drunk in the Spirit, holy laughter, visions, tongues, prophecy and the like. True, I'm sure exaggerated examples can be found for each phenomena, which is to be expected. Yet to deny the countless testimonies of the overall authentic move of the Spirit in the light of historical observation is to deny the most potent spiritual force to propel the church in the twentieth century.[31]

Summary

To embrace the phenomena accompanying the most recent wave of the Spirit released in 1993 and 1994 is to embrace revival history. As more and more research is being provoked because of this worldwide renewal, it is surprising to realize that Solomon was right all along: "There is nothing new under the sun. Is there anything of which one can say, 'Look! This is something new'? It was here already, long ago; it was here before our time" (Eccl. 1:9-10).

SECTION THREE

The Prophetic and a
Visitation of the Holy Spirit

11

PROPHECY AND A VISITATION OF THE HOLY SPIRIT

Worship God! For the testimony of Jesus
is the spirit of prophecy.
Revelation 19:10

It was the final meeting of the Indonesian conferences. Prayer ministry was taking place all over the auditorium. A pastor approached me and said that a young lady had a prophetic word for me. As this sort of thing happens often, I wasn't overly anticipatory. I knelt down on the stage and introduced myself. Suddenly she began to shake and with her eyes fixed on mine, she began to prophesy in a strong, ecstatic form. When translated into English, the message come through loud and clear. Everything she said was right on and immediately bore a witness with me. She was speaking words from God. I was surprised and delighted. By now a crowd had gathered that was made up of many individuals I knew. I encouraged this young woman to also pray for some of them. Once again her accuracy was incredible.

After the crowd had left, I asked her, "How did this happen to you?

When were you released in this form of ecstatic prophecy?" Her name was Magdalena, a daughter of an Indonesian pastor. She had recently married, and now she and her husband were pastoring a church. As a child of nine, Jesus had once appeared to her and called her to be a prophetic vessel. From that time on she was prophetic and just knew things that were unknowable in the natural. Magdalena confessed that it had been hard growing up in an anti-Christian culture, and she had often suffered for her faith.

Desiring more, Magdalena had traveled to Toronto for one of the Catch the Fire conferences. During prayer she suddenly found herself shaking uncontrollably. For the rest of the conference whenever she went forward for prayer, she was shaken violently. Admittedly she did not know what was happening to her. Upon returning home to Indonesia, Magdalena made an amazing discovery. She found that the revelatory abilities she previously possessed were now greatly multiplied. She now knew who and what to pray for. It was like having a sixth sense. She testified that where her revelatory ability was previously functioning at a three out of ten, now it had suddenly jumped to an eight or nine out of ten. Strangely enough, Magdalena's story is not an isolated case. Similar examples are beginning to surface by the thousands from all over the world.

The Shaking Hippopotamus

Before the renewal began, Colorado pastor James Ryle wrote a book about how God speaks to His people in dreams, revelations, the quickening of Scripture and the "small still voice." The book's title, *Hippo in the Garden,* was taken from a pronounced revelatory dream he received in 1989. In the dream James was standing in his house looking out at an English garden in his backyard. Everything was in place, and it was peaceful. Then a movement to the right of the garden caught James' attention. An uninvited man entered the garden followed by a huge hippopotamus. The man was leading the animal by reins held firmly in his hands. James knew the man was there to stay. Outraged and somewhat flabbergasted, James demanded to know who the man was and what was he doing. James later told me he was so startled that he spoke right out loud and woke himself up.

Having had many previous accurate dreams and revelations, James knew God was speaking to him. Lying in bed awake, James asked, "Lord, what are You saying? What was the meaning of that?"

"I am about to do a strange, new thing in My church," He said. "It will be like a man bringing a hippopotamus into his garden.

Think about that."

"What is the strange thing You will do?" I asked.

He answered, "I will surely pour out a vast prophetic anointing upon My church and release My people as a prophetic voice into the earth. It will seem so strange and out of place — like a hippo in a garden — but this is what I will do."[1]

Reflecting on that dream, James wrote:

I realize now why the dream startled me awake as it did. It was exactly what the Lord intended to happen, for the uniqueness of what the Lord is about to do will likewise jar the church from her season of slumber. Isaiah prophesied, "The Lord will rise up as he did at Mount Perazim, he will rouse himself as in the Valley of Gibeon — to do his work, his strange work, and perform his task, his alien task" (Is. 28:21). I refer to this only to highlight the fact that it is not uncommon for the Lord to do uncommon things. We tend to think that we can dictate to God what He can and cannot do. But now, as always, God will arise and do His own bidding. He will enter our docile kingdoms — uninvited, if necessary — and bring His pet *hippo* with Him!...A vast prophetic movement inspired by the Holy Spirit within the church and a validated prophetic message preached through the church in the midst of the world resulting in an evangelistic ingathering — that is the "hippo in the garden."[2]

Just months after the renewal began and we compared notes on how many people were being released in the prophetic during this move, James said, "This is the dream — the hippo in the garden." But whoever thought that it would be a shaking hippopotamus?

The Spirit and Prophecy

As introduced in chapter 4, it is my observation that the release of prophecy is one of the primary aspects of an outpouring of the Holy Spirit. Therefore, it should not really surprise us that a vast prophetic movement was expected and is now unfolding in the church. Earnest Bible scholars have been predicting this for years based on the prophecy of the outpouring of the Spirit in Joel 2:28-3:3 and Acts 2:17-21.

In the last days, God says, I will pour out my Spirit on all people. Your sons and daughters will prophesy, your young men will see visions, your old men will dream dreams. Even on my servants, both men and women, I will pour out my Spirit in those days, and they will prophesy. I will show wonders in the heaven above and signs on the earth below, blood and fire and billows of smoke. The sun will be turned to darkness and the moon to blood before the coming of the great and glorious day of the Lord. And everyone who calls on the name of the Lord will be saved (Acts 2:17-21).

Vinson Synan, dean of the school of divinity at Regent University, is an authority on Pentecostal history. As such, he was one of the theologians interviewed by *Time* magazine in the article "Laughing for the Lord."[3] In Synan's book, *In the Latter Days,* he states that the Acts 2 outpouring was not a total fulfillment of Joel's prophecy. At the time of Pentecost the gospel was only beginning to be preached. Pentecost did not touch all people because segments of the world had not yet been evangelized and had no Christian witness for the Spirit to be poured upon.[4] Even after Pentecost groups and individuals continued to be baptized with the Holy Spirit for many years (see Acts 8:14-17; 9:17; 10:45; 19:6; 2:38-39). Furthermore, the Spirit's deluge was to be followed by cataclysmic signs in the heavens and on earth leading to Joel's "great and dreadful" day of the Lord, and the coming of Peter's "great and glorious" day of the Lord (Joel 2:31; Acts 2:20). It is after or at least during this time that the great harvest occurs when "everyone who calls on the name of the Lord will be saved' (Acts 2:21). Most scholars believe this is yet to be fulfilled and spans a time up to and including "the end" — whatever that looks like.

We might say that the outworking of the Holy Spirit being poured out on all flesh began at Pentecost and will continue all the way until the second coming. As such, conservative evangelicals and cessationists believe that, like those at the time of Pentecost, we who now believe are also baptized with/in the Spirit (Acts 2:38-39). This general and permanent positional filling now essentially has become a theological conception. And if this is all that Pentecost means to us today, it is a view that is sadly lacking.

Today many settle for a positional baptism with the Spirit later expounded by Paul (1 Cor. 12:13; Rom. 8:9). The unspoken attitude is, "If you have believed, you are already baptized with the Spirit whether you felt it or not. Just accept it positionally and get on with it." But that is not the biblical emphasis of the classic texts from the books of Joel and Acts. To the early disciples, Pentecost was the coming of the active presence of God. The baptism and subsequent fillings initiated momentary demonstrations of divine power through a special work *of* the Spirit, for a special work *by* the Spirit.

Peter's answer to the onlookers who asked, "What does this mean?" was not to say, "Oh this is a one-time positional filling." Rather, Peter answered a question about the obvious phenomenon of speaking in *tongues.* Peter told them that the phenomena they were asking about was what Joel said would happen when the Holy Spirit was poured out on all flesh. In the case of Pentecost, prophecy via tongues was the primary manifestation of the outpouring of the Spirit. Later, when Paul found some uninformed disciples in Ephesus and baptized them in the name of the Lord Jesus, the Holy Spirit came on them, and they spoke in tongues and prophesied (Acts 19:5-6). Throughout the book of Acts dynamic works of power and inspired words of God are associated with being filled with the Spirit, or influenced (possessed) by the Spirit. A few of the many examples cited throughout Acts can be found in the following texts: Acts 2:4; 4:8,31; 6:3,8,10; 7:55; 8:6,15-18; 10:44-46; 13:2, 9-12; 19:6.

Paul warned: "Do not put out the Spirit's fire; do not treat prophecies with contempt. Test everything. Hold on to the good" (1 Thess. 5:19-21). By linking these terse statements together, Paul is implying that the Holy Spirit and prophecy have an intimate cause-and-effect relationship.[5] The same cause-and-effect relationship of the Holy Spirit and prophecy was also understood in early Judaism. According to Hebrew scholar David Aune, the title "man of the Spirit" used in Hosea 9:7 was a popular term for a prophet in the eighth century.[6] The title referred to one who was overcome by the Spirit of God and thereby caused to prophesy. This can be seen in the example of the Lord coming down to take of the Spirit that was on Moses and transfer it onto the seventy elders so that "when the Spirit rested on them, *they prophesied*" (Num. 11:25, italics added).

There was an apparently widespread view in early Judaism that at the end of the present age or in the age to come the Spirit of God would be poured out on all Israel, and all Israelites would have the gift of prophecy. In Numbers 11:29 Moses is quoted as saying: "Would that all the Lord's people were prophets and that the Lord would put his Spirit on them!" In the rabbinic commentary on that passage, Numbers Rabbah 15:5, we read: "In this world some men have prophesied, but in the world to come, all Israelites will prophesy." The same comment is made of Joel 2:28

148

(Masoretic text 3:1)."[7]

The ramifications of this are monumental. Scripture models much more than Christians paying mental assent to a general positional filling and going on with life as normal. They also expected the manifestations of divine power as demonstrations of this dynamic filling. And what are the manifestations of the Spirit's filling?

> Now to each one the *manifestation of the Spirit* is given for the common good. To one there is given through the Spirit the message of wisdom, to another the message of knowledge by means of the same Spirit, to another faith by the same Spirit, to another gifts of healing by that one Spirit, to another miraculous powers, to another prophecy, *to another the ability to distinguish between spirits,* to another the ability to speak in different kinds of tongues, and to still another the interpretation of tongues. All these are the work of one and the same Spirit, and he gives them to each man, just as he determines (1 Cor. 12:7-11, italics added).

Just as Joel prophesied that revelation coming in the forms of prophecy, visions and dreams, were to be the manifestations of the outpouring of the Spirit (Joel 2:28-29; Acts 2:17-18), so now Paul maintains that prophecy (among other revelatory and miraculous gifts) is a "manifestation of the Spirit." Even the angel speaking to John during the apocalypse rebuked John for worshiping him because of the magnitude of the revelation. The angel emphatically said, "Worship God! For the testimony of Jesus is the spirit of prophecy" (Rev. 19:10). Therefore a testimony that Jesus is in His church should be the release of the spirit of prophecy.

In one of the most comprehensive works to appear on early Christian prophecy, Dr. David Aune summarizes that "the ability to prophesy, which was closely associated with the presence of the Spirit in Judaism, was also regarded as a natural manifestation of the presence of the Spirit in the church, a view reflected in both Acts and 1 Thessalonians."[8] Is it any wonder then, that in the present move of the Spirit, tens of thousands of believers are receiving physical fillings with power; that many are being released in prophecy, dreams, visions, tongues and ecstatic utterances; that these fillings are experiential as well as positional; that the prophet is considered a fool, and the "man of the Spirit" a maniac (Hos. 9:7)?

12

FACILITATING AND RELEASING THE PROPHETIC

Follow the way of love and eagerly desire spiritual gifts,
especially the gift of prophecy.
1 Corinthians 14:1

We love the gifts of the Holy Spirit even though they can be like a double-edged sword — one side bringing great good and the other some pain. As mentioned earlier when the Lord first moved on our church, the prophetic gifts came with fairly wild and violent manifestations and various forms of physical phenomena. As Baptists we did not have a clue what to do with everything that was happening. There we were, up in the hinterlands of Canada with the moose and grizzly bears. We felt all alone and yet we were experiencing a spiritual awakening in our midst.

We had never heard about manifestations, spiritual phenomena or ecstatic prophecy. We didn't even know these things existed. We were Baptists! For sheer survival, we banded together in little meetings to try to figure out what was going on. In the course of time, God helped us understand some things. One of our primary discoveries was that most often these fillings were "unto something." In other words, it was not shaking for shaking's sake. A deeper, more purposeful work was going on. We had to search it out. As described in chapter 4, these anointings most often resulted in times of refreshing, impartation and empowerment. In our case, clearly the most prominent aspect was impartation unto revelation or prophetic utterance.

In this section, I have chosen to concentrate on the prophetic and a visitation of the Holy Spirit because this was one of our primary discoveries. Also, the prophetic tends to be more controversial as well as the most difficult to release and administrate. By prophecy I mean the ability to "give a word or oracle revealed by God, through the inspiration of the Holy Spirit, as delivered through a willing medium or participant sometimes designated a 'prophet' or 'one who prophesies.'"[1] It is not limited, as some would maintain, to merely good preaching — the "forth-telling" of inspired biblical truth with application. It is much more than that. Prophecy may include the forth-telling of inspired declaration, but it is not limited to that. In the tradition of the Old Testament function, prophecy also includes foretelling and the revealing of the secrets of the soul (1 Cor. 14:25). New Testament prophecy has the function of building up, encouraging and comforting (1 Cor. 14:3), as well as direction (Acts 13:1-4) and the revealing of secrets (1 Cor. 14:25; 12:8; Mark. 2:8). Rather than developing this further, I will presuppose a working knowledge of simple prophecy.[2]

The observations I share both on releasing prophecy and pastoring the prophetic are the things we have learned through trial and error. Some of the principles we have learned via the deductive method. That is, we have observed and arrived at certain conclusions based on the way things appear to be. We believe that what we pass on is implicit from Scripture, even though it may not always be explicit in Scripture.

Spirit-Filled and the Presence of God

Before applying the principles we have gleaned, a brief theological framework is necessary. In the Old Testament a primary understanding relating to the filling is the example of the Holy Spirit *coming upon* individuals.[3] Gradually the teaching begins to unfold that a new day is coming when the Lord will place His Spirit *in* us.[4] It will not be just a special few but all who possess the Spirit. By the end of Jesus' ministry the great anticipated event is not far away. Immediately after the crucifixion

151

and resurrection, Jesus appeared for the first time to His disciples and "breathed on them and said, 'Receive the Holy Spirit'" (John 20:22). In another post-resurrection appearance, Jesus told His disciples, "Do not leave Jerusalem, but wait for the gift my Father promised, which you have heard me speak about. For John baptized with water, but in a few days you will be baptized with the Holy Spirit" (Acts 1:4-5).

This promise of the Father would be like being "clothed with power from on high" (Luke 24:49). The power Jesus spoke of would follow the Holy Spirit coming upon them and would thereby enable the disciples to be His witnesses (Acts 1:8). Pentecost brought this long-awaited Spirit baptism and the same promise was extended to all who are afar off who will believe (Acts 2:38-39). Today the promised Comforter dwells *in* all of God's people (John. 14:14-17).

Over the years the prevailing evangelical notion is that the primary difference between the eras of the Old and New Testament is that whereas in the old covenant, the Holy Spirit *came upon* some of God's people, now in the new covenant the Holy Spirit *indwells* all of God's people. But is it that cut and dried? According to David Aune, an authority on prophecy in the ancient world, it isn't. He writes:

> Many texts in the New Testament and in early Christian litera-
> ture indicate that the Spirit of God was regarded as the com-
> mon, permanent possession of all Christians. At the same time,
> many other texts indicate that the Spirit of God was also
> regarded as God's power bestowed on particular individuals for
> special occasions. Although these two ways of conceptualizing
> the presence of the Spirit appear contradictory, they were never
> so regarded by early Christians...There is little reason to deny
> that both conceptions of the presence of the Spirit — as a gen-
> eral endowment of all Christians, and as an exceptional mani-
> festation of divine power in certain situations — are very old,
> and neither one can claim precedence over the other.[5]

In the context of renewal/revival, an inclusion of both dynamics better facilitates biblical theology as well as observed historical renewal/revival practice. That is, the Holy Spirit will both be *in you* and at times *come upon you*. Setting the two models of filling in opposition toward each other does not encompass the real-life tensions of how the Spirit life works. Biblically speaking, the amount of post-Pentecost biographical material is minimal as compared to pre-Pentecost Old Testament biography and New Testament gospels of a similar genre. Even so, examples still exist of post-Pentecost ministry that demonstrates the power of the Holy Spirit coming upon, as well as filling up. Like the Old Testament situational anointing, God continues to act externally with His own power coming down and/or around, dispensing extraordinary fillings and special power enabling the spirit man to act.[6]

There is no way to prove that the fillings enjoyed by Peter, Paul and the others were the same as the Old Testament fillings, but there is good reason to believe they were. When Christians experienced those extraordinary times of power where the Holy Spirit seemed not only to be in them, but all around them (Acts 5:12-16; 8:6-8; 19:11-12), these are reminiscent of Old Testament times where the Holy Spirit came upon the champions of God. Most assuredly it is similar to the anointings on Jesus.

As the prototype of all we will be, Jesus was the Spirit-filled man par excellence. Certainly Jesus was endued with that which He promised us. He said we would be filled with the Spirit, and He was "filled with the Spirit without limit" (John. 3:34). He said we would be "clothed with power from on high" and that He was the express glory of the Father (Heb. 1:3). Even though Jesus was filled more that any man, it appears that the Holy Spirit still acted outside, on and around Him. Luke records:

> One day as he was teaching, Pharisees and teachers of the law...were sitting there. And the power of the Lord was present for him to heal the sick (Luke 5:17).

> And the people all tried to touch him, because power was coming from him and healing them all. (6:19).

> [Jesus cast out] demons by the finger of God (11:20).

All this Spirit activity sounds a whole lot alike, whether it is found in the Old or New Testaments. In the Old Testament, "the hand of the Lord came upon Elisha, and he said, "This is what the Lord says..."(2 Kin. 3:15; Is. 8:11; Ezek. 8:1; 33:21-22). The Old Testament's account of the way Elisha was filled and worked wonders under the Spirit's control sounds the same as the way Jesus cast out demons in the inauguration of the kingdom of God (Luke 11:20). People have often puzzled over the curious story concerning Elisha's bones.

> Elisha died and was buried. Now Moabite raiders used to enter

the country every spring. Once while some Israelites were burying a man, suddenly they saw a band of raiders; so they threw the man's body into Elisha's tomb. When the body touched Elisha's bones, the man came to life and stood up on his feet (2 Kin. 13:20-21).

How could this happen? My opinion is that the presence of the Spirit was so mightily upon Elisha that long after he was dead and gone the Holy Spirit still lingered over his bones. The presence of God rested on a tangible, inanimate thing. When this dead man's body then touched the bones of Elisha, where the glory of God rested, the man was raised to life.

The way Jesus operated with power coming out of Him and around Him is similar to the description of Peter's anointing: "People brought the sick into the streets and laid them on beds and mats so that at least Peter's shadow might fall on some of them as he passed by" (Acts 5:15). The way healing was transferred through Elisha's inanimate bones is similar to the way healing was transferred through Paul's handkerchiefs and aprons (Acts 19:12). Why? Because the Holy Spirit is not bound by our bodies. He is both in us and comes upon us. He moves through us, and He moves upon others independent of us.

It is precisely this ongoing tension of theology which accounts for the great controversy of the "second blessing." Early second blessing proponents believed that a special post-conversion endowment of power from on high was necessary for sanctification and power. Many testify to having received it: Thomas Aquinas, George Fox, Finney, Moody and Smith Wigglesworth, to name a few. Experientially the idea was right, but the semantics were wrong. We need more than a post-conversion baptism in the Spirit or second blessing. We need a third blessing, and a fourth, and a fifth and so on. Many fillings. But like these earlier pioneers in the Spirit we have found these many fillings, anointings or impartations may come down from above for a work of power as well as bubble up from within. We should expect more in the new covenant — not less. As the old-time Pentecostals used to say, "The Holy Spirit may be *in* you, but is He also *on* you?"[7]

So What?

The obvious question is, "So what?" Why dig for bones in this yard? Because theology determines practice. Whereas the old question was, Have you received? another question may be, How do you receive? If

Christians believe that all they have to do to be filled more is to yield more, then that will be reflected in what and how they pray. "Come, Holy Spirit," will seem like a ridiculous prayer. "More, Lord," does not make sense. But if our understanding is that proactive power demonstrations which accompany fillings are facilitated by *both* yielding more *and* the Lord coming upon you in power, then our prayers will reflect that. Prayers like, "More, Lord," and, "Come, Holy Spirit," now make a lot of sense.

One theology is saying, "Wait on the Lord for His Spirit to come upon you" while the other is saying, "What are you waiting for — the Spirit is already in you." One theology is asking for the endowment of gifts and power, while the other is confused, wondering why we cannot just move in the promise that has already been given. So it is this realization of a "both/and" theology that encompasses the real-life tensions of how the Spirit life works. A theology of "both/and" does this. And it is this same realization that affects our practice of how we facilitate and release gifts of prophecy.

Facilitating and Releasing Prophecy

Based on the rubric that the Holy Spirit already indwells every believer, and yet may come upon believers for special fillings, impartations or works of service, the following are some practical realities which we have observed:

Faith

Faith is important in releasing the power of God. When the woman with the issue of blood touched the edge of Jesus' cloak, power went out from Him to her (Luke 8:44-48). Jesus' response to this miracle was that her faith had healed her. That is, her faith released the power without Jesus even being aware that it was going to happen. In the same way, lack of faith can shut down the miraculous flow of the Spirit. For example, when Jesus visited His own hometown, Matthew tersely writes, "And he did not do many miracles there because of their lack of faith" (13:58). Mark says "he could not" (6:5).

The Scriptures tell us to "follow the way of love and eagerly desire spiritual gifts, especially the gift of prophecy" (1 Cor. 14:1). If we are to be "eager to prophesy" (1 Cor. 14:39), then we ought to have faith God will release that which He tells us to pursue. And, since thousands of believers are presently being imparted with gifts of revelation as predicted and

155

announced in Acts 2:17-19, why should you not expect to receive? Faith is the starting place in releasing the presence of God, even for believers

Pray for everyone.

There is a comical story in 1 Samuel 16:1-13 that illustrates the principle of praying for everyone to receive. After God had rejected Saul as king, the Lord directed Samuel to go to the house of Jesse of Bethlehem and anoint one of Jesse's sons as king. The interesting thing is that while the Lord had narrowed His selection down to one specific family from one specific town — out of all of Israel — Samuel was not told which son was the chosen one. When it came time to anoint the next leader:

> Samuel saw Eliab and thought, "Surely the Lord's anointed stands here before the Lord." But the Lord said to Samuel, "Do not consider his appearance or his height, for I have rejected him. The Lord does not look at the things man looks at. Man looks at the outward appearance, but the Lord looks at the heart."
> Then Jesse called Abinadab and had him pass in front of Samuel. But Samuel said, "The Lord has not chosen this one either." Jesse then had Shammah pass by, but Samuel said, "Nor has the Lord chosen this one" (1 Sam. 16:6-9).

This same process was repeated seven times as Jesse had seven of his sons pass before Samuel. But God had not chosen any of them. Finally Samuel asked, "Are these all the sons you have?" Jesse said he had one more. David was sent for, and "then the Lord said, 'Rise and anoint him; he is the one.'" So Samuel took the horn of oil and anointed him in the presence of his brothers, and from that day on the Spirit of the Lord came upon David in power" (1 Sam. 16:12-13).

A pragmatic thinker would ask, "Why all the drama? If God can reveal the one family out of all the thousands of families in Israel, can't He also reveal ahead of time which son is the right one?" Technically yes but practically no. God wants to keep us dependent upon Him. The Bible says that some will prophesy. The problem is that we don't know who they are. There is only one way to find out — pray for everybody! At every renewal conference I try to have one night where everyone receives prayer for the impartation of prophecy. In these days of the outpouring of the Spirit, thousands of "Jesse's youngest" are being released. You will never know whether you are meant to be released in the gift of prophecy unless you come in faith asking for the spirit of prophecy to come upon you.

Epicenters of the Spirit's power

When we pray for people to be filled and released we have found that some times are hotter than others. Accepting for the moment that the Holy Spirit both fills us from within but may at the same time act independently of us, whole new models of prayer are opened up to us. We can pray that the Spirit falls on an entire area in power. There are accounts of that happening in renewal/revival history. More than that, these examples have happened in the Bible. In our experience, we have seen epicenters of Spirit power, similar to the model recorded in 1 Samuel 19:19-24.

> Word came to Saul: "David is in Naioth at Ramah"; so he sent men to capture him. But when they saw a group of prophets prophesying, with Samuel standing there as their leader, the Spirit of God came upon Saul's men and they also prophesied. Saul was told about it, and he sent more men, and they prophesied too. Saul sent men a third time, and they also prophesied. Finally, he himself left for Ramah...So Saul went to Naioth at Ramah. But the Spirit of God came even upon him, and he walked along prophesying until he came to Naioth. He stripped off his robes and also prophesied in Samuel's presence. He lay that way all that day and night. This is why people say, "Is Saul also among the prophets?" (1 Sam. 19:19-24).

This story is absolutely amazing. King Saul had many soldiers, but only those who came into the proximity of Samuel and the prophets experienced the Holy Spirit coming upon them along with the subsequent manifestation of prophecy. The implications are vast. Can people, Christian or not, come into the presence of the Holy Spirit and be moved upon and filled with accompanying manifestations? Can transference of the Holy Spirit, in the external sense, happen? Can the spirit of prophecy jump from one person or group onto others who previously have never prophesied (Num. 11:25)? Evidently so. I have personally watched people just walk across the floor through an area where some major fillings had previously taken place. They were physically thrown by the power of God. The more faith and presence of God, the more likelihood of that being your moment of release.

The laying on of hands and the transference of fire

Closely linked to the reality of epicenters of the Spirit's power, is the teaching of the laying on of hands and the transference of "fire." Just as God's presence may fill a temple and make it impossible to stand (1 Kin. 8:11), so He may fill people who will have the same effect on others. Jesus often touched people as He healed them. Simon the Sorcerer saw that the Spirit was given as the apostles laid their hands on people (Acts 8:18). Ananias laid hands on Saul of Tarsus and said, "Be filled with the Holy Spirit" (Acts 9:17). "When Paul placed his hands on the Ephesian disciples, the Holy Spirit came on them, and they spoke in tongues and prophesied" (Acts 19:6).

Throughout the Bible the laying on of hands is an important form used by God to facilitate release. Twice Paul reminded Timothy not to neglect his gift which was imparted through prophecy and through the laying on of hands (1 Tim. 4:14; 2 Tim. 1:6). By the time the book of Hebrews was written, the doctrine of the laying on of hands was considered a foundational doctrine (Heb. 6:1-3).

The idea of people acting as spiritual lightning rods may be new to many, but it is an old principle. Some people are so conducive to God's Spirit that when they touch others God may use them for impartation or to release others. One summer night our church's top street evangelist was punched in the face while trying to witness to a young gang kid. John, our street worker, was a triathlon runner and very strong, but the blow crushed his spirit.[9] He came to the house where we were praying, discouraged and broken of heart.

After a brief discussion we placed him in the middle of the room and began to pray. Soon the room was charged with the power of God. All at once David Ruis became like a Holy Spirit power lifter. David was physically trembling with the power of God emanating out of him. He stepped back with his arms raised and shouted, "Receive the power of the Lord!" With that he lunged forward and grasped the back and torso of John who was sitting on the floor with legs extended. John's body jolted with power.

David stepped back and with even more intensity, shouted, "Receive the power of the Lord!" Again he lunged forward and embraced John around the back and torso. The room was electric. Almost everyone present immediately began to shake violently. Then one final time David stepped back and shouted again. This time when David gripped John's body, John's entire six-foot frame was zapped with the tangible power of God. His teeth chattered, and his whole body shook as he vibrated across the floor with his legs fully extended.

Needless to say, John received a major infilling. All discouragement left, and he was lifted to spiritual heights never before experienced. For months afterward a radiance of God was visibly evident as he led worship and preached with a new boldness. It is our experience that these fillings do not last a lifetime but rather for a moment, a situation or a season. They are fillings to help us go higher. As my brother-in-law Steve said, "It wasn't when I was by myself yielding but when I was touched by others that I received an impartation and release for prophecy." We need to lay hands on one another and watch for the transfer of "fire."

Waiting

When we combine faith, the presence of God, and those gifted for impartation, we have an explosive combination. Still we may have to wait for the wind to blow, and the presence of the Lord to come. Like Elisha who called for a harpist to play as he cultivated the worshipful resting place for the Holy Spirit — we wait. We are told to "fan into flame, the gift of God in us" (2 Tim. 1:6). A fan blows wind on a small flame and the flame burns brighter. The blowing of the wind is analogous of the way the Spirit of God works.[10] The Arnotts call this "soaking" — prolonged prayer that soaks the recipient.[11]

The Holy Spirit is power, but He is also a person — the person of the Holy Spirit. We invite Him to come to us. The Quaker practice was to wait upon God until His Spirit moved upon them. The moving of the Spirit would cause the Quakers to quake and prophesy. The analogy of waves is a good description of how the Spirit comes. We wait, and then we feel the waves of the Spirit. If we remain focused and intent, another wave of the Spirit will come — only this time more intense. Then another and another. We have had many meetings where the weight of glory so increased that by one or two o'clock in the morning people could not even walk to their cars to drive home. They were grounded by "sober intoxication."[12]

Sometimes we have to wait even after the prayer time is over. An interesting discovery was made in a recent survey conducted by Margaret Poloma, a sociologist from the University of Akron in Ohio. The study was derived from responses of more than five hundred respondents who had visited the Toronto Airport Christian Fellowship and who represented more than thirty denominations and many countries. Of the respondents, 50 percent were church pastors or leaders with an average age of forty-five years. When asked if they were more in love with Jesus now than ever before in their lives, a whopping 88 percent said yes they were. Eighty-two percent communicated that talking to their families and friends about Jesus is more important to them now than ever before, and 92 percent said they were now encouraging others to visit the Toronto Airport churches. The unexpected discovery was that many testimonies began to come in which revealed the critical aspect of waiting. Testimony after testimony said they experienced physical manifestations of the Holy Spirit not at the renewal meetings, but later when they returned home after having been prayed for in Toronto. Many reports of healing reflected the same process. People were prayed for and found themselves better the next day even though the illness had persisted for years. Time is important in the process of prayer ministry.

One young lady in our church was from a very conservative cessationist missionary background. At first she was very leery of this prayer ministry. When one pastor, who was greatly used in impartation and release, prayed for her, to her own surprise she began to shake violently. For months all she could do was shake. To her knowledge nothing else was happening. We kept praying for her and she kept shaking. After some months she began to have prophetic dreams. Then a few months later she began to have waking pictures. Then she began to get prophetic phrases. Within eight months of the first impartation a full-blown prophetic gift blossomed. This lady became one of the most revelatory persons in our whole church and continues to prophesy regularly to this day, nine years later.

Read the signs.

One of the noticeable aspects of this present worldwide renewal is the abundance of manifestations associated with it. While manifestations are a response of our limited human frame to the mighty power of God, manifestations can also act as signs. What do you do with signs? You read them. At Pentecost the people asked, "What does all this mean?" Peter responded with, "Let me explain this to you." Personally I have found manifestations useful in helping me to know how to pray. I ask God and others who have had experience in this arena to help me interpret the signs.

For instance, in the last eighteen months I have witnessed people everywhere overcome with groaning and pains in their stomachs when prayer teams prayed for them. Early on in our renewal experience we learned what this manifestation often means. One evening the Lord said,

"Tonight I am going to teach you." He instructed us to bring a quiet and deeply sensitive lady into the middle of the room for prayer. She was the type who never drew attention to herself and never wanted to make a spectacle. The Lord then said, "I am going to show you the burden of intercession." As we began to pray for this young mother, she began to double over in pain. She groaned and heaved. In front of us all it was as if she were going through hard labor. The Lord said, "This is the burden of prayer I want you to carry. I want you to travail over the lost until My Son is formed in them." That was nine years ago, and I never forgot that night.

Today I see similar scenes taking place in the lives of thousands of people at renewal meetings. Often, but not always, shaking precedes an impartation unto revelation and prophecy. By understanding the sign, I know how to pray, what to bless and how to ask for more. In order to release to full term everything that the Lord wants to do, we try to discern the intentions of God by reading the signs or various manifestations as best we can. Then we pray for more!

Prophecy according to your faith

The last aspect that I have found to be critical in the releasing of prophecy is simply the encouragement to do it. You learn to ride a bike by getting on and pushing the pedals. In the same way, people will not be released in prophecy unless they actually begin to prophesy. An often mistaken assumption is that if one is going to operate in spiritual gifts, then one will always operate in them to the fullest degree. In other words, an individual with the gift of healing will always be able to pray for the sick and they will always be healed. Surely Paul had the gift of healing,[13] and yet even he left Trophimus sick in Miletus (2 Tim. 4:20), and did not receive a miraculous healing for Epaphroditus (Phil. 2:26-27).

Similarly some have a superficial understanding of prophecy. They think each person endowed with a prophetic, or budding prophetic, gift should prophesy like an Old Testament seer. In fact the New Testament gift of prophecy is much different than the Old Testament office of a prophet. In the New Testament we are instructed to prophesy according to, or in proportion to, our faith (Rom. 12:6). Paul said, "We see through a glass darkly" (1 Cor. 13:12). Therefore, "Two or three prophets should speak, and the others should weigh carefully [judge] what is said" (1 Cor. 14:29). We no longer stone those who give a non-prophecy; we judge it and try to mature the gift and encourage the individual as maturity in the gifting develops.

161

So it still remains that when learning to ride a bike, ultimately you have to get on and start pedaling. The person released in the flow of prophecy must be encouraged to exercise that gift. Even if it is only one word, they should be encouraged to say it. Yes, it needs to be under the supervision and care of pastors and leaders, but it must start somewhere. As Paul says, "Since we have gifts that differ according to the grace given us, let each exercise them accordingly: if prophecy, according to the proportion of his faith" (Rom. 12:6, NAS). In time each gift will grow and mature. Every great oak tree was once a little acorn. Early on in our church's visitation of the Holy Spirit, the Lord told us to greet one another by name and say, "Prophesy in the name of the Lord!" So I say to you, "Prophesy according to your faith."

13

PASTORING THE PROPHETIC

It was he who gave some to be apostles, some to be prophets,
some to be evangelists, and some to be pastors and teachers,
to prepare God's people for works of service, so that
the body of Christ may be built up.
Ephesians 4:11-12

One of the big challenges arising from current renewal is how to integrate what God is initiating into the daily flow of church life. How do we pastor a visitation of the Holy Spirit? How do we pastor the outbreak of the prophetic? These are critical questions and deserve greater treatment than can be covered in one chapter. Still, an overview, however incomplete, is helpful to point one in the proper direction. As the church is moved along in the process, people will learn as they go. In our experience we have had to overcome significant hurdles as we grappled with hard lessons during nine years of pastoring in the midst of a phenomenal (literally) outpouring of the spirit of prophecy. Some of this we pass on to you.

Welcome Prophecy

If any church or group is going to pastor a prophetic move, they have to welcome prophecy. I always say to pastors, "You gotta want it!" The Bible treats prophecy as normal in the context of Christian living. The letters to the Thessalonians are considered among the earliest books of the New Testament. In them Paul tells us: "Do not put out the Spirit's fire; do not treat prophecies with contempt. Test everything. Hold on to the good" (1 Thess. 5:19-21). This Scripture sandwiches prophecy in the middle of such ordinary things as prayer, giving thanks, testing everything and avoiding evil. It is clear in Scripture that prophecy is for the church, and we're not to forbid it (1 Cor. 14:39-40).[1] The New Testament acknowledges the prophetic office (Acts 13:1; Eph. 2:20; 4:11; Rev. 16:6; 22:9), prophetic giftings (1 Cor. 12–14; Rom. 12:6), and momentary prophetic empowerings according to the will of God (Acts 2:11; 16-19; 8:29; 19:6).

Going beyond the warning not to forsake prophecy, the Bible teaches that we are to "eagerly desire" it (1 Cor. 14:1,39). This is the place to begin. I do eagerly desire prophecy and welcome it in the church. I believe in it, have faith for it and have received great benefit from it. Direction, programs, callings and even the acquiring of large church facilities are all due to the prophetic gift operating in our midst. We have scores of incredible testimonies to illustrate the truth that prophecy builds up (see 1 Cor. 14:3). As a result, I welcome prophecy, and we continue to see it blossom. John Arnott always says to me, "You love this, Wesley," and it's true. I do.

So the first principle, which is so simple but can't be stressed enough, is this: "How badly do you want it?" If you really want prophecy and pray earnestly desiring it, the Lord will grant it. You don't have to be prophetic yourself to see it birthed in your group. You simply need to have a heart for God, a heart for the prophetic and a heart for prophetic people. I love the prophetic ministry. Someone said the main criteria for raising children is to love them! The same goes for prophecy. Pray for it; be around people who do it; encourage them, and they will become as your children. Paul said, "Eagerly desire spiritual gifts, especially the gift of prophecy" (1 Cor. 14:1). Why? Because prophecy edifies and comforts. Prophecy is a gift that can build up the entire church.

Expect Problems

Recently I had a sobering, yet confirming, talk with John Wimber. He sat on one side of the table and I on the other. "Wesley," he said, "you need to stress the problems of the prophetic more than you do, or people will be set up for disappointment and trouble."

"What do you mean?" I asked.

John elaborated, "You are a strong leader with a good biblical background, mixed with a healthy dose of common sense. On top of that, you have a very pure form of the prophetic in your midst. This has resulted in great blessings for your church. Because you love and believe in the prophetic, your faith is infectious. But it may not go so well for others who desire an experience similar to the one you have had."

I nodded, and John went on, "Wesley, I've had many, many prophetic or so-called prophetic words given to me — hundreds of them. I can count on two hands those words that were actually the Word of the Lord in season. Unless a pastor is strong enough and well-grounded enough to pastor this through, it may prove more of a bane than a blessing."

Whether Wimber's ratio of accuracy is exact or speaking in hyperbole, the point is clear: Much of what is given in the name of the Lord isn't! Yet when it is the Lord, it is powerful. It is God speaking through the darkness. The tension of expecting a mess along with blessing should not surprise us. At the end of the day, someone has to clean the fish that were so eagerly caught. The writer of Proverbs wryly states, "Where there are no oxen, the manger is empty, but from the strength of an ox comes an abundant harvest" (Prov. 14:4). The meaning is obvious. If you don't want a mess, don't have any oxen in the stall. But the very oxen that make the mess are the same oxen who work to produce an abundant harvest. If we are going to do the works of the kingdom we must expect problems along with the harvest.

Of course the problems are legion. There are the problems of more gifting than character (1 Cor. 13). Of jealousy and quarrels. Of people wanting to be what they are not (1 Cor. 12:14-30). Some will feel that God doesn't love them because they don't manifest, and others wonder why they are manifesting. There is the offensive odor of ambition and those who are trying to find their significance through the gift. At times the church body will shut down the prophetic person through criticism and judging. At other times the person with revelation will so intensely feel the burden or warning of the prophecy that they internalize the word and actually turn against the body. These are all messes, and we have not even gotten out the big shovels.

It takes an even larger shovel to scoop up the mess of wrong prophecies or non-prophecies. There are always those who think they are prophetic when they aren't. Then there are those who have a mixture of true revelation and their own "stuff." If that isn't bad enough, an even worse situation develops when those who are in the place of weighing the word (1 Cor. 14:29), make a call that the word is off, but the speaker will not receive it. Convinced he has heard from God, the revelatory person will not lay it down. This creates more of a mess.

Finally there are the problems of revelation, interpretation and application. Let's define these terms. Revelation is discerning what is seen or heard in the Spirit. Interpretation is determining what is meant by what is seen or heard. And application is understanding how to apply that which was seen or heard. There are times when a prophetic word or picture must be exegeted and then skillfully pastored into the life of a church or individual. These are all potential minefields — messes in the stall.

I once watched a documentary called *Yellow Fever*. It was about Brazilian miners in pursuit of gold. Men left wives and children to go deep into the jungle and live in harsh conditions. Their job was to blast the side of a large mountain with pressurized water. As the water dislodged the dirt, it formed a river of mud which drained down the hillside. Thousands of men, standing up to their knees in muck, were busily scooping up huge buckets of the mud, which they carried to the rinsers. The mud was then rinsed over and over again. Panning ever so delicately they hoped in the end to be left with a little gold dust or, better yet, a few small golden nuggets. This search for gold motivated the entire human ant pile.

After the documentary I thought, *That's what we are doing!* All the muck and troubles for a few small golden nuggets. Prophetic nuggets. Apples of gold in pictures of silver. Words fitly spoken from God (Prov. 25:11). It takes a lot of wading and washing to get to the gold. Maybe this is why Paul wrote, "Do not treat prophecies with contempt. Test everything. Hold on to the good" (1 Thess. 5:20-21). To pastor the prophetic, we begin by realizing that, in spite of the pitfalls, we must nurture and not despise prophecies.

Prophets Prophesy, But Pastors Pastor

> It was he who gave some to be apostles, some to be prophets, some to be evangelists, and some to be pastors and teachers (Eph. 4:11).

Both the prophet and the pastor may be sorely tested whenever there is an outbreak of renewal and prophecy.[2] Simply put: the prophet is not the

166

pastor; the pastor is not the prophet. We cannot presuppose that people with prophetic giftings also possess pastoral abilities. While some may, most revelatory people are not gifted to carry the weight of leadership or pastor that which they are seeing. As mentioned previously, the prophetic person will have their fair share of problems. But the pastors and leaders will be tested as well. Will they continue to lead in the outpouring, or will they abdicate to others? The answer to that question will determine the effectiveness and life expectancy of a visitation.

Pastor More, Not Less

People do not handle change well. The more activity there is, the more need for pastoral care. The more movement, the more need for more guidance. Picture a floating or drifting sailboat. Very little guidance is needed. However, if the winds are high and the boat is moving fast, constant vigilance is essential. As the early church in the book of Acts grew, the apostles were forced to pastor more. Paul's entire section on the gifts in 1 Corinthians 12-14 is pastoral in nature. The church needs to be pastored; the prophetic people need to be pastored, and the prophecies or prophetic messages need to be pastored.

Early in the process we learned an axiom: Pastors pastor and prophets prophesy. There is a difference. Pastors cannot relinquish their role even when — might I say, especially when — the prophetic voice is strong. A very real danger is that the revelation of prophetic people can be so powerful and so accurate that it appears as though the prophets have the entire mind of Christ on the matter they are prophesying about. And if indeed it is God speaking, ought we not listen? Yet it is also true that "we know [see] in part, and we prophesy in part" (1 Cor. 13:9). Letting the Spirit lead does not mean that the Spirit's leading is antithetical to His own complementary, but distinct spiritual gifts of "leadership, governance, and administration" (Rom. 12:5-8). Structure is not the great enemy of being led by the Spirit. On the contrary, it is the bipolar extremes of too much structure or too much free form that create the problems. Riverbanks actually increase the speed of the water, and containers increase the water's usefulness. Thus, when God is speaking through people, we must understand He is also leading through people. We all are co-laboring with Him, all using our gifts until we come to the unity of the faith (Eph. 4:11-13).

167

Lead More Than Before

Closely linked to pastoring is leadership. Again, you do not have to be prophetic to lead the prophetic. Although I do hear from God, I am not nearly as prophetic as those I have had the privilege of working with. In our church we have many people who are very prophetic. The first thing that can happen to pastors is that they become extremely intimidated. What are you going to say to these people who "hear from God"? One can almost feel like saying, "They hear from God, but who do I hear from, Ann Landers?" Unfortunately, when intimidation sets in, pastors lay down their gifts — to the detriment of the body of Christ.

This is illustrated in a humorous, real-life story from our own church (that I described earlier in the book). Initially, we were having many meetings in the back room or in homes where a great deal of shaking and prophesying was taking place. We were very excited, but we didn't know how to bring it into the church at large. We also were scared that if we took it into the Sunday services it would blow the church apart. One night as we were meeting in a small, cloistered group, the Lord spoke loudly through the other pastor, saying, "Take Me out of the back room!" God wanted to expand what He was doing to more people. This was to take the form of the church-wide night of repentance mentioned in chapter 4. With fear and trembling we told the church all that God had said, and although we weren't sure what it would look like, we invited everyone to come.

Surprisingly, hundreds of people showed up. News had leaked out that something big was happening. We began the meeting without any agenda. David Ruis led the worship from his keyboard. Things were going beautifully and the presence of God was in the place when all of a sudden the power of the Holy Spirit fell on David. He began to shake violently and instantly he broke into spontaneous prophecy. Leaving the keyboard, he roared out, "On your face!" Immediately all the people in the church dropped to their knees. Six or seven other people were hit with ecstatic shaking and fell in line behind David, forming what looked like a human train with seven boxcars. David was moving through the congregation shouting out prophetic exhortations.

Other than the few who had already been initiated in the small prayer meetings, no one had ever seen this before. A long-haired, backslidden fellow brought by his girlfriend happened to come to church that night for the first time. For a moment he stood petrified as if glued to the back wall. Then, like a man aflame, he ran to the front, prostrated himself on the carpet and began to cry out in repentance. He rededicated himself on the spot and is still active in church to this day. All around him people began to wail and cry out. The noise was like a herd of bawling cattle.

I did not have a clue what to do. It was so intimidating. I was the pastor, and people were looking up at me, questioning if this was OK or not, and wondering what they should be doing. But I was busy following behind David wondering if I was to get on my face. As this surreal picture unfolded, I was abruptly yanked back to reality by a man pulling on my pant leg. It was a deacon in our church. He had a look of panic on his face. Desperately he asked, "Wesley, can I go to the bathroom?" I whispered in a hushed tone, "Yeah, sure, go to the bathroom."

Although humorous now, this incident furnished a lesson in leadership. The man was so awe-inspired, he didn't know how to fit real life into the equation. God had said, "On your face," but this man had to go to the bathroom. I realized something that day. When the supernatural intersects with the natural there exists the possibility for tension. That is why there must always be a leader. Renewal or no renewal, somebody has to be there to say, "It's OK; you can go to the bathroom!" Seriously, I learned a lesson: Never abdicate the leadership of the floor.

Prophets Prophesy

While it is essential that pastors pastor and lead, it is equally essential that prophets prophesy. Scripture says, "Two or three prophets should speak, and the others should weigh carefully what is said" (1 Cor. 14:29). Notice, the "prophets should speak." Getting the prophetic people to speak is an art. I have discovered that prophetic meetings need a conductor. Paul put it very aptly when he likened the church to instruments of an orchestra (1 Cor. 14:7-8). An orchestra has a conductor! A conductor is helpful because the people who ought to speak often don't, and the people who ought not to speak, always do. I've often found that godly and gracious people are less inclined to push themselves forward. Yet they may be the very ones the Lord is speaking through. But there are others who say too much, and by their audacity they destroy credibility and shut down the authentic gift of prophecy in the group. So a prophetic administrator or conductor has to come along to govern the amount of volume being produced. They have to silence the part of the band that is too noisy and increase the volume of other instruments.

Once the prophets speak, "the others should weigh carefully what is said" (1 Cor. 14:29). Judgment of the words lies with the hearers. In our context we stress that all prophecies come under the judgment of the leaders and the listeners. Prophetic people are not necessarily responsible for the interpretation of their words and definitely not responsible for the application of them. That responsibility lies with the leaders or with the individual(s) to whom the prophecy is given. In one respect that is freeing, but it's also where conflict comes into play. All prophetic people must cultivate a heart of submission. This is sometimes easier said than done.

One reason for this is that prophetic words often come with intense feelings. Like the little bird in *Chicken Little,* the prophet can feel as if the sky is falling or as if there will be disaster if immediate obedience doesn't follow his or her prophetic word. Nobody wants to disobey God, but there are always many angles that the prophetic person doesn't see because they are not speaking from the perspective of leadership. Often it is not that easy to instantly implement the directives of a given word. In fact, when the Lord deposited prophecy in our church nine years ago, there were many directives given, some of which we are just now getting around to implementing. Others, like the acquisition of our church facility, took more than five years before it was fulfilled.

Prophetic people need to know that they are only responsible before God to give what they feel the Lord is saying. They are not responsible to see that directional words are carried out. These words may, in fact, be rejected. However, if a prophetic person does not cultivate a submissive attitude, they will begin to hold an offense and feel as if leadership is being disobedient to God. A serious division can be the eventual result, which is exactly the opposite of what prophecy is supposed to do (Eph. 4:12-13).

Building a Prophetic Nest

Early on we found that if we wanted the prophets to prophesy we had to provide a safe place where this could happen — a nest where young prophetic eagles could grow. We began a group where prophecy could be nurtured on a regular basis and called it Prophet Sharing. This group met for five main reasons: relationship, pastoral care, pooling of revelation, practice and prayer. After eight years of consistent prophetic ministry, these prophetic people say it has been their lifeline.

I now tell church leaders, "If someone in your church does not oversee a group like this, you probably will not have a mature prophetic ministry in your church." Whatever a pastor wants, talks about, believes in and nurtures, that is what will happen in the church. Anyone can say, "Oh, I honor it, and I like it," but if they don't put energy into it, it will not happen. This does not mean that the senior pastor has to oversee such a group. But it does mean that someone tied into leadership must be involved. Our church attendance has been more than a thousand for many years. Even so, Stacey and I personally lead the various prophetic groups meeting virtually every week since prophecy broke out in 1988.[3] That is a high degree of commitment for a large church. By investing a high level of commitment, we have also been blessed with a high level of prophetic ministry. There's no shortcut to pastoring the prophetic. It's the long way home.

It is hard to describe what a typical Prophet Sharing meeting looks like, but I can say what they include over a given time. Rarely do all the elements happen in each meeting. Formal teaching has not often been a main emphasis of the meeting but is present on an as-needed basis. There are several key ingredients necessary for building a prophetic nest. They include:

1. Relationship

Part of the long way home is developing relationships. Without relationship with leadership in the church, it is doubtful whether the prophetic ministry will be a long-term blessing. There are too many things to go wrong. Relationships are developed over time. So we hang out just to hang out. The people of my church want me to relate to them as people, not just as prophetic gifts. When we gather, the first thing we do is have coffee and visit for twenty or twenty-five minutes. And it's wonderful fellowship It's not irrelevant. It's part of the program. This is where our group often gathers vision. What's happening? How has everyone been? What is God doing? Many times we never leave this phase as it leads into a talk about our group, an individual in the group or the church and the kingdom of God.

This is also where the alarm bell sounds, warning us of problems. People do not work together without problems. We try to maintain a rule that if there is a problem we will talk about it. Without this system a fire could start, and you will have no advance warning. Then a single bucket of water wouldn't be able to put out the fire. Soon a great amount of water would be needed. Communication is best facilitated within a relationship setting. Over the years the relational component has proven to be the most important part of meeting together. Without it there would not even be a group to work with.

One day a group leader came to me upset because people in his group were so busy talking he could not get the meeting started. This same leader was also in the habit of leaving as soon as the structured part of the meeting was over. Soon he was no longer the leader. The people had stopped following him. Remember, the people *are* the meeting. Leadership works best in relationship.

2. Worship

If there is a worship person present, it is good to have a time of worship. Often we glorify God by just speaking scriptures out to Him and telling Him how great He is. Or we may just talk of the great things God has done and stir ourselves up with Holy Ghost stories. Often the Lord comes right into the midst of it. We pray and glorify Him, and then we wait for direction.

One time we were praying with Jim and Ann Goll from Kansas City. Jim has listed one hundred names of God, and at this particular meeting he began to extol the Lord by calling out His names. We came to the name Friend of Sinners. Out of nowhere came a fervent spirit of prayer for evangelism. It increased as groanings and travailings spontaneously broke out in the room. We continued to pray on the subject of evangelism for about an hour or more. In the midst of prayer, many prophecies came forth. It was glorious, and yet no one had any idea that the meeting was going to go in that direction. This illustrates how the Spirit may lead within a structure. The stronger the leader, the greater his capacity to lead freely.

3. Pooling and interaction of revelation

The pooling of revelation is especially unique. In the meeting mentioned above, the worship time launched us into a great time with God. At other times, however, you could declare all one hundred names of God, and there may be no special anointing on any of them. At those times we may choose to be quiet for a time to see if there is some revelation that the Lord wants to give us. If we ask the Lord for revelation and don't hear anything specific right away, the leader must now exercise leadership. The normal question is, "Has anyone been hearing anything through the week that we ought to pray on?" Often the reaction is the same. Like an ancient tribal custom we invariably go through our 'prophetic extraction dance.' Everyone in the group will feign deafness. Body language says, "No, we have not heard anything this week." It's always the same. Again I will prod, "Anything?" Heads lower and the group does not make eye contact. Feet shuffle silently. Usually there's nothing! An inexperienced leader may be tempted to give up at this point, but this is all part of the dance.

Then I say, "Well, have any of you had any specific dreams in the last few days?" Again no one speaks. Now I begin to ask by name. "Cathy, have you had any specific dreams?" "Well, yes, but I don't think it's relevant." So she'll tell her dream and say "But I don't know what it means." We go through the whole process with the next person who might venture, "Well actually, I was praying the other day, and I did have this thought come through my mind." After a few more people have been pooled someone says, "This is amazing! Just this morning I was thinking the same thing, but I thought it was just me." The leader, by taking the initiative to go through this process, will generally gather a theme out of the pooled revelation, which we never would have had if the leader hadn't extracted it. It is a divine treasure hunt where we are usually delightfully surprised by the complex revelation and direction that was unearthed.

Another benefit gained from pooling revelation is that it clears the slate. It is not healthy for revelatory people to carry heavy burdens around for long periods of time. Once shared with the group, revelation can be prayed through, and it may even act as a warning from the Lord. It also helps beginners to grow in confidence by the simple act of seeing that they are actually hearing the same things as the rest of the group. Unless there is this type of objective measuring process most people would not even know that God had been trying to communicate with them.

4. Practice

Like all the other spiritual gifts, prophecy can atrophy by lack of exercise. The muscle must be continually used in order to stay strong. One day I was taking a group of prophetic prayer people out to help minister at a conference. On the way there I asked a newly released prayer person, "Sarah, how's it going with the prophetic?"

Sheepishly she said, "Oh, you know, it hasn't been going too much."

"Well, don't you think it ought to be?" I persisted.

Remembering back to the night when she was prophesied upon and received an initial impartation, Sarah began to unravel her theory. "Maybe the Lord just touched me for that month, and now it has lifted."

I listened for a while and finally said, "I don't believe that at all. I believe it's just gone dormant through lack of use. What we need to do is stir it up again. Use the gift."

Unconvinced, she mumbled, "Well, maybe."

I insisted, "I believe that when the Holy Spirit gives these gifts, they are actually without repentance. That means they are there if you step out in faith and exercise them."

The next meeting, when it came time for prayer ministry Sarah was at the back. Vexed in my spirit, I called, "Sarah, come on up here!" We got a group around her and began to pray. "Lord, more! Come Holy Spirit!" In moments she began to quiver. We continued, "Lord, empower Sarah to prophesy." Suddenly God ignited her like an electric rod. Grabbing her hands I placed them on people's heads and encouraged her to pray! Before long Sarah was flowing again. As the intensity increased she would pray for a few moments and then fall to the ground. Now the people coming up for prayer began to pick her up and ask her to pray for them. Sarah would pray some more and then fall right out in the Spirit.

Later that night Sarah grinned, "I guess it's not gone away." It has been a year and a half since her initial impartation. She now meets regularly in a small group, and her revelation continues to increase by the week. Recently her mother said, "From the first night Sarah was prayed for, God literally added prophetic and creativity all at once. Sarah is a different girl."

There are many reasons why prophetic people shut down, including lack of use, criticism, fear or lack of confidence. It's one thing when the Holy Spirit comes on someone in a meeting with great power, but then there is "the morning after." They think, "Did I really do that? Oh, I've embarrassed myself. Maybe I made it up. I'll never do that again as long as I live." This is the time they need a group that will say, "Hey, that was great. We loved it. You're hearing God speak." They need to be told that over and over again. And they need to continually get up on the horse and keep riding. Exercise the gift weekly in a safe place where the prophetic gift can be measured, blessed and matured.

5. Prayer on a theme

The possibility always exists that truly no one has any prophetic revelation that is relevant. If that happens, then the leader should suggest a theme or direction. The leader should always come prepared to pray about certain themes, either from Scripture or from needs within the church. But such themes are not injected unless there's an absence of a theme from the prayers of the group. During intercession a prophetic theme may or may not come, but it doesn't really matter. I encourage everyone to pray whether or not they are moved by a prophetic prayer. From time to time emphasis should be on praying one for another in a prayer ministry mode.

Summary

Although the preceding material is not exhaustive, it gives a general idea of the basic structure of a "prophetic nest," outlining what a prophetic group might look like. I wanted to de-mystify the shroud that goes along with prophetic meetings to demonstrate that a successful prophetic group, like all successful groups, has basic and practical steps that are taken to assure its success.

Of all that I have mentioned in this section, probably the two single most important aspects in pastoring the prophetic are 1) providing a structured setting or "prophetic nest" for the prophetic eagles to gather; and 2) strong pastoral leadership that loves the prophetic. I cannot stress these two enough. You don't have to be prophetic to be a leader. But you do have to have a heart for God, a heart for the prophetic and a heart for prophetic people.

I exhort you to pray for prophecy. Be around people who do it. Why? Because prophecy edifies. Prophecy comforts. Prophecy builds up the entire church.

SECTION FOUR

Where to Go With
a Visitation of the Holy Spirit

14

THE MAIN THING IS
THAT THE MAIN THING
REMAINS THE MAIN THING

He answered: "'Love the Lord your God with
all your heart and with all your soul and with all
your strength and with all your mind;' and,
'Love your neighbor as yourself.'"
Luke 10:27

When I was in Toronto in August 1994, I came upon an interesting newspaper item. It read as follows:

This Tuesday marks the hundredth anniversary of one of the strangest events in Toronto's history. On August 16, 1894, people in Buffalo watched with astonishment as an image of the city of Toronto appeared hovering over Lake Ontario.

The image was so detailed that witnesses could actually count downtown church spires. Here is a description of the event as recorded in the August 25, 1894, edition of *Scientific American* magazine:

"The citizens of Buffalo, N.Y., were treated to a remarkable mirage between 10 and 11 o'clock on the morning of August 16. It was the city of Toronto, with its harbor and small island to the south of the city...The mirage took in the whole breadth of Lake Ontario. A side-wheeler steamer could be seen travelling in a line from Charlotte (a suburb of Rochester, N.Y.) to Toronto Bay.

Two dark objects were at last found to be the steamers of the New York Central plying between Lewiston and Toronto. A sailboat was also visible and disappeared suddenly. A close examination of the map showed that the mirage did not cause the slightest distortion, the gradual rise of the city from the water being rendered perfectly. It is estimated that at least twenty thousand spectators saw the novel spectacle. [1]

Today's Move of God, a Mirage or the Real Thing?

Was the Toronto apparition a hundred years earlier an ironic foreshadowing or just coincidence? Today the world is watching again as church spirals are seen on Toronto's skyline. Is it just coincidence that the word *Toronto* is the native Indian word for "meeting place?" After only one year into the renewal, *Toronto Life* magazine, in naming the best and worst of Toronto, named Toronto Airport Christian Fellowship as the city's top tourist attraction in 1994.[2] Customs officials shake their heads in wonder as hundreds of thousands of visitors have come from all over the world to Toronto. Whereas once their destination was the mighty Niagara Falls, now it is the mighty spiritual water falling from heaven.

Taxi drivers know the church and the phenomena equated with it. One taxi driver was known to say to a laughing customer, "Don't worry. I know where you are. I'll be right over." Hotel revenue around the Toronto airport strip increased by 25 percent over 1994 and 1995 as an extra four hundred rooms a night continued to be booked on an ongoing basis due to visitors coming to go to church. Curious as to why a church has been responsible for their increase in business, some hotel owners have come to the meetings and wound up getting saved. As John Arnott says, "You know something is happening when hot dog vendors set up shop at the entrance of the church parking lot and end up finding Jesus."

Where Is This Renewal Going?

After two and a half years, more than one million people from all over the world have come to one renewal center to be touched by God. The question asked most often is, "Where is this renewal going?" Or better yet, "Where should it be going?"

Sense of an imminent worldwide revival is everywhere. The title of David Bryant's latest book says it all: *The Hope at Hand: National and World Revival for the Twenty-First Century*. Bryant quotes such Christian leaders as Billy Graham, Paul Cedar, Bill Bright and many others. They all concur: "We are on the verge of the greatest spiritual awakening in Christian history."[3] Of course the even tougher question is, "How do we get from here to there?"

Let the River Flow

The old adage still rings true, "It's hard to live on cake." After the renewal meetings then what? Once while on a ministry trip to Hamburg, Germany, I heard a phrase that stuck with me. It went like this: *"die Hauptsache ist, dass die Hauptsache, die Hauptsache bleibt!"* The English equivalent is, "The main thing is that the main thing remains the main thing." It has been stressed over and over again that this renewal is to renew us to "live out the main and plain commandments of Scripture."

After the initial news of what was happening in Toronto had rippled through the entire movement of Vineyard churches, Wimber came to speak to the Canadian pastors. The occasion was the first national Canadian Vineyard pastors' conference in August 1994. En route to Canada, John asked the Lord, "What should I say to the Canadians with respect to this recent visitation?" As John continued praying the Lord gave him an open vision. The following is how Wimber conveyed his vision to the group.

> In the vision the Lord showed me a magnificent mountain lake. Beautiful sunshine reflected off water that was fresh and inviting. The water of the lake spilled over a dam and cascaded into a river and came down the sides of a mountain into a large plain. In the plain, there were thousands and thousands of acres of vineyards. I saw men working in the fields, digging irrigation ditches. Then the vision ended.
>
> So I said, "Lord, what does it mean?" In my mind, He gave me, "The lake is the blessing I'm pouring out. Isn't it beautiful? Isn't it fresh?" I was so touched, I began to cry. He then said, "The cascading stream is the church. I'm pouring it first into

the church." I wept more. I just thought, "Oh thank You, Lord. Thank You for the blessing on the church."

Then I saw again how the water came down to the bottom of the mountain into the plain where the workers were tending the irrigation ditches. I recognized these irrigation ditches as ministry to the poor, ministry to the weak, sick, broken and lost. There were different kinds of vineyards with different kinds of fruit growing on the vines. Then He said, "That's My people. This blessing can either stay in the church, with great meetings that eventually end. Or we can pull the gates up and let the water begin flowing. If you want, you can direct the water, the blessing, into the fields."

I got the clear impression of co-laboring. God was pouring out His blessing. But if we don't dig the channels, if we don't go out into the highways and by-ways, if we don't put evangelism forward, if we don't do the things God calls us to do, revival won't spread.[4]

Renewed Unto Seven Main Things of Scripture

Wimber's main exhortation was, "We can direct the water!" Where we dig the ditches, the water will go. We have a little joke in our church. Occasionally a person who has been moved by the Lord will repeatedly come up for prayer with the request, "What is this shaking unto?" Their question is always same, "What's it unto; what's it unto?" Not that we don't honor the sincere seeker, but sometimes you get the feeling that one is just wanting affirmation of the more visible anointings. In such cases we laughingly say, "It's unto tithing and service."

But there is more truth to that answer than it may seem. These special anointings or graces are really divine favors to enable us to be better Christians. Our preoccupation with spreading the fire should be so that believers will be renewed unto the main and plain things of Scripture. At the risk of oversimplifying I want to concentrate on what I believe to be the main and plain troughs where we are to direct this refreshing. Based on historical precedent the following seven emphases embody the elements necessary for any renewal or visitation to blossom into localized or full-scale worldwide revival. These seven main things flow out of the two great commandments (Matt. 22:37-40; Mark 12:29-31; Luke 10:27) and God's holy intention for a mature church (Eph. 4:11-13).

The remaining chapter contains the directions in which I believe any renewal or visitation has to go in order for it to become a full-scale, world-wide revival.

These directions include renewing our passion for the first great commandment to love God. Then we must work for the unity of the faith. We want to equip individuals to flow in the ministry gifts of the spirit, especially prophecy and healing (1 Cor. 14:1). Lastly we must seek to fulfill the second great commandment "to love our neighbor as ourselves," which includes taking the blessing to the streets by way of *mercy* and *mission*.

1. Spreading the renewal of loving God

Through overwhelming feedback we see that the renewal is facilitating a grace for loving God and creating a greater thirst for the spiritual disciplines of "mere Christianity." As such, continuing to spread renewal is a legitimate end in and of itself. By spreading renewal we can keep from spending all the refreshment on ourselves. Give the water away, and keep digging the ditches to bring water to other dry areas. My observation of churches who have experienced dramatic renewal is that they begin to stagnate if they are not continually giving it away. Once we are refreshed in our love for God it is then time to do something with it. Renewal meetings for meetings' sake lose their vitality if new people are not coming to be filled. Having said that, the ministry of giving the refreshment away to parched believers is valid.

While the oil is flowing, we need to get everyone under the flow of the Holy Spirit. Elisha told a distressed widow to gather all the clay pots she could find and then was warned, "Don't ask for just a few" (2 Kin. 4:3). As she went inside and shut the door, the oil began to flow. Interestingly the oil stopped flowing when there were no more jars to fill. We need to bring in the people just as the widow woman brought in the pots to be filled. Without more empty vessels to fill, the flow of oil stops. Without fresh wood, the fire goes out. This is one of the major reasons churches must monitor closely what God is doing and ask what their own unique calling will be. If they are not capable of or called to be a watering hole, then they must turn the emphasis to renewed workers carrying water out to the thirsty.

Steve and Doug are from a small town of about ten thousand in California. In June 1994 Steve and his wife, Becky, were on holiday in Kelowna. As God would have it, he drove by our church and saw the prayer pole we had erected during our twenty-one-day prayer and fasting time. Slightly put out he thought, "What a bunch of exhibitionists." On his long drive back to

California the Lord began to convict him. "Would you do it?" the Holy Spirit's voice said to his spirit. Steve didn't answer. The voice went on, "If not, why not?" In his own words, Steve later said, "I was brought face-to-face with my own coldness of heart."

About a hundred miles down the road, Steve came to the conclusion that he had to resign from pastoring his small Foursquare church. Later he told me, "I realized I had lost my first love, and my church deserved better." As they drove along, Steve woke his wife and told her what he was thinking. She said, "Steve, don't be hasty. What else would you do?" They drove on in silence. Upon returning home, try as he might, Steve could not shake his conviction. He decided, "If God does not come and refresh me, I'll quit the ministry."

Within a few weeks the situation came to a head. Steve had spent ten hours preparing a sermon on the Holy Spirit. He was in church on Sunday morning laboring to get it out when he felt he couldn't hide it any longer. He hung his head and right in the middle of his sermon said, "I can't take this any more. I'm so dry that if God doesn't do something to me, I have to resign as pastor. You deserve better than I am giving you." A hush went over the congregation. Steve slowly left the pulpit and made his way to the place of prayer in front of the altar. There were sniffles in the crowd, and some came and joined him in prayer. All in all it was not a victorious service. People left confused, scared and wondering what was going to happen.

The next day in desperation Steve phoned his friend Doug, who had pastored the same church before him. Doug confessed, "I can't help you, Steve. I resigned myself. But maybe we could both be helped by going to a Let the Fire Fall conference at the Anaheim Vineyard." On Tuesday they were both on their way to the conference.

What happened next is the same story that is being played out in thousands of pastors' lives. Steve and Doug received a mighty touch of God. They fell, shook, laughed and cried. At times they were so full of God that they were incapable of walking or talking. But it is the rest of the story that really excites me. In recent letters Steve and Doug described in outline form what God did in their lives over the next twelve months.

1. More than one thousand people came to faith during a crusade manned and staffed by the renewal leaders from their small church.

2. Doug and Steve have spoken in more than fifty churches and

pastors' meetings.

3. Their church has been sought out by other denominations for advice in prayer and renewal.

4. They have hosted monthly Pastor's Renewal Fellowship meetings with more than sixty pastors from thirteen denominations.

5. They participated in a Foursquare pastors' camp with more than four hundred pastors and their wives, where many were mightily renewed.

6. Steve has become a divisional superintendent in his denomination and oversees fifteen churches.

7. In their city of Dinuba, Steve has been asked by other churches to become the president of the city's ministerial association, specifically for the purpose of leading other churches in renewal.

8. Their small church of two hundred has maintained weekly renewal meetings for more than one year with many hundreds of people coming and receiving ministry from the Lord.

In a word, Steve and Doug have never been so excited in the things of God! These two pastors are now on a mission, doing the main and plain.

2. Unity in the faith

Another of the items high on the agenda of the main and plain purposes of God is that of the unity of His children. In Jesus' great prayer at the last supper He pleaded:

My prayer is not for them alone. I pray also for those who will believe in me through their message, that all of them may be one, Father, just as you are in me and I am in you. May they also be in us so that the world may believe that you have sent me. I have given them the glory that you gave me, that they may be one as we are one: I in them and you in me. May they be brought to complete unity to let the world know that you sent me and have loved them even as you have loved me (John

17:20-23).

Unity is a fruit of the commandment that we love one another, just as Jesus has loved us (John 15:12). It is a tragic twist of Scripture for some to label the unity that God is initiating worldwide as an end-time conspiracy of Satan to set up the church for an antichrist. Whatever else the religious conspiracy warnings mean (Matt. 24:24; 2 Thess. 2:3-12; Rev. 13), they are not describing the unity of true Christians with other Christians that Jesus prayed for. Paul is very clear in saying that the deception will be swallowed by those who are perishing.

> They perish because they refused to love the truth and so be saved. For this reason God sends them a powerful delusion so that they will believe the lie and so that all will be condemned who have not believed the truth but have delighted in wickedness (2 Thess. 2:10-12).

And yet even with all this spiritual and occultic deception gathering momentum, God will be enacting His own revival of unity until the end. An often-missed end-time passage is Ephesians 4:11-13, which says:

> It was he who gave some to be apostles, some to be prophets, some to be evangelists, and some to be pastors and teachers, to prepare God's people for works of service, so that the body of Christ may be built up until we all reach unity in the faith and in the knowledge of the Son of God and become mature, attaining to the whole measure of the fullness of Christ.

Unity will come before Christ returns for His bride who will be mature, clothed in glory, holy and blameless (Eph. 5:27). In fact, the unity that Christ prayed for is a precursor to evangelism. As believers from every church love one another, it is this display to the people of the world that causes them to believe there really is a God, and He really did send His Son to love us because He Himself loves us as His own Son (John 17:21,23).

Once, when asked about the union of the United States of America, Benjamin Franklin was heard to say, "My advice is that we hang together, or we'll all hang alone." Franklin said much with little. He recognized that the states needed each other for their own well-being. For far too long the Christian church has not hung together and has, in effect, "hung alone."

Without realizing how much the isolation and division have hurt us, we have chosen to cut off our noses to spite our faces. One of the great virtues of a worldwide renewal is a new and real unity.

Everywhere Christian churches of every denomination and persuasion are beginning to work together with a new love and appreciation previously unheard of. During eight months of the renewal meetings at The Tabernacle Church in Melbourne, Florida, cessationist Presbyterians worked hand in hand with interdenominational charismatic churches. Southern Baptists preached in the same pulpits as Vineyard church pastors. As a result, thousands came to Christ in just a few months, and refreshment came to hundreds of churches.

One of the significant fruits of the Toronto Airport Christian Fellowship is their continual determination to work for city unity. Before they were two and a half years into the renewal they were networking with more than six hundred local pastors and churches. At an inter-church rally held in October 1995, one hundred Toronto churches participated as more than five thousand believers came together from all denominations to worship and celebrate their corporate love for Jesus Christ. Earle Cairns, in his treatise on awakenings and revivals, lists one of the main fruits of historical revival: a revival of an ecumenical spirit.[5] I would add that Christian unity is no small matter, nor an addendum to the faith. It is the embodiment of the second great commandment.

3. The spiritual disciplines of prayer and intercession

Both before and after a personal visitation in 1984 (mentioned in chapter 2), Mike Bickle committed himself to pray. He felt compelled to pray along with God's intended purpose to visit the earth. The mode it took was absolutely amazing. For the next seven years Mike and many of his staff personally spent five hours a day praying for a future revival. Then in the subsequent three years they averaged about three hours a day in devotional prayer and intercession. They built into the genetic code of their church, the Metro Vineyard in Kansas City, three prayer meetings a day, six to seven days a week. Prayer became a calling and a "gracelet" (as John Wimber says) for them. Yet during a time of special renewal and grace, surely some of this grace should rub off in the prayer room.

The example of Daniel in Babylon typifies this activity. He writes:

> In the first year of his reign, I, Daniel, understood from the Scriptures, according to the word of the Lord given to Jeremiah the

> prophet, that the desolation of Jerusalem would last seventy years. So I turned to the Lord God and pleaded with him in prayer and petition, in fasting, and in sackcloth and ashes (Dan. 9:2-3).

When Daniel understood through prophecy that God was about to visit his people, he set himself to pray. Prophetic forecasting produced a confidence to pray in or "win" the known will of God. Daniel's model of prayer and intercession is something for us to emulate. It is worth mentioning that the bulk of the prophetic words with respect to this present outpouring do not stop with renewal. As mentioned earlier, many world leaders believe that God's intention is full-scale revival — now! As yet we have not seen worldwide revival rains.

One statement which has always convicted me greatly is the pithy description mentioned by James, "Elijah was a man just like us...and he prayed." None of us ever really think about Elijah being a man just like us but praying earnestly. James goes on to say, "He prayed earnestly that it would not rain, and it did not rain on the land for three and a half years. Again he prayed, and the heavens gave rain, and the earth produced its crops" (James 5:17-18).

The actual account in 1 Kings 18:22-46 says that "Elijah climbed to the top of Carmel, bent down to the ground and put his face between his knees." He took the birthing position and began to travail for the rains. Sending his servant to "go and look toward the sea," the report came back, "There is nothing there." But Elijah had heard the sound of heavy rain. He assumed the birthing position again. Again the servant went and looked. It was seven times until faith gave way to sight. Seven times Elijah prayed. The seventh time the servant reported, "A cloud as small as a man's hand is rising from the sea." Then "the sky grew black with clouds, the wind rose, a heavy rain came on and...the power of the Lord came upon Elijah...and he ran."

Before we can run, we have to bend down and pray. As mentioned in chapter 3, there is a growing momentum of prayer beginning to ascend up to heaven. Surely the prayer of faith is one of the fruits of this renewal, and a main and plain command of Scripture that must be pursued.

4. Prophecy, and 5. Praying for the sick

A mature renewal church will operate in the gifts of the Spirit, especially those modeled and called for by Jesus. Jesus heard from the Father and moved to heal the sick. Jesus was called "a prophet, powerful in word and deed before God and all the people" (Luke 24:19). Jesus commissioned His disciples to disciple all future believers in the things He had taught them (Matt. 28:20). They did. The church of the New Testament did hear from the Father and prayed regularly for the sick. The empowering of Pentecost was given as a promise for all future believers to be like the ones described throughout Acts.

> Peter replied, "Repent and be baptized, every one of you, in the name of Jesus Christ so that your sins may be forgiven. And you will receive the gift of the Holy Spirit. The promise is for you and your children and for all who are far off — for all whom the Lord our God will call" (Acts 2:38-39).

In section 3 I dealt extensively with the gift of prophecy, which the early church considered a regular part of their spiritual arsenal. To be renewed in the main thing of prophecy I refer you back to the previous section. But the other main thing the early church did well was praying for the sick. Indeed so many were healed that praying for the sick became a primary means of evangelism. Hence, Wimber's thesis in his book, *Power Evangelism,* asserts that conversion and church growth rarely occur from preaching alone. Rather it was signs and wonders, namely, healing and demon expulsion, that brought about the great results.

Randy Clark, the fire-starter God used to ignite the Toronto fire, spoke at both the one- and two-year anniversaries of the Toronto Blessing. Each time he brought forth a powerful message on healing. When I first met Randy, healing was in the category of "we had hoped..." At both anniversaries he stood up with confidence in front of thousands of people saying God can use anyone for healing because he used "little ol' me." Recounting several miraculous stories, Randy talked for hours of God's present power to heal. In the last two years Randy has personally prayed for and witnessed incredible healings, many of them in this last year, including cancers, tumors, Parkinson's disease, scoliosis of the spine, asthma and even a completely debilitating fused back.[7] These were desperate situations. He says, "Not all are healed, but I do pray for all, and some are healed."

The same is true of Gord Whyte in our own congregation. When he first came on staff, Gord had his own design and carpet installation business. He came from the tough world of construction workers and building developers. But when the Holy Spirit's power fell on us, Gord was renewed. Now, eight years later, he moves in incredible words of knowledge and prays regularly for the sick. He says he has seen hundreds of healings.

Recently Gord received a letter from a young lady he had prayed for. For a year-and-a-half she had been experiencing chronic fatigue. On top of that she was plagued by a severe case of plantars warts. The evening of the meeting her feet were so sore she could barely walk, but her mother implored her to go for prayer. When the ministry time came she asked for prayer for her fatigue. Gord and his wife, Jan, prayed and within moments she felt a marked improvement. Excited and feeling better she stayed late and a whole group went out to the restaurant late in the evening.

At the restaurant conversation came around to healing, and it was then that the young lady revealed her terrible bout with plantars warts. Just two months before she had gone to the doctor to have them surgically removed. The doctor cut out fifty warts on her left foot and twenty-five on her right. Sadly they had already begun to grow back. Gord began to relay how he prayed for his own daughter's warts, and they had vanished within days. Gathering faith from the stories, they prayed right there in the restaurant and committed it to the Lord.

Within two days all of her warts had literally dried right up. She said the skin on the soles of her feet was so new and tender that for a time she had to wear special socks until the skin could toughen up. She said her feet had became like those of a baby. Six months later she was writing to verify God had indeed done a healing, and she was thankful for the servants He had used.

Summary

Loving the Father, prayer, unity, praying for the sick — these are the ministries of Jesus. This is where the river has to flow.

15

EMPOWERED FOR MISSIONS AND MERCY

As long as it is day, we must do the work of him who sent me.
Night is coming, when no one can work.
John 9:4

As an illustration of the second greatest commandment in action, Jesus told the famous parable of the Good Samaritan. At the end He asked a religious inquirer a very pointed question: "Which one was neighbor to the man who fell among thieves?" The only response possible was that the real neighbor to the Samaritan was "the one who showed mercy on him." The story was obviously designed to demonstrate to the listeners what loving ones' neighbor actually looked like — true goodness as opposed to imagined goodness. Then, with penetrating application, Jesus said, "Go and do likewise." In other words, love is practical. It is amazing that, in spite of all of our learning and correct doctrine, there are still two things the church appears to have trouble doing, namely, loving God and loving each other.

6. Mercy, and 7. Mission

If we are to truly love our neighbors as ourselves, we will find ourselves being pulled towards mercy and mission. Mercy, because we are moved for the temporal needs of others here on earth, and mission, because we are moved for the spiritual needs of those both here and after they have left this earth. It should sober us to think that the same Jesus who enjoined us to love God and then our neighbors also taught that each and every one of us will give an account of our own lives and sins. The result of that account will be that some "will go away to eternal punishment, but the righteous to eternal life" (Matt. 25:46).

I believe it is difficult to assert that we actually do love our neighbors if we are not just as concerned about their eternal well-being as we are about their earthly well-being. Paul's missionary thrust was motivated by this concern. He said, "Knowing the terror of the Lord we persuade men" (2 Cor. 5:11). And it was for good reason that Jesus commanded His disciples (and us) to "go into all the world and make disciples of all the nations or peoples" (Matt. 28:19). In light of these two concerns for the well-being of mankind, the temporal and the spiritual, Christians must engage in the dual aspects of mission and mercy. Broadly defined, mission would include evangelism (saving the lost), foreign missions and church planting. It is natural that Christians who have been renewed or revived flow toward these directions of missions and mercy.

An encouraging sign that we are on the threshold of a great move of God is that while people in the renewal are being refocused onto evangelism, church planting and missions, there also appears to be an inexplicable worldwide receptivity to the gospel. Many are praying and believing for a great harvest. David Bryant writes, "I believe — with unshakable conviction — that we are on the threshold of the greatest revival in the history of the church. This is what I hope. I have no doubts that it is coming."[1] Apparently he is not alone in his convictions. Bryant quotes several Christian leaders as saying that we are on the verge of the greatest spiritual awakening in Christian history.[2] The really tough question, however, is, How do we get from here to there?

Camp Meetings and Circuit Riders

A peek at the past may help to stimulate faith for the future. In both the first and second Great Awakenings, two dominant components — open-air meetings and circuit riders — helped to fuel the refreshing stream until it became a mighty river of salvation. In England during the Great Awakening (the late 1730s to 1740s), the three most famous personalities were the Wesley brothers — John and Charles — and their friend George Whitefield. What these three men did was unheard of in their day. They took church outside! In fact, they began to preach every day, many times a day, wherever they could get an audience. This was scandalous due to the fact that in those days clerics were strictly confined to their own dioceses. Therefore, evangelism, discipleship and missions conducted outside of one's own diocese would be considered anathema.

Whitefield was the first to take this novel idea of preaching to the marketplace. In time he would be preaching forty to sixty hours per week. Initially John Wesley abhorred the idea of preaching outside of a church in the open air and/or in another's diocese. Eventually, however, Wesley followed Whitefield's example. He recorded his first endeavor in an entry in his April 1739 journal. It read, "I submitted to be more vile, and preach the gospel out-of-doors." That day Wesley stood on a little hill and preached to Bristol shipyard workers. It became the first of thousands of outdoor sermons. As a consequence, when asked later in life, "Where is your parish?" John Wesley was able to truly say, "The world is my parish."

What the Wesley brothers accomplished in their lifetimes is virtually superhuman. It is reported that during John Wesley's fifty years of ministry he traveled an incredible 250,000 miles on horseback — a distance equal to ten circles of the globe. He preached more than forty thousand sermons to crowds sometimes in excess of more than ten thousand persons at a time. All of this was done outdoors. For all the power of his voice and endurance, John was only five feet three inches tall and weighed 128 pounds. John Wesley also wrote five thousand sermons, tracts or pamphlets of some kind. His brother, Charles is credited with writing more than sixty-five hundred hymns, an equivalent of one a day for twenty years, many of which are still sung today. Together these brothers were used of God to transform the English world in their lifetimes.[3]

Inspired by their model, hundreds, and then thousands, of ardent preachers began to preach outdoors to whomever would listen. Two American examples were Francis Asbury and Peter Cartwright. Asbury's long career spanned forty-five years. Like Wesley, he wore out six faithful horses traveling 270,000 miles. He visited every state in the union once a year and crossed the Allegheny Mountains sixty times. One biographer estimated that Asbury stayed in ten thousand homes. He preached more than sixteen thousand sermons and ordained more than four thousand preachers.[4] Because of this, Asbury became the father of the American circuit riders and provided a workable example. The circuit riders traveled and preached two sermons per day on average. On top of that, they wrote, counseled, exhorted, led Bible classes and established churches and local ministers.

Cartwright's legacy is just as amazing. Starting in 1803 as an eighteen-year-old single man, Cartwright began to preach a grueling schedule of two to three sermons a day for twenty years. Marrying in 1808, he altered his pace slightly but kept "beating the ground." Despite marriage, children and poverty, he also preached an unbelievable fifteen thousand sermons, as well as baptized eight thousand children, four thousand adults and received ten thousand into church membership. His autobiography is colorful and feisty — the stuff American frontier folklore is cut from.[5] Peter and his saintly wife, Frances, ultimately had nine children. When Cartwright died in 1872, his descendants included fifty grandchildren, thirty-seven great-grandchildren and seven great-great-grandchildren. To their credit, all of the Cartwright children became active adult members in the Methodist Episcopal Church and brought their children up in the same.[6]

The American counterpart of the Wesley and Whitefield open-air meetings were the camp meetings. The first one was the Cane Ridge Revival camp meeting. It seemed to spring out of nowhere and caught everyone off guard. Instead of the few thousand who were expected, crowds of upwards to twenty thousand descended on this small town in Kentucky. The event began a phenomenon. Desperate souls, hungry for God, fainted, cried, laughed and shook. Before the week was over, three thousand people had found new faith in Christ. Observers described it as a "second Pentecost." It is worth noting that this great revival, which went on to transform American society, "displayed more physical manifestations than any other revival in history. Indeed they seemed to be an integral part of the awakening."[7]

Many Preachers Preaching Many Sermons to Many People!

In less than a hundred years the world would feel the impact. An irreligious population was brought face-to-face with Christ. Many have asked why. Why did the Great Awakenings bring so many people to true, saving faith? The answer may be more obvious than we think. Could it be that there were just so many preachers, going to so many places, preaching so many sermons to so many people? Everyone knows that if we are going to catch any fish, we have to go fishing. And the more we fish and the more fishermen involved in fishing, the greater the yield of fish. Yes, it's true that God has to anoint the preaching and the hearers, but that is His responsibility. Nevertheless, His command to preach is clear. The reason the Great Awakenings woke up so many was because so many preachers were preaching so many sermons to so many people.

The data can well support this theory. The Methodists did become the fastest growing church in post-Revolution America.

> Between 1770 and 1820, American Methodists achieved a virtual miracle of growth, rising from fewer that one thousand members to more than a quarter million. In 1775, fewer than one out of every eight hundred Americans was a Methodist; by 1812, Methodists numbered one out of every thirty-six Americans. At mid-century, American Methodism was almost ten times the size of the Congregationalists, America's largest denomination in 1776. The key to the Methodist success was a dedicated contingent of itinerant preachers, or circuit riders.[8]

Even though it was called a time of Great Awakening, it appears that each group did not receive the same blessing respectively. No, it was the Methodists and the Baptists that were awakened and grew more than others. Why? Because they put out more fishermen. Similarly today, it will be the ones preaching and not the ones criticizing who will see the converts.

It is especially encouraging that of those surveyed after attending renewal meetings in Toronto, 83 percent report that "talking about Jesus to my family and friends is more important to me now than it has ever been before."[9] So it holds that if this renewal leads individuals, laypeople and pastors to preach the gospel more than they ever have before, then we can speculate that it may lead to full-scale revival.

Ironically, the worldwide refreshing and awakening that began in earnest in 1994 has produced its own style of camp meetings and circuit riders. Renewal conferences have replaced the old camp meetings, and pastors who have experienced a fresh touch from God have added itinerant circuit riding to their job descriptions. In just two years after the 1994 renewal began, millions of thirsty Christians from around the world have attended these modern camp meetings. Renewal conferences and local church renewal meetings are taking place all over the world. England's summer Bible weeks have seen record crowds as more than twenty thousand at a time congregated to meet Jesus and be touched by His Spirit. For the modern circuit riders, jets have replaced horses and personal computers hum as the Internet conveys the latest statistics to all those who are plugged in.

One day in Toronto a number of us sat together to discuss this concept. As we counted and compared meetings and conferences, we found some interesting parallels to the old camp meetings and circuit riders. John Arnott conducted approximately one thousand meetings in the first two years of renewal. These meetings ranged from small groups of a hundred or so pastors and leaders to larger general gatherings of one thousand to ten thousand persons. By year two there were as many as twenty circuit riders from the Toronto Airport Christian Fellowship who were carrying the renewal message to different parts of the globe. When we added up all the other renewal centers with their respective pastors conducting renewal conferences, we realized that in our circles alone, circuit riders numbered more than a hundred people who were cumulatively conducting thousands of renewal services a year. The river was flowing in the direction it needed to flow. And the result of more fishermen fishing for fish is that more fish are caught. Renewal is begetting salvations and a ground swell toward revival is forming.

From Hollywood to Argentina

One hot summer night in Pasadena a man came up to me with tears in his eyes and said, "Thank you for what you guys are doing with these meetings." The man, Clayton Golliher, was director of Hope for Homeless Youth and had been working Hollywood's inner city for fourteen years. He said, "I don't know how to explain it, but ever since the nightly renewal meetings began here in Pasadena I have seen more conversions in the last few months than in any other period in our fourteen years of ministry. We are now pushing the three hundred mark of conversions in Hollywood of even the hardest of street gangs." Clayton told me that he often took gang members to the renewal meetings, and many would run down to get saved. Instead of being turned off by the manifestations and visible displays, Clayton says they "sensed God" and wanted His touch.

Recently Marcello Marioni, one of the pastors from Buenos Aries who is well acquainted with the Argentine Revival, was ministering at a small town in Oregon. As he addressed a group of pastors, someone asked him, "What did it look like before revival broke out in your country? Spiritually what was happening?" His answer was not what some of the more conservative pastors were waiting to hear. He said, "The revival was preceded by three years of many of the things you are presently seeing happen in North America. There were the manifestations, the laughter and the spiritual drunkenness. Finally it was as if the sponge had reached a saturation point. Then suddenly revival came and millions of salvations occurred. In Buenos Aries, my city, two million people were saved over a two-year period. Meetings would start in the morning and continue non-stop until early in the next morning."

Mercy

Even a casual look into church history reveals how intricately tied to revival is the aspect of showing mercy. In some cases revival fell, and then with new eyes the revived Christians began to demonstrate extraordinary acts of mercy as they transformed society from the bottom up. At other times the seasons of refreshing revived only segments of the church, who, with a renewed zeal, began to show mercy. The result was the same — revival. Where does this river of refreshing have to flow? It has to flow where it has flowed so many times before in classic revival — to the streets.

The examples of revived Christians who revitalized the larger church by showing mercy are plentiful. Early Christians were known for rescuing abandoned Roman babies and then raising them as their own. Orphans and the poor could always find help from the church (James 1:26). For centuries monks and nuns gathered together in communities called monasteries. The majority of these monasteries became centers for learning, hospice or medical work, care for the poor and evangelization. Entire religious orders were organized throughout the Middle Ages with a focus on preaching the gospel and helping the poor. Some of the most famous are the Order of the Franciscans, founded by the radical St. Francis of Assisi, and the Poor Clares, a female order started by "Gentle" Clare, also of Assisi.

Besides the more strict religious orders of monks and nuns, there were voluntary lay movements made up of Christians totally devoted to preaching the gospel and serving the poor. A mass women's movement called the Beguines was one such organization that affected Christian Europe for hundreds of years. At times the numbers of these volunteer women reached as high as 10 percent of a city's population as they banded in semi-communal structures to work for the good of others.[10] A modern day equivalent would be to see cities with as high as 10 percent of the population living together in communal context like a Youth With A Mission base or some other parachurch organization in order to serve the poor. The great Catherine of Siena was a tertiary and member of one of these lay movements who practiced selfless sacrifice to the poor, the sick and the dying.

Revival and Mercy

Again, looking at the examples of the awakenings over the last 250 years, we find the pattern is the same. In a sweeping historical overview of revival and social reforms, Earle Cairns maintains that "revival goes hand in hand with the application of Christian principles to government, and with antislavery, antiwar and temperance activities."[11] Revival historian J. Edwin Orr found the same. Of the great revivals from John Wesley on, they all resulted in huge thrusts of ongoing evangelization and social action.[12]

In England it was the Quakers and then Wesley and the Methodists who were the first to oppose black slavery. Although Wesley and his converts ministered in prisons, hospitals and work houses, they also tried to abolish slavery. At age eighty-eight, six days before he died, Wesley wrote his last letter, which was to William Wilberforce, an evangelical member of Parliament. With faltering hand Wesley exhorted him to keep on fighting that "execrable sum of all villainies — slavery, until it shall utterly vanish away." Wilberforce did keep up the fight, and with the help of the rest of the Clapham Sect — evangelical leaders in business and politics — they brought bill after bill to bear in the House of Commons. For forty years they fought through the government systems with Wilberforce losing most of his money amid his deteriorating health. In the last year of his life he saw the reward of his suffering as the Emancipation Act of 1833 freed 781,000 slaves throughout the British colonies.[13]

The list of charitable works, organizations and accomplishments done by those revived Christians who literally obeyed Jesus' command to show mercy are so numerous as to boggle the mind. John Howard, founder of the John Howard Society, was encouraged by John Wesley to reform England's prisons. Elizabeth Fry, mother of eleven children, became a Quaker preacher as well as a prison reformer. Even the Young Men's Christian Association (YMCA) was founded to provide religious services and culture in a "home away from home." Florence Nightingale said that God had called her with an audible voice to help the sick. She impacted an evangelical named Henri Dunant who went on to found the Red Cross. Even the Royal Society for the Prevention of Cruelty to Animals (RSPCA) was founded by an Anglican cleric — Arthur Bloome, with the aid of Wilberforce and friends.[14]

Mercy to children has always been a focus of the church. Lord Shaftesbury became a member of Parliament in 1826 and wrote in his diary that he would found his "policy on the Bible" and practice "active benevolence in public life" in order to advance religion and "increase human happiness."[15] Shaftesbury spent most of his time fighting the evils of child exploitation in the factories, mines, brickyards and chimney sweeps. It was rightly called "the white slave trade." Children as young as four were spending up to fourteen hours a day in pitch black mines. Little orphans picked up off the street were forced up chimneys to clean in the choking, claustrophobic dark. Shaftesbury enacted the Ten-Hour Act which prohibited factories from working children thirteen to sixteen hours a day. He passed legislation prohibiting the use of children as chimney sweeps and children under ten from working in the mines. Shaftesbury enacted government on behalf of the oppressed.

George Müller got revived and turned his attention to caring for orphans. He eventually was caring for up to 2,050 children at one time. Thomas J. Barnardo was the product of the revival in 1859. Lord Shaftesbury influenced Barnardo to become a missionary to the slums of London. Barnardo opened homes for children who were homeless because of drinking parents. Before Barnardo died he had cared for sixty thousand children.[16]

In America the Second Awakening commenced under the ministry of Francis Asbury and the circuit riders as well as through the camp meetings. It continued right into the ministry of Charles Finney and created a virtual tidal wave of mercy ministries. It is said:

> This Awakening had a greater impact on secular society than any other in American history through its vast social concern...Christian laypeople organized thousands of societies that touched every phase of American life. Slavery, temperance, vice, world peace, women's rights, Sabbath observance, prison reform, profanity, education — all these and more had specific societies devoted to their betterment.[17]

The instrument formed for doing this was a vast network of volunteer societies all united under one great banner called the Benevolent Empire

By 1834 the total annual income of the Benevolent Empire was about today's equivalent of 130 million [American] dollars, which rivaled the entire budget of the federal government in those days![18] They succeeded in bringing Christian values into the mainstream of American society.

Few people realize that out of the first 119 colleges founded in America, 104 were started by Christians to acquaint students with the knowledge of God. These colleges and universities include Princeton, Dartmouth, Columbia, Harvard and Yale. Furthermore, out of a graduating class of forty thousand in 1855, ten thousand went on to become ministers — more than 25 percent![19] So whether it was schools, hospitals, politics or the evils of society, revived Christians always let their religion flow out to the streets in mercy.

Mercy Ministries Can Grab You, Too

When God moved powerfully on our church, we became incapacitated by our newfound love for Him. All we wanted to do was to gather together, worship and pray. During the first six months of our outpouring, we did little else but meet and pray — sometimes for up to thirty and forty-five hours a week. I remember thinking, "Nothing else matters but this." Then later, after we had spent much time in the Lord's presence yearning to just know and love God, a subtle shift began to take place. We began to love the things He loved. Directly traceable to our renewal, we became involved with social concern and mercy ministries. God's choice of vehicles was most surprising.

One night a no-nonsense businessman named John had set up an appointment to see me. He and his wife, Sandra, had been attending our church for only a short time. They had come from a Dutch Reformed and conservative Baptist background. At the last minute I called him to say that I would have to cancel because an emergency had come up. He asked what the emergency was. Reluctantly I told him that it was a serious deliverance situation that couldn't wait. I offered that he and his wife were welcome to come along if they liked, but this had to be done. Fear told him not to come, but curiosity got the better of him. He decided to join me on my trip, even though he didn't know whether he believed in demons, let alone in confronting them. Later he said, "That night I was thrown into a radical learning curve."

The night was wild enough by anyone's standards, and John went home very impacted by the whole exposure. He also developed a whole new appreciation for prayer. He and his wife began to pray all the time. One night he jumped out of bed thinking they were in an earthquake. Surprisingly, when his feet hit the floor, he found that it was not shaking. Quickly turning on the light he realized it was Sandra who was physically shaking and had caused the bed to shake. Now John was getting even more concerned. *What was it with this new church? First I see people with demons, now my wife is shaking in bed.* He cried out to God for understanding.

Through a series of encounters, the Lord began to deal with John. First, by speaking to his heart and then by baptizing him with His love. Then God began to speak to John's conscience. For the next two to three months John began to hear audible bells whenever he would lie or bend the truth. This could happen at board meetings or at home. Finally the Lord said, "Now I want all of you! I love you, and I have called you to serve. You will be a servant to others. I want 30 percent of your time, your belongings and your finances! After that I want you to move it to 50 percent."

This all translated into a Good Samaritan-type lifestyle. It began slowly at first as John got creative and hired single mothers to pray for his business and spiritual life. Soon his whole family became very active in the abortion fight. As young mothers began to deliver the babies they had been counseled against killing, more needs were presented to John to be dealt with. Some of those mothers and their children moved into John and Sandra's home. His family had as many as five to eight extra people living with them at all times for the next six years. In time a scheme to help with housing opportunities and progressive employment was born. It would be called the Society of H.O.P.E.

With a team of dedicated laypeople, John and others spearheaded their own mercy-oriented society. Before long they had accumulated entire apartment buildings and large houses worth millions of dollars. The society now owns and manages subsidized housing for single parents in need. If that wasn't enough, H.O.P.E. for the Nations was developed. Under that organization the leadership team began by partnering three orphanages in underdeveloped areas, changing the lives of scores of children. Today everyone believes this is just the beginning. This is only a snapshot of one family affected by renewal. It may have started with shaking, but it didn't end there. For our church, renewal became the fuel that directed hundreds of committed Christians towards a new focus of mercy — the ministry of Jesus. Mission and mercy — that's where the river has to flow.

Conclusion

After eight years of firsthand experience with a real visitation of the Holy Spirit, I know I would not want it any other way. Early Methodism was called "a boiling hot religion." Jesus said of John the Baptist, "He was a burning and a shining light: and you were willing for a season to rejoice in his light" (John 5:35, KJV). That heart burning with passion for God and that shining light, which was such an extraordinary witness, preceded the greatest revival in Jewish history — the birth of the church. The prayer everywhere is that the present visitation of the Holy Spirit will likewise set our hearts aflame with the fire of God so that we become shining witnesses and see an even greater revival in our day.

Amen!

APPENDIX A

THE ASSOCIATION OF VINEYARD CHURCHES STATEMENT OF FAITH

The Association of Vineyard Churches' statement of faith is a thoroughly evangelical document. It is derived from a position that the Bible is our final authority for faith and practice. The following excerpt is just one section of fifteen major sections, with this one concentrating on the person of Christ. There are also thirty-four cross-references of Scripture that back up what is affirmed. These have not been included. Obviously there are other statements about Jesus Christ in the other fourteen sections, but brevity of space allows for only this point. A full statement of faith may be obtained by writing to the Association of Vineyard Churches, P.O. Box 17580, Anaheim, CA 92817.

WE BELIEVE that in the fullness of time, God honored His covenants with Israel and His prophetic promises of salvation by sending His only Son, Jesus, into the world. Conceived by the Holy Spirit and born of the Virgin Mary, as fully God and fully man in one person, He is humanity as God intended us to be. Jesus was anointed as God's Messiah and empowered by the Holy Spirit, inaugurating God's kingdom reign on earth, overpowering the reign of Satan by resisting temptation, preaching the good news of salvation, healing the sick, casting out demons and raising the dead. Gathering His disciples, He reconstituted God's people as His Church to be the instrument of His kingdom. After dying for the sins of the world, Jesus was raised from the dead on the third day, fulfilling the covenant of blessing given to Abraham. In His sinless, perfect life Jesus met the demands of the law and in His atoning death on the cross He took God's judgment for sin which we deserve as law-breakers. By His death on the cross He also disarmed the demonic powers. The covenant with David was fulfilled in Jesus' birth from David's house, His Messianic ministry, His glorious resurrection from the dead, His ascent into heaven and His present rule at the right hand of the Father. As God's Son and David's heir, He is the eternal Messiah-King, advancing God's reign throughout every generation and throughout the whole earth today.

APPENDIX B

A CONTROVERSIAL PROPHETIC WORD

One aspect of the renewal that continues to arouse criticism is the prophetic. Probably no prophetic word that Stacey has delivered has been more trumpeted and more vilified than the "Choose! Choose! Choose!" word delivered at the Toronto Airport Christian Fellowship's Catch the Fire conference in October 1994. Many say it is one of the most gripping words they have ever heard. Others, such as Hank Hanegraaff and the Christian Research Institute, purport it to be the epitome of false prophecy and everything bad about the prophetic stream of the renewal movement. I have chosen to include this prophetic word in this book as an example of how prophecy is to be weighed and judged.

The Context of the Word

The word was given directly to a specific group of people — those present in the conference. These people had already witnessed an electrifying night of testimonies, worship, exhortative preaching and some prayer ministry. They had been brought to a place of action. They had seen and heard it all. Now would they really go all the way — even if embracing this move of the Spirit came with a stigma, even if it meant that people might criticize them or call them crazy? Or even if division became the inevitable result of the malicious attacks of others? Would they still go for it?

Stacey felt in the spirit that some were there for the express purpose of finding fault, gathering intimidating evidence and becoming pawns of division.

She delivered the word with strong shaking manifestations, and it was accompanied by a dread of the Lord that many had never felt in their lives. It was ecstatic and given direct without faltering or thought of what would be said next. The thousands present knew it was God speaking. The following is the word in its entirety.

The Transcript of the Prophecy

And as Elijah spoke on Mount Carmel, immediately after showing the power of God, immediately after great displays of His power, He did not stop with the display of His power; He said, "Choose! Choose! Choose you this day whom you will serve!" And in the days of power and in the days of sight, when many miraculous things are being done around you and many signs and wonders are happening, and many outpourings, and much joy and many good things are given, the Lord would say, "Choose! Choose! Choose!"

Will you be like Job, who said, "Shall I accept good from the hands of the Lord and not evil?" (see Job 2:10) Will you take both the good and the bad? For I am telling you, grab all you can while you can get it. Take what you can while you can have it. For the days are coming, says the Lord, when a great division will begin in the church. And a man's enemies will be those of his own household. Your parents will criticize you and speak evil of you and fear they have lost you to a cult. Your sons and your daughters will say, "My parents have gone crazy!" There will be mourning in the house of God. And I tell you there are those even among you now who are here simply to spread discord among the brethren.

There are seven things that the Lord hates, that are an abomination to Him. One of them is a man who deliberately comes seeking to spread division in His church, seeking to destroy and divide, who in the name of truth, abandons love and stirs up hate, who does not understand that love covers a multitude of sins. The Lord says, the word of correction is to be brought in love. The Lord does correct. The Lord does like correction and He calls for it to happen. But the Lord hates — *hates* — division! For the one who comes to bring division, to divide the church of Christ, to cut off His arm from His leg and the toes from His feet, the Lord says, it will be better for Sodom and Gomorrah than it will be for that one on that day. But I tell you nonetheless that division will come! And it is even now brewing like a leaven in the church.

So the Lord calls you right now this day — seeing what you are seeing, hearing of the miracles you are hearing of, seeing the fruit of God that you are seeing — to call it [these things] God and endure to the end and be saved; or to follow after human wisdom and reasoning that kills the word of faith and brings division and justifies, in self-righteousness, the dividing of the church. The Lord wants you to purpose in your heart this night: Is it God or isn't it? And stand by your commitment as you are called to stand by your confession of faith. Amen.

The Main Emphasis of the Word

Over the years I have heard this prophetic word being interpreted everywhere from saying that, "Wesley and Stacey Campbell believe that anyone who doesn't accept the Toronto Blessing will be worse off than those of Sodom and Gomorrah," to others saying that this was the most awesome word they had ever heard. The following is the main emphasis of what was meant by what was said.

Having seen the power and testimony of God, the people were called to make a stand. It is not in context to take this word as a broad brush pronouncement to people who were not at the meetings. It is not fair to interpret this as James Beverly does when he writes, "Readers are then told they have a choice: Accept the Toronto Blessing and 'call it God' or follow after human wisdom and reasoning."[1] This was not said to readers who were not there, but rather it was a rhetorical question to people who were there and knew the overall gist of what they were seeing and what they were being asked to decide on. Clearly what the people witnessed was of God and many of them were being called to take a stand even if it cost them later.

The Second Main Point

There were those who had already determined in their own minds that that which was taking place at these Catch the Fire meetings was heresy. Their intention was not to correct or help the pastor but to stop it and stamp it out. Thinking we are dangerous, they "in the name of truth, abandon love and stir up hate." If in fact we turn out to actually be the body of Christ, in their blindness they will find themselves to have been fighting against Him. Later we were confronted by Christian Research Institute workers. Yes, the tape did make it to Hank Hanegraaff, and yes, even this prophecy has been derided and condemned continuously for two years. The result is more fear, more suspicion, more hate and more division. That is what God hates.

The phrase in paragraph two about "taking both the good and the bad" dealt with the authentic things of God versus the regular fleshly issues that must be pastored in every movement. There is no intention there to say that errors and excesses should not be corrected. The word said, "for the Lord does correct." But God's method of correction to His children is "correction brought in love."

The next time you hear a critic, listen to his criticism. Is it correction brought in love for the sake of building up the body? Or has the protagonist already determined that those he is attacking are heretics who must be stamped out, divided from the rest of Christianity and shunned. If they are wrong, and in their self-righteous truth campaign actually stumble the little ones, where does that put them?

The New Testament references to Sodom and Gomorrah quoted in the prophecy have to do with those who reject authentic, Christ-inspired works because they believe they are inspired by the devil (see Matt. 11:20-24), and those who reject the message of the kingdom complete with healing the sick, raising the dead, cleansing lepers and casting out demons (see 10:7-16). Like the Pharisees of old they persecute the messengers, thinking they are doing God a favor and make division of households (see 10:17ff.). Notice this continues until the Son of Man comes (see 10:23). So for the one who deliberately comes seeking to spread division in His church, seeking to destroy and divide, who in the name of truth, abandons love and stirs up hate — it will be better for Sodom and Gomorrah than it will be for that one on that day.

This is only a brief and incomplete mention of the Stacey Campbell word of October 1994. For a greater treatment please contact the author at the address provided in the back of the book.

NOTES

Chapter 1
Welcoming a Visitation of the Holy Spirit

1. Daina Doucet, "What Is God Doing in Toronto?" *Charisma* (February 1995): 20-26. The author also has a working knowledge of the Toronto Airport Christian Fellowship Church records.

2. John Wimber, article in the *Vineyard Reflections* (May/June 1994): 2-3. The entire account is an adaptation of the *Reflections* article intermixed with personal interviews with John and Carol Wimber. *Vineyard Reflections* is a publication of the Anaheim Vineyard.

3. Ibid., 3.

4. John Wimber, article in the *Vineyard Reflections* (July/August 1994): 7.

5. Eleanor Mumford, recorded message at Holy Trinity Brompton Church, 29 May 1994.

6. *HTB in Focus*, 12 June 1994. *HTB* is the newsletter of Holy Trinity Brompton Church.

7. Sandy Millar, introductory words to Mumford's recorded message.

8. At a holiness conference in Anaheim, Calif., February 1990, Paul Cain announced to more than nine thousand people that revival would begin in England. On July 14, 1990, in a private meeting with John Mumford, several associates and John Wimber, Paul Cain declared, "Revival will be released in England in October of 1990...Tokens of revival will come in October 1990." John Wimber remarks that Paul Cain meant revived people and revived churches. Wimber summarized the prophecy in this way: 1) The "first shot" of revival would come to England in October 1990. (Wimber held five major conferences in England during that time, ministering to eighty-five thousand people with significant results); 2) "Tokens" of revival would be the firstfruits of a greater revival; and 3) It would affect individuals and whole churches. Wimber went on to remark that past revivals have tended to come in two stages: the first stage is internal — affecting the church — the second is external — affecting the community.

9. Mumford, recorded message.

10. *National and International Religion Report* 9, no. 8 (3 April 1995).

11. Mona Johnian, "Flowing With Revival," *Charisma* (February 1995): 14.

12. *National and International Religion Report* 8, no. 15 (11 July 1994).
13. *National and International Religion Report* 9, no. 7 (20 March 1995).
14. *The Baptist Standard* 107, no. 10 (8 March 1995).
15. *National and International Religion Report* 9, no. 8 (3 April 1995).

Chapter 2
Prophetic Forecasting of God's Visitation

1. J. Edwin Orr, *The Flaming Tongue* (Chicago: Moody Press, 1973), 11.
2. Richard M. Riss, *A Survey of Twentieth-Century Revival Movements in North America* (Peabody, Mass.: Hendrickson, 1988), 32.
3. Eifion Evans, *The Walsh Revival of 1904* (Bridgend, Mid Glamorgan, England: Evangelical Press of Wales, 1969), 79.
4. Orr, *Flaming Tongue,* 8.
5. Ibid., 7.
6. Ibid., 28.
7. For a brief but succinct overview of the twentieth-century expansion of the Pentecostal/charismatic Third Wave movement as traced from the Azusa Street Revival, see "Church Growth" and "Statistics, Global" in *The Dictionary of Pentecostal and Charismatic Movements,* ed. Stanley M. Burgess and Gary B. McGee (Grand Rapids, Mich.: Zondervan, 1988), 181-191; 810-830.
8. Unfortunately space does not permit a background description of these prophetic personalities or the many other predictions and personal words which they have given under the sanction of pastoral accountability. Yet even an awareness of these specific prophecies as they relate to God's present timetable will prove to be faith building.
9. For instance, in the case of Marc Dupont's word as he originally submitted it, it was four pages in length and even then needed interpretation and explanation as to its application. The same is true for most of these words.
10. Mike Bickle with Michael Sullivant, *Growing in the Prophetic* (Lake Mary, Fla.: Creation House, 1995), 33-49. The complete prophetic story has been shared numerous times and is available on various tape series, including *The Prophetic History of the Kansas City Fellowship,* 1984. The brief overview related here is from the message "Revival Now," by Mike Bickle and Wesley Campbell, given at the Catch the Fire conference in Dallas, Texas, on July 18, 1996.
11. Howard Pittman, *Placebo* (Foxworth, Miss.: Self-published, 1982), 53, 43.

12. In August 1995 myself and a team conducted a Catch the Fire conference in Jakarta, Indonesia, the fourth most populated country in the world. Virtually the entire Christian church of Indonesia has heard about the Toronto Blessing, and many of the leaders say that it has facilitated some of the greatest moves of the Holy Spirit in their nation in the last twenty-five years. This is directly traceable to 250 Indonesian pastors and leaders traveling personally to Toronto and being touched by the Spirit of God.

13. Larry Randolph, *Why God Is Moving Powerfully in the Nineties,* a message spoken and taped at New Life Vineyard, Kelowna, British Columbia, June 1994.

14. Ibid.

15. John Paul Jackson, letter to author, June 1996.

16. Randolph, *Why God Is Moving,* as well as *Paul Cain's Life Testimony,* a four-tape audiocassette series available from Metro Vineyard Fellowship, 11610 Grandview Rd., Kansas City, MO 64137.

17. Mike Bickle, *Introduction to Prophecy Series,* tape 4 of the audiotape series, 1989.

18. Patrick Dixon, *Signs of Revival* (East Sussex, U.K.: Kingsway Publications, 1994), 81-112. Dixon gives an extremely thorough response to the background of the events that led up to the reviving of the English Church in 1994. He especially explains Paul Cain's prophetic word and documents how he believes it was fulfilled. A complete discussion of Paul Cain's prophecies, as well as John Wimber's comments are written up in *Equipping the Saints* 5, no. 1 (winter 1991): 10-12.

19. A prophetic word given by Marc Dupont in May 1992. Recording available through Toronto Airport Christian Fellowship, 272 Attwell Drive, Toronto, Ontario, Canada M9W 6M3.

20. After two and a half years of continuous meetings John Arnott said that they were networking with over six hundred pastors in the Toronto and South Ontario area. Considering the state prior to 1994 that is an amazing turnaround.

21. Randy Clark, conversation with author and Toronto Airport Christian Fellowship first anniversary message, 20 January 1995.

22. Cho's quote is contained in *Spread the Fire* 1, issue 3 (May 1995).

23. Orr, *Flaming Tongue,* 19.

Chapter 3
How to Prepare for a Visitation of the Holy Spirit

1. Phillip Schaff, *Nicene and Post-Nicene Christianity,* vol. 3 of *History*

of the Christian Church (Grand Rapids, Mich.: Wm. B. Eerdmans, 1978), 191-195.

2. Ibid., 194.

3. David Bryant, *The Hope at Hand* (Grand Rapids, Mich.: Baker Book House, 1995), 31.

4. Orr, *Flaming Tongue,* 188.

5. Bryant, *Hope at Hand,* 25-35.

6. Jean Seligmann, "Talking to God," *Newsweek* (6 January 1992): 38.

7. Bryant, *Hope at Hand,* 31.

8. Ibid., 15, 233, 237 respectively.

9. Ibid., 32.

10. Orr, *Flaming Tongue,* 18.

11. Ibid., 20.

12. At Toronto Airport Christian Fellowship's two-year anniversary service, R. T. Kendall of Westminster Chapel, Gerald Coates and other speakers affirmed this. See *Anniversary Messages,* audiocassettes including Gerald Coates, Paul Cain, R. T. Kendall and Ted Haggard, 18-21 January 1996.

13. Ibid., 10-11.

14. The testimony of Martin Buhlmann was written and sent from Switzerland for the express purpose of chronicling the spread of the Toronto Blessing. Used by permission.

Chapter 5
Interpreting the Bible

1. The following excellent books describe the principles of interpretation: Gordon D. Fee, *New Testament Exegesis* (Louisville, Ky.: Westminster/John Knox Press, 1983); Gordon D. Fee and David Stuart, *How to Read the Bible for All It's Worth* (Grand Rapids, Mich.: Zondervan, 1993); Jack Deere, *Surprised by the Power of the Spirit* (Grand Rapids, Mich.: Zondervan, 1993). Deere's book illustrates how these principles come to bear within the whole topic of the Holy Spirit and the supernatural.

2. Ibid., 21.

3. The majority of the section on exegesis and worldview was written by Roger Helland and appeared in a manual that Roger and I co-wrote entitled "Welcoming a Visitation of God," July 1995. These sections are used by permission.

4. John Wimber, *Power Evangelism* (San Francisco, Calif.: Harper Collins, 1992), 75-96.

5. Deere, *Surprised by the Power,* 46.

6. Wimber, *Power Evangelism,* 77.

7. Wherever the Western church has cultivated an operating belief in the supernatural, it has produced great results. Oxford researcher David Barrett states that in just ninety years, the Pentecostal/charismatic/Third Wave persuasions already constitute the largest Protestant body in Christendom worldwide. See "Church Growth" and "Statistics, Global" in *Charismatic Movements.*

8. Campbell and Helland, "Welcoming a Visitation of God."

Chapter 6
Manifestations of the Holy Spirit

1. The three lists of physical, emotional and spiritual phenomena are taken from Campbell and Helland, "Welcoming a Visitation of God." Definitions were developed by Helland and are used by permission.

Chapter 7
A Biblical Basis for Present-Day Phenomena

1. Every group who elevates their teaching or revelation to the place of Scripture has inevitably contradicted Scripture. Witness for instance, papal bulls and the private revelations of Joseph Smith.

2. Association of Vineyard Churches, board report, September/October 1994.

3. Henry M. Morris, *The Genesis Report* (Grand Rapids, Mich.: Baker Book House, 1976), 52.

4. David E. Aune, *Prophecy in Early Christianity and the Ancient Mediterranean World* (Grand Rapids, Mich.: Wm. B. Eerdmans, 1983), 87, 370.

5. John White, *When the Spirit Comes With Power* (Westmont, Ill.: Inter-Varsity Press, 1989), 25.

6. See "Slain in the Spirit" in *Charismatic Movements.*

Chapter 8
Holy Spirit Apologetics

1. William DeArteaga, *Quenching the Spirit* (Lake Mary, Fla.: Creation House, 1992), 52.

2. Ibid., 45-57.

3. Ibid., 53.

4. Orr, *Flaming Tongue,* 23.

5. Ibid., 23.

6. Ibid., 17.

7. John F. MacArthur Jr., *Reckless Faith* (Wheaton, Ill.: Crossway Books, 1994), 155-158.

8. Ibid., 159.

9. Ibid., 160.

10. John Wimber, *Vineyard Reflections* (May/June 1994).

11. MacArthur, *Reckless Faith,* 160.

12. Wimber, *Power Evangelism,* 5.

13. MacArthur, *Reckless Faith,* 27-29.

14. Cecil M. Robeck Jr., *Prophecy in Carthage* (Cleveland, Ohio: Pilgrim Press, 1992), 9.

15. MacArthur, *Reckless Faith,* 91-117.

16. Hank Hanegraaff, *Counterfeit Revival,* recorded message given at Calvary Chapel in Costa Mesa, Calif., 1995. (Unfortunately Hanegraaff wilfully and consistently misrepresents both the Toronto Blessing and the current worldwide renewal using the platform of the Christian Research Institute. His daily broadcasts consistently talk about it and have often deliberately misrepresented or twisted the views of those who are involved in the renewal. I would encourage anyone who listens to his outlandish claims, even when supposedly quoting someone, to check first with the source before believing him.)

17. Ibid.

18. In Jesus' denunciation of Judaism, He said that it produced "twice the sons of hell" as the blind guides were already themselves (see Matt. 23:15). Jesus said they looked good on the outside, but they were full of dead man's bones and all uncleanness on the inside (see Matt. 23:27). Clearly this was the bad fruit being referred to, not a missed prophecy or an unorderly manifestation.

19. Association of Vineyard Churches' Statement of Faith, Vineyard Christian Fellowship, Anaheim, Calif., 1994. See Appendix A for the section detailing the official Vineyard position regarding Jesus Christ.

20. An expansion of the issue of spiritual fruit is discussed in chapter 9.

Chapter 9
You Will Know Them by Their Fruit

1. Personal interview of statistics with John Arnott, July 1995.

Chapter 10
The Corporate Witness of Church History

1. Deere, *Surprised by the Power*, 68-70, 145-146, 272. Deere gives many examples of healing and shows how the reality of the gift destroys the cessation theory.

2. White, *When the Spirit Comes*, 225.

3. For more examples of manifestations and phenomena in salvation history see Guy Chevreau, *Catch the Fire* (London, U.K.: Marshall Pickering, 1994), 70-144; Dixon, *Signs of Revival* (East Sussex, U.K.: Kingsway Publication, 1994), 113-198; David Pytches, *Prophecy in the Local Church* (London, U.K.: Hodder and Stoughton, 1993); Rob Warner, *Prepare for Revival* (London, U.K.: Hodder and Stoughton, 1995), 37-65; White, *When the Spirit Comes*, 34-102.

4. Special thanks to Roger Helland, who gathered some of the historical examples from their original sources for "Welcoming a Visitation of God." Used by permission.

5. Cecil M. Robeck Jr., *Prophecy in Carthage* (Cleveland, Ohio: Pilgrim Press, 1992), 107.

6. Ibid., 20.

7. Ibid.

8. Johannes Jorgenson, *Saint Catherine of Siena* (London, U.K.: Longmans, Green and Co., 1938), 15.

9. Edith Deen, *Great Women of the Christian Faith* (Uhrichsville, Ohio: Barbour, 1959), 102-103.

10. *The Life of Teresa of Jesus,* trans. E. Allison Peers (New York: Image Books, 1960), 177-178.

11. Henry Baird, *The Huguenots* (Charles Scribner, 1895), 186-187.

12. "John Wesley," *Christian History* 2, no. 1 (1983): 4.

13. Dixon, *Signs,* 122.

14. Ibid., 122.

15. John Wesley, *Journal,* 28 July 1762.

16. Ibid., 8 September 1784.

17. Ibid., 5 August 1959.

18. George Fox, *The Journal of George Fox* (London, U.K.: Friends Tract Assoc., 1901), 23.

19. *The Journal of George Fox,* ed. Rufus M. Jones (1908; reprint, Richmond, Ind.: Friends United Press, 1976), 215-216.

20. "Jonathan Edwards and the Great Awakening," *Christian History* 4, no. 4 (1985): 18.

21. Chevreau, *Catch the Fire,* 75-88.

22. *Jonathan Edwards on Revival* (Carlisle, Pa.: Banner of Truth, 1965), 151-154.

23. "George Whitefield," *Christian History* 12, no. 2, issue 38 (spring 1993).

24. "Spiritual Awakenings in North America," *Christian History* 8, no. 3, issue 23 (summer 1989), 26.

25. Winkie Pratney, *Revival* (Springdale, Pa.: Whitaker House, 1984), 125-126.

26. Quoted from Peter Cartwright's autobiography by Keith J. Hardman, *The Spiritual Awakeners* (Chicago: Moody Press, 1983), 145-146.

27. "Charles Grandison Finney," *Christian History* 7, no. 4, issue 20 (fall 1988), 2-3.

28. Richard M. Riss, "The Manifestations Throughout History," paper presented at a Catch the Fire conference, St. Louis, Mo., May 1995.

29. Helen Wessel, ed., *The Autobiography of Charles Finney* (Minneapolis, Minn.: Bethany, 1977), 57-58.

30. Frank Bartleman, *Azusa Street* (South St. Paul, Minn.: Logos, 1980), 59-60.

31. See "Church Growth" in *Charismatic Movements.*

Chapter 11
Prophecy and a Visitation of the Holy Spirit

1. James Ryle, *Hippo in the Garden* (Lake Mary, Fla.: Creation House, 1993), 259.

2. Ibid., 261-262.

3. Richard N. Ostling, "Laughing for the Lord," *Time,* 15 August 1994, 38.

4. Vinson Synan, *In the Latter Days* (Ann Arbor, Mich.: Servant Publications, 1984), 4.

5. Aune, *Prophecy in Early Christianity,* 191.

6. Ibid., 83, 369.

7. Ibid., 193.

8. Ibid.

Chapter 12
Facilitating and Releasing the Prophetic

1. Gerald F. Hawthorne, Ralph P. Martin and Daniel G. Reid, "Prophecy,

Prophesying" in the *Dictionary of Paul and His Letters* (Westmont, Ill.: Intervarsity, 1993), 755.

2. There are many excellent books on the subject of prophecy. A brief scanning of the books dealing with prophecy which are mentioned in the endnotes and bibliography will provide ample material concerning the subject.

3. There are numerous examples in the Old Testament of the Holy Spirit coming upon God's people: Judg. 6:34; 14:6,19; 15:14; 1 Sam. 10:9; 16:13; 19:20; 2 Kin. 3:15.

4. See Num. 11:29; Jer. 31:31-34; Hos. 2:16; Joel 2:28-29.

5. Aune, *Prophecy in Early Christianity,* 200.

6. See Acts 2:4; 4:31; 5:15; 7:55; 8:6,15-18; 10:44-46; 11:15; 19:6,11-12.

7. See "Baptism in the Holy Spirit" in *Charismatic Movements.*

8. Ibid., 42.

9. John is not his real name.

10. See John 3:8; Acts 2:2.

11. John Arnott, *The Father's Blessing* (Lake Mary, Fla.: Creation House, 1995), 96.

12. "Sober intoxication" is the term used by Philo to describe the sleep of the senses when the soul is awakened to the appearance of God. *Philo's Commentary on the Canticles,* fifth and eleventh homilies, paragraph 44, 873d, 990b and col. 993 ac.

13. See Acts 14:3,8-10; 19:11-12; 20:10; 28:5-6; 1 Cor. 2:2; 2 Cor. 12:12; Gal. 3:5; 2 Tim. 4:20; 1 Tim. 5:23.

Chapter 13
Pastoring the Prophetic

1. It is not my purpose here to debate the cessationist position on whether or not prophecy is operational for today's church. For a more complete treatment on the subject see Gary S. Greig and Kevin N. Springer, *The Kingdom and the Power* (Ventura, Calif.: Regal Books, 1993) and Deere, *Surprised by the Power.*

2. I use the term *prophet* loosely. In my context I am referring to those with a prophetic ability or gifting. I am not using the term in the strict sense of the office of a prophet.

3. With the spread of the renewal I have been devoting my time to helping other groups get started in their locations. Therefore my time at home has been cut down.

Chapter 14
The Main Thing Is That the Main Thing
Remains the Main Thing

1. "The Day Toronto Was a Big Mirage," *The Toronto Star,* 14 August 1994.

2. "Best and Worst: A Year in the Life of the City," *Toronto Life Magazine* (January 1994).

3. Bryant, *Hope at Hand,* 22-32.

4. *Vineyard Reflections* (July/August 1994): 6-7. This was also reiterated at several meetings and in personal conversations and interviews.

5. Earle E. Cairns, *An Endless Line of Splendor* (Wheaton, Ill.: Tyndale House, 1986), 267-274.

6. Wimber, *Power Evangelism,* 116, 181-182.

7. See Randy Clark's anniversary messages given at Toronto Airport Christian Fellowship, including "God Can Use Little ol' Me." Randy is writing a book on renewal and healing that will include many of his eye-witness accounts, which will by supported by medical documentation.

Chapter 15
Empowered for Missions and Mercy

1. Bryant, *Hope at Hand,* 42.

2. Ibid, 22-32.

3. "John Wesley," *Christian History* 2, no. 1 (February 1982): 4.

4. "Spiritual Awakening in North America," *Christian History* 8, no. 3, issue 23 (summer 1989): 23.

5. Peter Cartwright, *Autobiography of Peter Cartwright* (Nashville, Tenn.: Abingdon Press, reprint 1984), 339.

6. Ibid., 9.

7. *America's Great Revivals* (Minneapolis, Minn.: Bethany House Publishers, 1994), 45.

8. Camp Meetings and Circuit Riders," *Christian History* 14, no. 1, issue 45 (winter 1995): 22.

9. Margaret Poloma, *By Their Fruits: A Sociological Assessment of the Toronto Blessing* (self-published, 1995), 22.

10. "Women in the Medieval Church," *Christian History* 10, no. 2, issue 30 (spring 1991): 14.

11. Earle E. Cairns, *An Endless Line of Splendor* (Wheaton, Ill.: Tyndale House, 1986), 275.

12. Orr, *Flaming Tongue,* 9 14.

13. Cairns, *An Endless Line,* 277-284

14. Ibid., 305.

15. Ibid., 290.

16. Ibid., 303.

17. "Spiritual Awakening," *Christian History,* 31.

18. Ibid., 31.

19. Roy Abraham Varghese, *The Intellectuals Speak Out About God* (Dallas, Tex.: Lewis and Stanley, 1984), 23.

Appendix B
A Controversial Prophetic Word

1. James A. Beverly, *Holy Laughter and the Toronto Blessing* (Grand Rapids, Mich.: Zondervan Publishing House, 1995), 146.

SELECT BIBLIOGRAPHY

Arnott, John. *The Father's Blessing*. Lake Mary, Fla.: Creation House, 1995.

Aune, David E. *Prophecy in Early Christianity and the Ancient Mediterranean World*. Grand Rapids, Mich.: Wm. B. Eerdmans, 1983.

Baird, Henry. *The Huguenots*. New York: Charles Scribner, 1895.

Bartleman, Frank. *Azusa Street*. South St. Paul, Minn.: Logos, 1980.

Beougher, Timothy and Lyle Dorsett. *Accounts of a Campus Revival: Wheaton College 1995*. Wheaton, Ill.: Harold Shaw Publishers, 1995.

Bickle, Mike. *Passion for Jesus*. Lake Mary, Fla.: Creation House, 1993.

———. *Growing in the Prophetic*. Lake Mary, Fla.: Creation House, 1996.

Bouyer, Louis, Jean Leclercq and Francoi Vandenbroucke. *A History of Christian Spirituality*. Vols. 1–3. New York: Seabury Press, 1982.

Bryant, David. *The Hope at Hand*. Grand Rapids, Mich.: Baker Book House, 1995.

Burgess, Stanley M. *The Spirit and the Church: Antiquity*. Peabody, Mass.: Hendrickson, 1894.

Cairns, Earle. *An Endless Line of Splendor*. Wheaton, Ill.: Tyndale, 1986.

Carson, D. A. *Showing the Spirit*. Grand Rapids, Mich.: Baker Books, 1987.

Cartwright, Peter. *Autobiography of Peter Cartwright*. Nashville, Tenn.: Abingdon Press, 1984.

Chevreau, Guy. *Catch the Fire*. London, U.K.: Marshall Pickering, 1994.

———. *Praying With Fire*. London, U.K.: Marshall Pickering, 1995.

DeArteaga, William. *Quenching the Spirit*. Lake Mary, Fla.: Creation House, 1992, 1996.

Deen, Edith. *Great Women of the Christian Faith*. Uhrichsville, Ohio: Barbour, 1959.

Deere, Jack. *Surprised by the Power of the Spirit*. Grand Rapids, Mich.: Zondervan, 1993.

Dixon, Patrick. *Signs of Revival*. East Sussex, U.K.: Kingsway Publications, 1994.

Douglas, J. D. ed. *The New International Dictionary of the Christian Church.* Grand Rapids, Mich.: Zondervan, 1974, 1978.

Edwards, Jonathan. *Edwards on Revival.* Carlisle, Pa.: Banner of Truth, 1965.

———. *A Treatise on Religious Affections.* Grand Rapids, Mich.: Baker Book House, 1982.

———. *The Works of Jonathan Edwards.* 2 Vols. Carlisle, Pa.: Banner of Truth, 1992.

Fee, Gordon D. *The First Epistle to the Corinthians. New International Commentary on the New Testament.* Grand Rapids, Mich.: Wm. B. Eerdmans Publishing, 1987.

———. *How to Read the Bible for All It's Worth.* Grand Rapids, Mich.: Zondervan, 1981, 1993.

Gillespie, Thomas W. *The First Theologians.* Grand Rapids, Mich.: Wm. B. Eerdmans, 1994.

Greig, Gary S. and Kevin N. Springer, ed. *The Kingdom and the Power.* Ventura, Calif.: Regal Books, 1993.

Grudem, Wayne. *The Gift of Prophecy in the New Testament and Today.* Wheaton, Ill.: Crossway Books, 1988.

Hardman, Keith J. *The Spiritual Awakeners.* Chicago: Moody Press, 1983.

Helland, Roger. *Let the River Flow: Welcoming Renewal Into Your Church.* South Plainfield, N.J.: Bridge-Logos, in press.

Jones, Brynor Pierce. *An Instrument of Revival.* South Plainfield, N.J.: Bridge Publishing, 1995.

Jones, Rufus M. *The Journal of George Fox.* Richmond, Ind.: Friends United Press, 1976.

Kraft, Charles H. *Christianity With Power.* Ann Arbor, Mich.: Vine Books, 1989.

Lovejoy, David S. *Religious Enthusiasm in the New World.* Cambridge, Mass. and London: Harvard University Press, 1985.

Lovelace, Richard F. *Dynamics of Spiritual Life.* Westmont, Ill.: Intervarsity Press, 1980.

Morphew, Derek. *Breakthrough: Discovering the Kingdom.* Cape Town, South Africa: Struik Christian Books, 1991.

Orr, J. Edwin. *The Flaming Tongue.* Chicago: Moody Press, 1973.

Poloma, Margaret, *By Their Fruits: A Sociological Assessment of the Toronto Blessing.* Self-published, 1996.

Pratney, Winkie. *Revival.* Springdale, Pa.: Whitaker House, 1983, 1984.

Pytches, David. *Prophecy in the Local Church.* London, U.K.: Hodder and Stoughton, 1993.

————. *Some Said It Thundered.* London, U.K.: Hodder and Stoughton, 1990.

Riss, Richard R. *A Survey of Twentieth Century Revival Movements in North America.* Peabody, Mass.: Hendrickson, 1988.

Robeck, Cecil M. Jr. *Prophecy in Carthage.* Cleveland, Ohio: Pilgrim Press, 1992.

Roberts Dave. *The Toronto Blessing.* East Sussex, U.K.: Kingsway Publications, 1994.

Ryle, James. *Hippo in the Garden.* Lake Mary, Fla.: Creation House, 1993.

————. *A Dream Come True.* Lake Mary, Fla.: Creation House, 1995.

Schaff, Philip. *History of the Christian Church.* 8 Vols. *Nicene & Post-Nicene Christianity.* Grand Rapids, Mich.: Wm. B. Eerdmans, 1910.

Stearns, Bill and Amy. *Catch the Vision 2000.* Minneapolis, Minn.: Bethany, 1991.

Stronstad, Roger. *The Charismatic Theology of St. Luke.* Peabody, Mass.: Hendrickson, 1984.

Synan, Vinson. *In The Latter Days.* Ann Arbor, Mich.: Servant Books, 1984.

Teresa of Avila. *The Life of Teresa of Jesus.* Translated by E. Allison Peers. New York: Image, 1960.

Tucker, Ruth A. and Walter L. Liefeld. *Daughters of the Church.* Grand Rapids, Mich.: Zondervan, 1987.

Varghese, Roy Abraham. *The Intellectuals Speak Out About God.* Dallas, Tex.: Lewis and Stanley, 1984.

Wessel, Helen, ed. *The Autobiography of Charles Finney.* Minneapolis, Minn.: Bethany, 1977.

White, John. *When the Spirit Comes with Power.* Westmont, Ill.: Intervarsity Press, 1988.

Whitefield, George. *George Whitefield's Journals.* Carlisle, Pa.: Banner of Truth, 1960.

Williams, Don. *Revival: The Real Thing.* La Jolla, Calif.: Coast Vineyard, 1995.

Wimber, John. *Power Evangelism.* San Francisco, Calif.: HarperCollins, 1985, 1992.

————. *Conference Notebook for Facing the 90s: A Prophetic Word for the Church Today.* Anaheim, Calif.: Mercy Publishing, 1990.

SUBJECT INDEX

If you enjoyed reading *Welcoming a Visitation of the Holy Spirit*
you'll also appreciate these other resources
from New Life Vineyard team members:

Music on compact disk

Various worship leaders are featured on CDs such as *God Rock I, God Rock II, Let There Be Dancing, Joel's Place,* and Andrew Smith's *Through My Emotions.*

Schools of ministry

New Life Vineyard offers two ten-week schools each year, focusing on themes such as Worship and Prophecy, Leadership and Church Renewal, Missions and Mercy, and Healing and Counseling.

Conferences

New Life Vineyard hosts two to four conferences a year. Wesley and Stacey speak at conferences together or separately.

Let the River Flow
by Roger Helland

Helland, associate pastor of New Life Vineyard, places renewal in its biblical, historical and theological context and shows how its fruit is always seen in changed lives, evangelism, service and renewal.

A complete list of cassettes, videos and books is available on request.
You may also receive information on the schools of ministry,
conference bookings for Wesley and Stacey Campbell
or conference bookings for other members of
the New Life Vineyard team by contacting:

New Life Vineyard Fellowship
2041 Harvey Ave.
Kelowna, B.C.
Canada V1Y 6G7
Telephone: 604-762-4255
Fax: 604-861-3844
E-mail: Newlife@silk.net

If you enjoyed *Welcoming a Visitation of the Holy Spirit,*
we would like to recommend the following books:

The Father's Blessing
by John Arnott

Since January 1994, hundreds of thousands of people have visited
John Arnott's church, the Toronto Airport Christian Fellowship, where
they experience powerful manifestations of the Holy Spirit. With
extraordinary firsthand testimonies and sound biblical insight,
John Arnott will speak to your heart and show you how you can
experience a fresh move of the Holy Spirit in your life.

Growing in the Prophetic
by Mike Bickle

As a young pastor not personally inclined toward prophecy
Mike Bickle was taken by surprise by the upsurge of the gift in his
own church. *Growing in the Prophetic* is Bickle's account of the journey
away from "prophetic chaos" toward a clearer understanding of God's
order. He writes for all those interested in seeing prophetic ministry
developed in the church today.

Hippo in the Garden
by James Ryle

Author James Ryle says that God speaks to us at unusual times
in unexpected places. Through his humorous personal anecdotes
and references to the Old and New Testament Scriptures,
you will discover that every circumstance of life becomes
an opportunity to converse with God.

Available at your local Christian bookstore or from:

Creation House
600 Rinehart Road
Lake Mary, FL 32746
1-800-283-8494